Got Solidarity?

The 21st century in the United States continues to be marked by persistent disparities between members of different classes, races, genders, and sexual orientations. Influencers of this society seem bent on polarizing citizens along their diverse identities, often blaming those already disadvantaged for the nation's apparent plights. Elite white men still benefit from a political, economic, and social hegemony, and some ardently resist an egalitarian society. Preserving American democracy rests in the hands of young Americans committed to equity and social justice.

In *Got Solidarity?*, Jörg Vianden reports the results from the Straight White College Men Project, a nationwide qualitative study of how heterosexual white college men experience or perceive campus and community diversity issues. In college, few white men tend to engage in majors, discussions, or courses on diversity, inclusion, equity, or social justice. Indeed, many white men say that they have "no place" in these discussions, and more commonly assert that "diversity is not about them." Using a sociological perspective, the author chronicles their upbringing in families and schools, their perspectives on race, gender, and sexual orientation, as well as their trepidations on challenging oppression they notice taking place around them. Their stories lead to a renewed understanding of how white disengagement constrains progress toward a just society. This book offers strategies for enhancing college teaching and learning, adds to the body of research on identity development theory, and provides implications for improving campus climates, fostering social justice advocacy, as well as re-designing programs promoting understanding of human differences.

Written especially for straight white male college students, as well as for educators at all levels, this book underscores the critical need for whites to raise consciousness, activate empathy, and build solidarity with members of minoritized social groups. Given the current American predicament, *Got Solidarity?* makes a timely contribution to our understanding of masculinity and endeavors to create a just society.

Dr. Jörg Vianden is Professor and Chair of the Department of Student Affairs Administration in Higher Education at the University of Wisconsin-La Crosse. Originally from Germany, he has lived in the United States for 25 years and received his doctorate from Indiana University. Vianden's scholarship focuses on men and masculinities as well as social justice issues in higher education. His research has been published in several national and international journals.

New Critical Viewpoints on Society Series
Edited by Joe R. Feagin

For more information about this series, please visit www.routledge.com/
New-Critical-Viewpoints-on-Society/book-series/NCVS

Got Solidarity?
Challenging Straight White College Men to Advocate for Social Justice

Jörg Vianden

Routledge
Taylor & Francis Group

NEW YORK AND LONDON

First published 2020
by Routledge
52 Vanderbilt Avenue, New York, NY 10017

and by Routledge
2 Park Square, Milton Park, Abingdon, Oxon, OX14 4RN

Routledge is an imprint of the Taylor & Francis Group, an informa business

© 2020 Taylor & Francis

Library of Congress Cataloging-in-Publication Data
A catalog record for this title has been requested.

ISBN: 978-1-138-65481-5 (hbk)
ISBN: 978-1-138-65483-9 (pbk)
ISBN: 978-1-315-62299-6 (ebk)

Typeset in Bembo
by Wearset Ltd, Boldon, Tyne & Wear

KD 11.20.2019 0750

Für meine Familie.

Contents

Preface

As the United States nears the end of the first two decades of the 21st century, partisan politicians have sharply divided Americans along racial, ethnic, class, gender, religious, and sexual orientation lines. While wealth and income gaps between the haves and the have nots hover at record highs, populist rulers blame already disadvantaged citizens and immigrants for the apparent perils of the nation. Not visible are the leaders' attempts to take responsibility for their own shortcomings or to advocate for equity among all Americans. As we're ensnared in this social predicament, elite straight white men continue to benefit from vast social capital, exorbitant economic worth, and enormous decision-making power. Not all but many of them are also most indifferent or offensive when it comes to issues of diversity or social justice. They either leave the educating or dissenting up to citizens who are already marginalized, or they do much of the blaming themselves. In so doing, they carelessly ignore the historical and current effects of living in a white supremacist, patriarchal, and heteronormative society on people of color, women, or individuals with different genders or sexual orientations. As America's ruling class continues to obstruct our nation's progress, young Americans need to step up and advocate for an equitable democracy and a just society.

The key to creating a pluralistic, open, and socially just union is to create civil discourse, to practice listening and dissent, and to allow and foster free thought. According to Bell (2007, p. 2), the goals of a socially just society should be, "democratic and participatory, inclusive and affirming of human agency and human capacities for working collaboratively to create change." An egalitarian society threatens the populists' power, plots, and policies, but helps *all* other citizens. Developing this kind of democracy depends on the participation and engagement of all citizens, including those with vast social privileges.

In *Got Solidarity?*, I share the thoughts, feelings, and questions of 92 ordinary straight white men on 10 different U.S. college campuses. Following phenomenological methods (Seidman, 1998), I trace the participants' upbringing in families, schools, and communities; their thoughts about engaging in and learning from diversity in college; their conceptualizations of their own identities; their ruminations about privilege and oppression; their trepidations about challenging social inequities; and their notions about their own responsibility to foster diversity and affect social change. A book for and about straight white men, *Got Solidarity?* encourages readers to develop their own consciousness and empathy, and to build solidarity with peers from minoritized backgrounds.

Once they move beyond college and into their careers, straight white men will hold social, economic, and professional positions of enormous influence in which they can affect real change. Hence, educators must challenge, support, and expect straight white college men to interrogate power and privilege, to develop capacity to build solidarity with others, and to help to engender social justice. Given our current American quandary, this book makes a timely contribution to our understanding of masculinity and our endeavors to create a more solidary society.

La Crosse, October 2019

Acknowledgments

I am indebted to several people without whom this book would not have been written. First, I want to thank my colleagues at the various institutions where we conducted the research for providing access to students to interview. These colleagues include Liz Gregg, Sarah Weiler, Adam Stafford, Keith Edwards, Lisa Erwin, Tamara Yakaboski, Ashley Grice, Brett Schieve, and Jenny Minsberg.

Next, I would like to thank the research team that first conceptualized the study, conducted literature searches and annotations, and collected, transcribed, and analyzed the data. They include my colleagues Dr. Ryan McKelley and Dr. Tori Svoboda, and graduate students Charles Martin-Stanley II, Kaylie Connaughty, Carrie Bero, Paige Kieler, Beck Hawkins, and Mitch Berry.

I couldn't have completed this book without Tony Docan-Morgan and Kate Parker, my colleagues and close friends who provided edits and comments on earlier chapters of the book, as well as providing insight and encouragement.

This book provides a glimpse into the hearts and minds of 92 straight white male college students around the country. These are regular men who simply participated in a research project. But through their participation they have given me and us access to their thoughts, perceptions, hopes, anxieties, shortcomings, vulnerabilities, fears, and dreams about living in a diverse nation like the United States. For that I will be forever thankful to them.

Finally, I thank the people most important in my life: my family. First, I thank my uncle and my aunt, their cousin, her partner, and my father for helping me reconstruct parts of our family history as it applied to this book. Second, and most especially, I thank my immediate family, my partner and our daughters, for supporting me throughout this process. During the research and writing of this book they endured countless hours of me hovering over my laptop or with my head in a book. Most of all, I appreciate their undying support and love. I dedicate this book to them.

1 Building Solidarity and Challenging Social Justice Advocacy in Straight White College Men

Ihr seid nicht verantwortlich für das, was geschah.
Aber dass es nicht wieder geschieht, dafür schon.
(You are not responsible for what happened.
But you are responsible that it doesn't happen again.)

Max Mannheimer, Czech Holocaust survivor

After a few days of torrential downpours that caused heavy flooding in nearby areas, the sun finally pushed its way through the clouds, and the rain subsided. Dipping into the mid-50s, the temperature felt cool for this time of year, but people were hopeful warmer days lay ahead. The ancient maples and oaks in the winding river valley were still lush green, but soon they would show first glimpses of the colorful fall foliage. In a fortnight, the grapes of the Riesling and Grüner Veltliner would be ripe, and local vintners were busy prepping for the harvest.

It was September 9, 1910. In Gars am Kamp, a picturesque Lower Austrian town a stone's throw northwest of Vienna, Johann Höbarth, a mason, and Maria, a homemaker, welcomed their new baby boy, Franz Seraf Karl, to the world. Franz was Maria's third boy in as many years; when he was born, his older brothers, Johann Jr. and Josef (Sepp), were three and one-and-a-half respectively. Between 1912 and 1919, Maria gave birth to three more children: the girls, Maria (Mitzi) and Aloise (Loisi), and Alois, a boy, who died at only 10 days of age. The family made their home in Thunau, a small village of 500 in the southern district of Gars.

The Höbarths were poor. Dirt poor in fact. At the turn of the 20th century, the Austro-Hungarian Empire, the second largest in Europe at the time, experienced a growing economy and industrialization; however, this growth hardly made it to Austria's expansive rural regions such as Thunau. Although Johann, the family's patriarch, had work, being a mason in a small community didn't guarantee a steady income. And, sadly, much of the money he made he squandered on liquor.

In the fall of 1918, when Franz was eight years old, Austria-Hungary, along with the German Second Reich, found itself on the losing end of

World War I. As the Empire collapsed, Austria ceded the fertile regions of Hungary and Bohemia and food supplies dropped dramatically. Agrarian production could only meet 50% of the pre-war mark, and in the frosty winter of 1918–19 Austrian coal yields met just one-fourth of demand (Gerwarth, 2016). Austria was demoralized by the human loss it incurred in the war – nearly two million deaths, including 120,000 civilians – and by the shame of not emerging victorious. The Höbarths didn't lose any immediate family members, but their disdain for those who weren't Austrians or Germans grew noticeably.

In the early 20th century, Gars served as *Sommerfrische*, a local summer recreation area for Viennese aristocrats. Franz and his brothers witnessed the lifestyle of the rich and famous as they perambulated through town dissipating their fortunes in lavish hotels and extravagant restaurants. After completing only an eighth-grade education, Franz started waiting tables full-time in one of the local establishments when he was 14 years old. All the money he made went directly to support the family and his father's alcohol addiction. One night, after Johann Sr. again abused his wife Maria in a drunken stupor, Franz, by now a tall and built teenager, stepped in: "If you ever touch my mother again, I will kill you!"

When the weather turned cold and dreary between the late fall and early Spring, restaurants downsized staffs and Franz found himself laid off from work for months at a time. Unemployment was generally high in Austria during this time as the young nation "staggered from one economic crisis to the next … dependent for its survival on financial assistance from the Western Powers" (Gerwarth, 2016, p. 249). Franz now had several people to loathe: his father for wasting the family's modest income and for beating his mother, the Viennese nobility for flaunting their riches, and the Allies for withdrawing their financial assistance from Austria by the beginning of the 1930s.

The Wall Street Crash and Great Depression in the U.S. had deleterious effects on Austria and Germany, and ongoing economic and political crises heightened the desire for new leadership among working-class, rural, and impoverished Austrians (Gerwarth, 2016). The level of extreme poverty, lack of government leadership, little faith in capitalist nations supporting Austria, and a slow recovery after losing a war created an environment ripe for the quick ascension and stardom of another working-class Austrian. By the time Adolf Hitler, born in Braunau, Austria, seized power as *Reichskanzler* (Chancellor of the German Third Reich) and head of the *Nationalsozialisten* (National Socialist Party, or the Nazis) on March 5, 1933, the Höbarth boys were between 22 and 25 years old. It didn't take long until Sepp and Franz became infatuated with Hitler's popularity (Crew, 2005).

Still dreaming of more and disillusioned by the current political situation, Sepp and Franz became more and more obsessed with nationalism. They believed most Nazi promises, including those of food "beyond a slave's ration of bread … an honorable life, decent earnings and the sanctity of [a farmer's] hard-earned property" (Crew,[1] 2005, p. 49). In 1933, the two Höbarth brothers joined the Austrian Legion, a paramilitary unit of the German Nazi *Sturmabteilung* (SA), along with 10,000 other Austrians. Despite its nationalistic leanings and earlier desires to join the German Reich after World War I (Gerwarth, 2016), Austria's new government prohibited any activity of the nationalistic party that same year. Sepp and Franz, now considered illegals and fugitives of their own country, crossed the border with the Legion into the German state of Bavaria, where they trained and were armed as SA men. In 1935, the brothers were separated as Franz received orders to join the newly established headquarters for the Austrian Legion, the *SA Hilfswerk Nordwest* in Bonn, Germany. Bonn, a city of about 100,000 at the time and located in the charming Rhine river valley, was nearly 550 miles away from Franz's home in Lower Austria. Shortly after arriving in Bonn, Franz met Änne, a local woman. It was nearly love at first sight and they married a year later. In the fall of 1937, their first-born son arrived.

After the annexation of Austria by Nazi Germany in 1938, both Franz and Sepp received orders to return to Vienna. This is where the brothers briefly reunited for what was to be the last time in their lives. Sepp and his wife, Stefanie, were assigned a luxurious apartment in a wealthy area of Vienna, one they couldn't have dreamed of affording when they lived in rural poverty. The previous tenant, a Jewish music storeowner, had been rounded up and sent to a labor camp with his family. Without as much as a qualm, Sepp and Stefanie moved in and enjoyed their lavish new digs.

Franz and Änne also moved into a new apartment. We don't know whether the previous residents met the same fate as the music storeowner's family, but it is highly likely. Franz was now an officer of the SA. He had reached what he always wanted: money, a lovely place to live, a beautiful young family, freedom, and authority. He was on top, and he hoped that those he disdained – including his father, the by-now widely detested Viennese aristocracy, and the foreign capitalistic democracies – would soon meet their fate. But it wasn't to be.

When World War II started in 1939, Franz left his wife and son for France, where he served the *Wehrmacht*'s infantry as an assistant on a *Flak*, an anti-aircraft cannon. The noise from the cannon and the images of burning, shot-down planes would haunt him for the rest of his life. Two years later, Franz joined the infamous *Afrika Korps*, a German expeditionary unit in support of Italian troops in northern Africa. Here, he saw action mostly as a motorcycle courier between Tobruk in Tunisia and El Alamein in Egypt. Photos he sent to Änne pictured him in the wide desert, usually posing by heavy weapons or machinery, shirtless, and just wearing a hat, dog tags, shorts, socks, and heavy boots. His skin, bronzed by the sun, was usually covered in dust. His six-foot-three, 190-pound frame appeared hardened from the war and cut from the wind and sand of the northern Sahara desert.

In Africa, Franz served under General Field Marshal Erwin Rommel, the so-called *Wüstenfuchs* (Desert Fox) – whom Franz adored – until the surrender of the *Korps* to U.S. forces in May of 1943. Franz was now a prisoner of war (POW) of the Americans. After his capture, Franz spent 10 days on a freighter to New York City with hundreds of other German POWs, many of whom did not survive the journey. He wrote to Änne about seeing the Statue of Liberty, getting de-loused by American officers, and spending three nights and three days on a cargo train to McLean, a tiny town in the Texas Panhandle, to be interned in the local POW camp with 3,000 other Germans.

Franz's time in the camp was spent working, on farms or roads, and when the officers learned he was a waiter and could cook, he was allowed to work in the kitchen. He wrote home:

> Darling, I prepared steak for the guards today. Because they knew I didn't speak English, they ordered me by making hand gestures. Two fingers, palm down, two fingers, palm up. That meant, I think, they wanted this thick steak on the grill for two minutes on each side. I smiled and thought, "if that's how you want to eat it, I'll cook it that way." Änne, when they cut into it, the blood must have been oozing out everywhere but I'm sure they loved it.

Franz was treated well by his captors. He never reported violent behavior by the guards, or any execution of German prisoners.

After the surrender of Nazi Germany in May of 1945, Franz was released from the Texas POW camp and slowly made his way back home to Austria. When he got there, he was sentenced to one year in prison for joining the illegal SA and fleeing Austria nearly 10 years prior. He also learned that both of his older brothers died in the war; he and his father were the only remaining Höbarth men. Franz was also stripped of his Austrian citizenship for joining the Austrian SA, a fate met by most of the Austrian Legionnaires (Kastner, 2002). In the early summer of 1946, he finally rejoined Änne and his now nine-year-old son. Slightly more than 10 months later, my mother was born.

Yes. Franz Höbarth was my grandfather. My beloved *Opa*.

My grandfather, the SA man.

My grandfather, the Nazi. Part of the worst mob of villains, perhaps ever, in the history of humankind, and, for sure, in modern European history.

Why?

I don't remember when I first found out, but I was likely in my 20s, perhaps even after my grandfather had passed away in 1997. I also learned very late about his incarceration after returning home. It wasn't something my grandparents, parents, or anyone else in the family wanted to talk about. We clearly weren't proud of our family's past, tried to avoid, forget. Taboo.

When I knew him, my grandfather was helpful, generous, caring, affectionate, even docile. He couldn't have hurt a fly, never raising his voice at my cousins or me. He would've done anything for his family, and he often did when any of us were in a bind. He was the kind of benevolent patriarch his father, my great grandfather, should have been. For the rest of his professional life, Franz lived in Bonn with his family, less than a mile away from where I grew up. He was a grocery truck driver, covering long distances, schlepping heavy loads, and providing for his family. My grandmother never worked outside their home, taking care of the four children. My grandparents spent a lot of time with me, picking me up from school or babysitting me at their house. I remember going on walks with my grandfather, playing in the park, skimming rocks on our beloved Rhine river, and playing cards with him for hours. I loved him so much.

Still I struggled. How could he? Did he kill anyone? Was he a major decision-maker or *just* a soldier? Was he a *Mitläufer*, a hanger-on or mere participant, swimming with the stream of thousands of fed-up Austrian men who had nothing and wanted so much more? Was he an inactive spectator when he learned of the atrocities of the Holocaust? Did he speak up, at least in his own mind or to his family? (Speaking up against the Holocaust while he was a soldier would have sealed his execution by guillotine, hanging, or firing squad for high treason.) Did he confront people later in life who made pejorative remarks about Jews, like his sister Mitzi did so fervently even in old age? Did he ever regret joining the SA in the early 1930s? Did he consider that he had a certain responsibility for how things turned out in his life and the lives of others? Would he have done anything differently? One thing I do remember clearly: in my presence, my grandfather never uttered a word of disrespect or oppression toward anyone else. My aunt and uncles also were raised without the hate with which Franz grew up. Despite all the disdain for others so prevalent during my grandfather's upbringing, he did not teach his children or grandchildren to hate the way he had done.

I'm sure the decisions Franz made as a young man in the 1920s and '30s he made for a variety of reasons. Primary among them was a dangerous mix of conviction, groupthink, poverty, despair, hopelessness, fervor, and even hate. I will never know the answers to my questions, but they're important in how I live with, engage, and accept my own history as a German, as the grandson of a former SA man and a Nazi. They're also essential to my identities as a father, a partner, and a man. After all, the identities that mattered in my grandfather's life still matter today: they are the identities used by today's seemingly ubiquitous American and European populists to divide, scare, and marginalize people, much like in Germany and Austria in the 1930s and '40s.

I've long forgiven my *Opa*, if there ever was anything to forgive. Our oldest daughter's middle name is Franziska in honor of his memory, and my uncle and aunt (Franz's two remaining children), my cousins, and I love to swap stories about Franz and Änne Höbarth whenever we get together. We still love them even though they have been gone for about 20 years.

Individuals or Members of a Collective Male Culture?

Why am I opening this book with a story about my grandfather? Because his story, despite beginning more than 100 years ago, is connected to my own search for my individual, cultural, and collective identities, as well as my awareness of systemic injustices to people all over. And my journey relates to how other straight white men in America (and perhaps Europe) conceive of themselves and of those with whom they interact. To begin, Franz reminds me of myself, but also of other white men in their early to mid-20s. We are impressionable. Some of us engage in critical thinking far too infrequently about the consequences of our own attitudes and behaviors, or the pain we may cause others with what we say and how we say it. We're optimistic, too, and often carelessly believe that hard work will get us somewhere – anywhere, in fact. Many of us haven't learned to speak out against the oppression of others, nor how to advocate for those who face daily stereotyping, prejudice, or hate. Many of us straight white guys often stand idly by when others are derided because we're not sure how to act. Or worse, we may tell racist, sexist, or homophobic jokes ourselves. Many of us struggle to confront friends and family for their attitudes and behaviors around race, gender, sexual orientation, or any other minoritized identity. And finally, we find ourselves unable to stem the tide of the time we don't see coming until it's too late, such as when ruthless leaders threaten our democracy. I hope most of you, regardless of how you conceive of yourself, can identify with some of these points. Franz must have felt some of this in his younger days; I know I did and still struggle at near 50 years of age.

My second point for opening this book with a story about my grandfather centers on the interrogation of our collective social and cultural identities as men. As a German citizen, and as the grandson of a former SA man, I was born into a nation and culture that, only a few generations ago, was single-handedly responsible for leaving most of Europe in ruins, for ruling its citizens with fear and hatred of others, and for murdering millions of innocent Jewish men, women, and children. The fact that I wasn't alive in the 1930s and '40s, or that I didn't participate in this inconceivable atrocity, doesn't mean that I can forget that it took place at the hands of my cultural ancestors. Germany's history doesn't make me a Nazi, but it makes me part of a culture that needs to critically explore its past and accept responsibility to educate self and others. As the opening quote by Max Mannheimer, Czech author and survivor of the Holocaust, suggests, we today are not responsible for what happened during the Third Reich, but we are responsible to never let it happen again. And we can certainly debate whether we're meeting that call these days, in the United States or in Europe.

When I became an American citizen in 2014, I accepted the credo that all men [women, and individuals of non-binary gender expression or identity] were created equal and that all Americans have the right to life, liberty, and the pursuit of happiness. For most Americans, these aren't empty words and they spell out attitudes and behaviors to live by. Do we, though, live by these mottos all the time and make sure we support others who can't live by them? Just like I can't dissociate with my German heritage, I also can't neglect being part of a country that committed, and continues to commit, many atrocities against minoritized citizens at the hands of European Americans. I won't compare these brutalities to the Holocaust; however, simply knowing of the present-day effects of slavery, Native-American genocide, Japanese internment camps, Jim Crow laws, a ban on Muslims, and separating children from families or holding them in metal cages at our southern borders, is a social, moral, and ethical obligation for all white Americans.

"But wait," some may say, "first you compare American white men to Austrian Nazis, and now you're saying we've had a role in the most shameful events in U.S. history." Consider this exchange from one of the focus groups at Southern State University on this topic.

> MARK: My great-grandparents came over here from Italy, my family never owned slaves, that type of thing. And that's not to say that that didn't happen.
>
> JUDE: I'm sorry for slavery. But yes, your family wasn't even in America at that time, even if you're an immigrant.
>
> MARK: What I meant to say is when you try to shame somebody, that doesn't encourage progress because you're always going to feel like you're doing something wrong.

You might add, "I am a straight white man, but I'm not racist, sexist, or homophobic. I have also never verbally or physically assaulted anyone based on their difference in skin color, gender, sexual orientation, religion, class, ability, age, or national origin." And I would agree. Most straight white men don't actively oppress fellow citizens, and earlier generations, not we, created America's social system. But we're a part of this system, we live in it, and by our actions and inactions toward social issues we perpetuate it. Feagin (2013, p. 94) has coined this behavior of whites as white virtuousness: "whites continue to view themselves individually and as a group as relatively good and virtuous." When racial matters surface in society or in their personal or familial environment, whites tend to insist on this general virtuousness and emphasize their position in life is not due to the oppression of others, but because they've worked hard and have earned what's theirs.

Even if we don't perceive ourselves as racist, sexist, or homophobic, we can't gloss over that systemic oppression exists, and that it systemically targets and hurts our fellow citizens, neighbors, friends, and family in this country. And systemic oppression hurts straight white guys as well; we just typically don't spend much time thinking about how and how much. The point is to recognize, engage, explain, and find ways to disrupt the perpetuation of this hegemonic, racialized, patriarchal and heteronormative culture. There are many whites in the United States who believe they're good, anti-racist citizens but who do little to interrogate their own or our society's actions, attitudes, and behaviors. Those who make the claim to be good whites without self-critique or self-interrogation may, in fact, help to perpetuate systemic oppression (Applebaum, 2005, 2010).

Forgive the oversimplified analogy, but Tim Wise (2003), American anti-racism activist and writer, relates being part of this social system to a pot of gumbo (stew with fresh seafood) left to sit out on a stove for days. When he was in college, one of Wise's roommates made a big pot of gumbo and offered some to his roommates. Wise didn't want any that night but asked his roommate to save him some and put the rest in the fridge. The next morning none of it had been saved for Wise and the pot was still sitting on the stove, gumbo still inside. He thought he should clean up the gumbo, but since he didn't cook it, he felt he didn't need to and left the house for work. When he came home that night the pot was still sitting on the stove, having turned into a rotting mess. After a brief conversation with his roommates, none of them felt it was their responsibility to throw the gumbo out. The gumbo sat on the stove for 36 hours before Wise decided to clean it up, now mad at himself and his roommates that no one had accepted the responsibility earlier. Certainly cleaning up a pot of gumbo is much easier than changing hearts and minds and eradicating the effects of centuries' worth of oppression. However, the key for straight white men is to see ourselves as part of that culture, not apart from it. And we need to take an active role in cleaning it up and to putting it away. For good.

Straight White Men's Solidarity

The first time I heard the word solidarity (for me it was the German *Solidarität*) was as a kid in the early 1980s. Lech Wałęsa, a Polish labor union leader and later President of Poland, founded the independent labor union *Solidarność*. I remember seeing him on TV speaking to thousands of people in Poland but I didn't understand the importance of the cause he led. Poland, as a Warsaw Pact country, was under communist rule, and creating an independent union was nearly unthinkable. *Solidarność* advanced the rights of Polish workers, and by 1981 some 10 million Poles had joined the union. This led to the Polish government banning *Solidarność* and imposing martial law. However, the union continued to gather influence, forcing politicians to negotiate with Wałęsa and other leaders, eventually leading to the first democratic elections in Poland after the dissolution of the Eastern Bloc.

The Polish people, much like inhabitants of other countries today, yearned for justice they didn't receive in a communist regime. Low wages, lack of freedom, restricted travel only to other Eastern Bloc countries, and no democratic elections included some of the hardships for people behind the Iron Curtain. The *Solidarność* movement was a way to fight that regime, to challenge inequalities, and to bring about social justice for all. Current American social movements like Black Lives Matter or #MeToo have similar goals of creating awareness, disrupting oppression, and advocating for equity for minoritized people who live under an oppressive regime.

Social justice can be defined as the opportunity and right of all citizens in a society to equitable access to and distribution of resources, including social, political, and economic. Achieving a socially just society means all people get to live dignified, safe, and self-determined lives (Goodman, 2011). Using this definition, ask yourself if the United States is a nation and society in which these tenets exist for all inhabitants. Straight white men typically don't struggle to realize social justice for themselves or their families based on their identities of race, gender, and sexual orientation, or at least not as much as members of minoritized communities. Realizing that others may have a much harder time to gain equitable treatment, straight white men must engage in building solidarity and advocating for social justice for all people.

Building solidarity for others in straight white college men is not a new concept. Quite a sizable body of research exists on the development of individuals as *social justice allies* (Boutte & Jackson, 2014; Broido, 2000; Davis & Wagner, 2005; Cabrera, 2012; Edwards, 2006; Fabiano, Perkins, Berkowitz, Linkenbach, & Stark, 2003; Linder & Johnson, 2015; Nash, 2010; Patton & Bondi, 2015; Reason, Broido, & Davis, 2005). Despite the many publications on this topic, much of what we know about men as social justice allies is somewhat dated. Also a bit dated is the term *ally* in the context of social justice advocacy of individuals with primarily privileged identities. The word ally tends to put the focus of action on the privileged person rather than the one who is minoritized. Straight white guys aren't allies simply because we say we are, or because we've participated in some training to document our ally identity. Allies are individuals who are identified by less-dominant social groups as longstanding supporters and advocates. There is also the potential for allies to behave in paternalistic ways toward members of communities of color or genders (Spanierman & Smith, 2017), especially when the allying behavior is short lived, such as during mission trips, Habitat for Humanity builds, volunteering at a women's shelter, or working in a soup kitchen once a year. The image of the straight white man riding in on a white horse comes to mind, trying to save poor people from their plight with his zealous humanitarian efforts. What we often don't realize is that when he rides away again, not much if anything has changed for the people he tried to save. Paulo Freire (1970), the famous Brazilian philosopher, educator, and author, called this behavior "false charity" and asserted allies must "shift their emphasis from saving people to transforming systems" (p. 45).

For the rest of this book I would, thus, like to focus on the word *solidarity* to signify straight white college men who are supporters, comrades, or accomplices in the fight for social justice. Solidarity, to me, connotes *with* not *for*, and places the focus on the task of disrupting or dismantling the system of oppression, not on the person helping or advocating. I expand here on Spanierman and Smith's (2017) definition of *white allies* to provide a suitable definition of someone who acts in solidarity with others. People who do so articulate an understanding of institutional oppression and their own social privileges, engage in a continuous process of self-reflection about how they may oppress or disadvantage others, express responsibility and commitment to use their privileges to advance equity, commit to disruptive actions to end systemic oppression, work collaboratively with members of minoritized communities, and challenge the resistance from other privileged individuals.

Methods and Data Sources

The foundation of this book is the Straight White College Men Project, a multi-institutional research study exploring the experiences and stories of 92 heterosexual white male undergraduate college students at 10 institutions around the country. The study started with a simple question many college educators have been asking for a long time: "Where are all, or most of, the straight white college men?" In this case, *where* refers to college courses, co-curricular programs, discussions, or other campus-based initiatives that focus on diversity, social justice, multiculturalism, equity, equality, power, privilege, or oppression from which many white men in college are typically absent (National Survey of Student Engagement, 2014).

Renowned sociologist Patricia Hill Collins (2008, p. 68) suggested using the "strategy of *dynamic centering*, a stance of foregrounding selected themes and ideas while moving others to the background." In the present study, I centered the categories of race, gender, and sexual orientation to limit the scope of the research, and to focus on the identities from which most often stem privilege (race, gender, and sexual orientation) and oppression (racism, sexism, and homophobia) in a U.S. context. The intent of the project was to focus on the ways in which participants think about, avoid, or engage in diversity or social justice initiatives on college campuses, the perceived benefits and drawbacks to their own salient identities on their campus, and their conceptualizations for their own responsibility in advocating for positive social change.

From 2013 to 2016, colleagues and I collected the data for this book during in-depth focus groups with straight white men. Groups ranged from three to eight participants, each group was moderated by a trained researcher, each was digitally recorded and verbatim transcribed, and each lasted between 60 and 90 minutes. We conducted a total of 21 focus groups with heterosexual white men on the 10 campuses. Participating in the focus group earned the students $10 in cash, or, at one research site, extra credit for an undergraduate course. Before each focus group began, participants completed both an informed consent form and a brief survey assessing demographic and campus engagement data.

Appendix A describes the 10 research sites (all four-year colleges and universities), the institution's affiliation, undergraduate enrollment, and percentages of white and male students. I assigned each institution a pseudonym to maintain confidentiality of the participants. The two largest institutions were Mountain State University, a public institution in the West enrolling 30,000 undergraduates, and Midwest University, a public university with 36,000 undergraduates. The smallest institutions, all in the Midwest and all private, were Danbury College (1,700 undergraduates), Callahan College

(2,000), Mason College (2,000), and Lucas College (2,500). All institutions were predominantly white and all but one (Danbury College) enrolled predominantly female-identified students. The highest percentage of white undergraduate students was present at Riverside State University (89%) and Lakeside State University (85%), both of them midsized public universities in the Upper Midwest. The lowest percentage of white students (50%) was enrolled at St. Margaret University, a private university on the West Coast. The only southern research site was Southern State University, with 15,000 undergraduates, 70% of whom were white.

Appendix B displays the mean age of the participants (21.3) and the overall type of engagement in campus life of the participants. I assessed engagement data to paint a picture of student involvement in educationally purposeful activities generally considered to engender outcomes of college student success. *Contact* describes how many hours per week participants estimated they spent in close personal interaction (longer than 30 minutes) with someone different than them (e.g., race, sexual orientation, ethnicity, religion). The average number of hours for the participants amounted to slightly more than five and a half per week. *Intramurals* (62%) and *Arts* (12%) capture the percentage of participants engaged in athletic or artistic activities at the time of data collection. *Student Organizations* reports the average amount of registered student organizations participants were part of; slightly more than one on average for the participants. *Office Hours* captures the average of how many faculty office hours over the past year the students had visited: slightly more than seven. *Diversity Programs* reports the average number of out-of-class activities related to diversity or social justice (1.7) the students participated during the academic year we collected data from them. *Diversity Electives* captures the average number of elective diversity courses in which the students enrolled beyond required diversity courses over their careers at their respective institution; on average, our participants enrolled in slightly more than one half of a diversity elective over the college career.

Data analysis of focus groups followed a systematic and sequential process (Krueger & Casey, 2000). A graduate student research team member and I conducted the majority of the data analysis. After each focus group was transcribed, we engaged in open coding using Dedoose, a cloud-based qualitative data analysis software. The round of open coding aimed to discover expected and unexpected participant perceptions, experiences, encounters, interactions, or other participant thoughts about diversity and social justice on their campus or in their communities. After the open coding process was complete, axial coding involved categorizing the data into larger themes (Creswell, 2014). The themes that emerged from the data provided the structure for the majority of the chapters of this book. The larger dataset emerging from the study featured more than 1,000 individual participant quotes or statements, often captured not in singular comments but in conversations between focus-group participants. I use these excerpts in this book to help the chapters come to life and to have you as the reader reflect on the perspectives of the participants. Whenever possible,

I will identify the specific participant by using a pseudonym and mention his institution. In some cases we couldn't identify exactly who made a specific comment or statement, but the quote was too important to leave out. So whenever you read a name (participant or otherwise), know that I changed them to protect the participants' confidentiality.

Why Study Straight White College Men?

"Isn't everything already about straight white men?" "Aren't you re-centering diversity and social justice around those in society who have key privileges, the loudest voice, and the most say?" These and other important questions I've faced since beginning the study that serves as the foundation for this book. The criticisms not only emanate from diversity or social justice educators, but also from those who fear a book on white college men is just another liberal attack on all whites in the United States. The androcentric notion that everything is already about white male collegians (Brooks & Elder, 2015) is not too farfetched, but it does not acknowledge that early higher education research studied white male participants *as* college students, not as white men who had a gender, a race, and other key identities (Davis & Laker, 2004).

Answering the question why I study straight white men in terms of diversity and social justice is relatively simple. First, I identify as a straight white man who is committed to fostering diversity and social justice. Second, not asking straight white men to engage in topics like racism, sexism, or homophobia – problems our cultural ancestors created and from which we continue to both benefit and suffer – leaves us without explanations about what we should do to help advance social justice. As Allan Johnson (2000, p. 10), American author and sociologist, notes in his book *Privilege, Power, and Difference*, "the simple truth is that [social injustice] can't be solved unless people who are heterosexual or male … or white or economically comfortable feel obligated to make the problem of privilege their problem and to do something about it."

It's not only necessary to study men who identify across gender, race, and sexual orientation saliency, but also how they benefit from unearned privilege based on those identities. This work should be done increasingly by white male researchers, teachers, and authors who must do their own part to disrupt white supremacy, patriarchy, and heteronormativity (Svoboda & Vianden, 2015). However, simply focusing on men's privilege alone would overlook how they feel about their own lived experiences, which don't always appear privileged. To this point, consider the following conversation with Tim during his focus group at Riverside State University.

> TIM: To me, sometimes it feels like white males, it's just assumed you have a family that supports you, and financial support, and stuff like that. And in my situation, I'm an independent student, and I'm

trying to go to school on my own cause of family problems. So, I can relate to what [students of color] talk about. But they still look at me like, "You're a white male, you don't have any problems kind of a thing." And I'm like, "Oh yeah, I do have problems. I know what you're going through."

JÖRG: And when you say that does that change the argument? Or do you not feel like saying that?

TIM: Yeah, I've just come to the point if they get upset with me because I bring that up, I go straight to the point. I'm like, "Yeah, my family's crap," and I explain to them really shortly. And they're like, "Oh, I'm sorry." And then we can talk about it and we, they, we kind of go back and forth and discuss if they want.

Tim's experience took place during a discussion in one of this classes, and his comments are important as they exemplify a host of key issues. First, straight white college men have identities that may be marginalized or overlooked; in Tim's case likely socioeconomic status or social class. These identities intersect with their primarily privileged identities depending on context and salience. Second, Tim's encounter confirms the fact, despite of what many may think, that not all straight white college men have easy lives. Third, his experience hints at the problem of equating or leveling class or socioeconomic minoritization with oppression because of race, gender, or sexual orientation. In Tim's case, some of his peers may feel he overstated his understanding of their concerns of racism or sexism because he has experienced a tough family life. White college men should engage in the conversation about potentially marginalized identities and also know that oppression isn't all alike in America. As Feagin (2013) and Bonilla-Silva (2014) make clear, discrimination based on race trumps all other forms of oppression in the United States, and we as white men should be keenly aware of that fact. However, and this is the final point Tim's account makes, white college men's conceivably marginalized identities may lay the foundation for conversations and identification with peers whose families have been oppressed for decades, perhaps centuries.

Straight White Male Vianden – My Position in Writing this Book

Qualitative researchers typically include a positionality or reflexivity statement in their work to show why they're interested or qualified to conduct the research, to announce their potential biases toward the topic, and to show how their personal and subjective experiences may affect their inquiry. There's no true objectivity in qualitative research and I appreciate the co-construction of knowledge with the research participants. As you read about my identities, experiences, and subjectivities, I invite you to reflect on your own story and your own encounters with the topics I discuss.

My Identities

I'm the proud father of three daughters who are the light of my life. For more than 20 years I've also been the partner to a wonderful woman who loves and gets me. I'm the son of a supportive father and grandfather and of a late mother and grandmother whose devotion to her family was unparalleled. I identify as a German-American citizen who immigrated from Europe 25 years ago. My mother tongue, national origin, cultural identity, and home country remain key staples in my life. My home town is Bonn, the former capital of West Germany, and I grew up with friends whose parents were from all over the world, including Turkey, Cyprus, Bolivia, Egypt, Ghana, Malawi, the Philippines, Malaysia, and the former Yugoslavia. In middle and high school, my best friend was originally from Iran, and I spent countless hours at his house, eating with his family and listening to Farsi, the family's native language. Growing up among friends with different races and ethnicities who spoke different languages with their parents was normal to me. I'm also privileged to be a college professor who's interested in the study of men and masculinities. I strongly identify as a teacher and am fortunate to spend the majority of my time with graduate students eager to engage in the study of higher education.

My family and professional identities are most important to me. But as you notice, none of them are typically minoritized or oppressed. Well, perhaps national origin, but I bet these days few people in the United States have strong feelings against Germans. I'm also a straight, cis-gender, white, able-bodied, middle-class man. Although I was born Roman-Catholic, I don't practice religion, nor do I belong to a specific denomination or faith group. Again, no marginalized identities here, except for maybe agnostic, but I would never call myself oppressed by someone not approving of the fact that I don't believe in a supreme being.

The fact that my identities are not oppressed is evidence of my privileges, specifically bestowed by my race, gender, sexual orientation, class, and ability. I'm also aware that I present to others as a white, six-foot-four, 230-pound man with a beard. Once I mention my female partner and kids, most assume I may also be straight, although sexual orientation is an invisible identity. My perceived race, gender, and sexual orientation as well as my perceived size mean that individuals with minoritized identities may identify me as someone who isn't initially to be trusted. I accept that fact not as disapproval of me, but as a result of my privileged identities, and I work to find ways to gain others' trust.

I didn't choose to be born this way or into my German family, but I also can't give back the unearned benefits I receive because of how I identify. I also can't transfer my privileges to others, or check them at the door of an institution, a bank, a store, a housing agency, or while walking down the street or driving a car. It's taken me years of education and professional development to become more self-aware and conscious of my position, and I recognize I've got much to learn. This book is an attempt to relay this story, to connect with others who may have similar experiences, and to be in solidarity with those who are minoritized in any way in this society, only because their stories and identities widely differ from mine.

When I was in college – the age of my participants – I didn't really know what race, gender, or sexual orientation privilege was, let alone how to articulate it. I was an international student who didn't always fit into the American cultural fabric. I moved 5,000 miles away from my home and family, and I was always the most homesick of all of my friends. Even though I spoke English fluently, most people figured out quickly that I wasn't American. (If I had a dollar every time I've heard, "I thought I detected an accent," well, you know ...) And despite receiving some financial aid from my institution, my family and I barely had enough money to cover the costs for the two years I attended my alma mater (Germans don't put away money for college because students don't pay tuition in Germany). Were those minoritized identities of cultural origin, language, and social class? Likely not, but in the mid-1990s I was certain that not everything came easy to me in life. Knowing what I know now, plenty of my fellow students' lives were much harder than mine. And as we know, the past 25 years have not been kind to people in the middle or working classes in the United States, so today's students face far more difficulties than I did more than two decades ago.

My Stance in Got Solidarity?

While I respect the opinions of straight white male college students and their potential difficulties in articulating, identifying with, feeling apart from, or directly resisting diversity and social justice initiatives in college, communities, or in society, I want to be clear about my position in writing this book: it's not neutral. I side with the overwhelming evidence, some of which I'll present here, that any substantive engagement in college diversity and social justice initiatives by straight white men improves their academic, professional, and personal lives (Hurtado, 2005; Sax, 2008, 2009; Spanierman, Neville, Liao, Hammer, & Wang, 2008). And that men who have been presented with, who have critically thought about, and who have raised their consciousness about identity, power, privilege, and oppression will build capacity to help engender social change in their future.

Let me speak directly to my audience of straight white college men. It's clear to me that our society will continue to afford us more opportunities than many of our fellow citizens, based on our social standing. It's also clear to me that many of us, especially younger straight white men in college, may struggle to understand their privilege and power at this moment in time. But I hope you will deeply and critically interrogate how diversity and social justice affect you, and how, in turn, you may be able to advocate for it. This kind of learning doesn't only happen in college classrooms but in dorms, fraternities, on sports teams, in libraries, in cafeterias, at work on our off campus, with family or loved ones, or while serving your community.

Even though I believe you will, in time, answer the call to build solidarity with others and advocate for social justice, the choice is entirely yours. I can only appeal to your heart and mind to heed it. From my personal experience, the journey to a more equity-minded, conscious, and empathic self is challenging, but the outcome is well worth it. Your future partners, children, family, friends, colleagues, neighbors, and fellow citizens will appreciate you having done this self-work, as well as your commitment to join others in the disruption of a system that continues to divide all of us. Whatever choice you end up making, please know that many of your peers who face frequent subjugation won't ever have the luxury to choose whether they get to care about privilege or oppression.

The Purposes of this Book

Presenting evidence from extant research as well as data from my own study, I aim to achieve the following goals: First, I hope to challenge but also support straight white college men to develop solidarity with minoritized people, to identify with issues of social inequities, discrimination, and oppression, and to pledge their responsibility to positively affect social change now and in the future.

Second, I aim to provide specific strategies for college professors and administrators, coaches, counselors, advisors, and teachers to change the way they reach and teach today's straight white male students about diversity and social justice. Specifically, we white male educators have been most ineffective in this work and have passed the baton to our already-minoritized colleagues. We can no longer ask our colleagues who are women-identified, queer, or of color to do the labor it takes to educate white men on issues of diversity, inclusion, equity, or social justice. We as straight white male educators and students have to do this work ourselves.

Third, I hope this book can incite a bit of a revolution, at least a cognitive one. The more we continue to perceive that only the most conservative factions of society are responsible for racism, sexism, or homophobia, the more we fail to recognize that oppression is a collective game in which all of us are players. For centuries, rich white men have succeeded in fooling Americans that "the other" is the enemy and responsible for the plight of everyone else. This white elitist politicians' strategy of turning citizens against one another still works today and 21st century populists have added to the list of whom to look down upon: lately, specifically transgender or gender-queer people, Muslims, Central American and Middle Eastern refugees, and gays and lesbians.

White college men should interrogate why they should support ruthless politicians just because they share gender identity, race, or sexual orientation (Feagin & Ducey, 2017). Some white guys in college have begun, and others should follow suit, to figure out what it feels like to live in solidarity with and develop empathy for peers who are more like them from an income-bracket standpoint, who are closer in age, or who share similar interests (e.g., what typical college students like to do). This kind of horizontal, not vertical, identification will include a wide variety of peers, many of whom will identify with minoritized social groups.

Finally, the book attempts to provide a lens on how American masculinity may be changing. More and more men break the boundaries set by the traditional rough-and-tough conventions of toxic masculinity and explore caring and empathic ways of living with partners, children, friends, and colleagues. Critics consider this caring or advocating individual as an outgrowth of the feminization of American men. They fear young men are in danger of being driven by equitable and collective values rather than rugged individualistic ones. Not all, but some of the stories you read in this book are indicative of what my colleagues Shaun Harper and Frank Harris call productive masculinities (Harris & Harper, 2014). The book attempts to help advance the transcendence from toxic to positive ways of enacting masculinity: by straight white college men finding ways of living in solidarity with others and by advocating for social justice.

Critical Whiteness

The target audience for this book is college students and college educators. As you may have gleaned, the purpose of the book is primarily to help with the practice of teaching, mentoring, or advising rather than to develop new theories. Nevertheless, a book such as this can't be written without highlighting the theoretical frameworks that build its foundation and that inform its findings.

In conducting the Straight White College Men Project, the analysis and interpretation of data, and in writing this book, I lean on critical theories. When we talk about critical theories, we are reminded of the work of philosophers like Karl Marx or Paolo Freire who used critical theory to call attention to and advocate for the struggles of minoritized people (class for Marx; mostly class and race for Freire) in states or systems dominated by capitalists or other oppressors (cultural, colonial, imperialistic). *Praxis*, the ancient Greek word for action, activity, or practice, was used by Marx and Freire to explain the synthesis between theory and action. However, praxis not only includes regular or typical practice (like day-to-day practice in teaching or advising college students for example), but must be revolutionary and aim to change society. Critical theories encourage learners to reflect on privilege and oppression so they can develop practice that is well informed by the experiences of all members of society, but especially those who are most marginalized by it.

This book is grounded in the scholarship and theoretical underpinnings of critical whiteness. Critical whiteness studies interrogate and disrupt the invisible structures that create, develop, and perpetuate white supremacy and white privilege (Applebaum, 2005, 2010). Due to the vast majority of white teachers and administrators, whiteness is so normative in education that it has gone unnoticed, even though it negatively affects the access, success, and equity for students of color (Matias & Mackey, 2015). Critical whiteness acknowledges that racism is inexorably linked to white supremacy and that white people may be complicit in racism unless they learn how to recognize and challenge the social system that is built on privilege and that condones oppression. Whiteness studies call attention to how whites continue to benefit from racial privileges and how they have amassed economic and political power (Matias & Mackey, 2015). Scholars also suggest that whites perform whiteness by evading questions of power, by proclaiming colorblind attitudes, and by asserting that individual actions of *good whites* are enough to end systemic racism (Johnson, Rich, & Castelan Cargile, 2008). Considering oppression an individual choice is especially problematic in the critical whiteness paradigm: "When White people view only one level of whiteness, the individual level, they may feel powerless yet have greater relative power than racially minoritized people" (Bondi, 2012, p. 398). I hope we as straight white men know that racism, sexism, and homophobia are not individual human pathologies, but structural and systemic problems of a society.

Critical race theory, one of the earliest theoretical critiques of systemic oppression in the United States (Crenshaw, 1989), can teach white educators and students that they should work collaboratively with others, including other whites, to disrupt oppression. Critical race theory should also encourage us as whites to confront the attitudes and behaviors of other whites regarding race, and to help them understand their racial privileges in places where people of color may not be heard. My good colleague Amy Bergerson (2003) suggested, and I concur, that critical race theory can help whites center race in their daily personal lives, that whites should acknowledge we perpetuate racism, and that we should be skeptical of concepts like neutrality, colorblindness, and meritocracy. Our role as white people is not to speak for people of color, but to raise awareness and action of other whites in understanding how systemic racism hurts our family, friends, and colleagues of color (Bergerson, 2003).

Part of the underpinnings of critical whiteness include examining the role white racial development plays in straight white men. The most prominent early scholar in this area was American psychologist Janet Helms (1984, 1990), who theorized that individuals develop their racial identity in a stage-like fashion in the socially constructed identity of race. White racial identity development specifically helps explain how whites move from fairly low levels of awareness of self and others to a more nuanced understanding of what it means to be a racial being with a racial background (Helms, 1984). Helms's (1990) model featured a continuum of six distinct stages from unawareness of racial identity in whites, to first noticing a white identity, to idealizing white identity and disparaging black identity, to intellectualized recognition of self and others, to a sincere understanding of racism and of whiteness as a privileged identity, to finally internalizing a multicultural identity.

In this book, I argue that engaging in positive development of one's racial identity leads to benefits, including raised awareness and understanding of self and others, which foster the creation of straight white men's solidarity with others in the fight for social justice.

Chapters Overview

The chapters that follow report on the most consistent themes emerging from the focus groups of the Straight White College Men Project. I will also share news, statistics, and empirical and theoretical research findings from existing published sources to illuminate the current understanding of the topics I discuss in each chapter.

Chapter 2 features participant perceptions of their experiences with diversity growing up in their families, schools, or communities. Despite growing up in the late 1990s and early 2000s, the participants hail from mostly white neighborhoods and schools. Even in larger cities, separation by race, ethnicity, socioeconomic status, or sexual orientation was significant. To make sense of this separation, the chapter explores the concepts of residential and educational segregation in the U.S. in more detail. Chapter 2 also discusses theoretical frames, most notably white racial frame (Feagin, 2013) and white habitus (Bonilla-Silva, 2014), as well as gender intensification (Smiler & Heasley, 2016). These frames underscore the socialized and inculcated separation of the white participants from their peers. The second chapter enables student readers to reflect on their own journeys and upbringing, and holds implications for college educators to understand college student attitudes or behaviors prior to enrolling in college.

Chapter 3 features participants' definitions and perceptions of diversity, privilege, and oppression, as well as sharing their perceptions of benefits and drawbacks of being straight white men on campus. I provide literature and data on what learning white college men take away from engagement in diversity initiatives, such as personal growth, openness, and future professional benefits. Next, the chapter features data on the participants' actual experiences with diversity on their campus, specifically in classrooms and with professors. The chapter ends with a description of the circumstances under which straight white men would consider engaging in diversity on campus, and a discussion of men's intersecting identities, resistance, and fragility. In Chapter 3, I invite college student readers to reflect on their own most important identities on their campus, and all readers to critically think about how they conceive of themselves in this society and which of their identities are most salient to them. Educators may use this information to explain attitudes or behaviors they encounter in their own work, or to involve their students in similar questions and discussions.

Chapter 4 begins with definitions of and a discussion on privilege, power, and oppression in contemporary America. Data from the study describe participant perceptions of drawbacks and benefits of being straight white men on their campus. The chapter ends with data on how participants identify oppression on their campus. Student readers can use this chapter to engage their own self-awareness and how they learn about or are taught about why diversity and social justice matter, or why they don't. Educators may use the information presented here to begin answering the question about how to engage more students from privileged backgrounds in conversations about power, privilege, oppression, and social change at their own school or institution.

The main concept underlying Chapter 5 is that of the straight white college man as bystander. The chapter begins with a discussion on straight white men's behavior on college campuses and their influence on the overall campus climate. Literature on men's inappropriate joking and the nature of bystanderism follows, before I share data on participant reactions to issues of racism, sexism, and homophobia in their campus or community. The chapter closes with a discussion on why straight white men may be hesitant to confront oppression. Educators can use the data in Chapter 5 to work with college students, specifically those with privileged identities, to conceptualize dissent, disruption, and advocacy to explore power and privilege and to end oppression. Because the roles of family members loom large in these pages, parents and other family should read this chapter to explore how they interact and communicate with their students relative to their support for social change.

The final chapter begins with a discussion on straight white college men's critical consciousness and social empathy after which a discussion featuring what the participants perceived their responsibility for social justice advocacy to be. The remainder of Chapter 6 provides literature-, author-, and participant–recommended strategies about how to increase the relevance of the topics of diversity, inclusion, equity, and social justice for straight white college men. Although the chapter is mostly for college educators or teachers, it allows all readers to move from dialogue to action by taking the information provided to increase straight white male engagement in diversity and social justice initiatives.

A Caveat

Before we jump in to the rest of the book, I have to offer an important caveat. This is critical for the study, analysis, interpretation, and reporting of research on college student perceptions of diversity and social justice. As much as I've tried to bracket or even abandon my privileged perspective in researching and writing this book (as a good phenomenologist should), I'll always remain a straight, white, male college professor. So my analysis, interpretation, and reporting are conducted and composed from that lens. In the book, I will use examples from a wide variety of sources, including other books, journal articles, research reports, news stories, blogs, websites, campus programs or initiatives, videos, or TV shows. In the end, I can't include all possible research because there's simply too much out there about race, gender, sexual orientation, privilege, and oppression. Honestly, the scope of this book allows for a mere smattering of content on each major issue. When you read *Got Solidarity?*, remember it scratches the surface of the complexities of today's social issues involving the intersections of masculinity and social justice. However, I hope this scratch will contribute to the overall canon of literature on these issues and that it itches you, the reader, long enough to engage more or differently in the work of diversity, social justice, and democracy.

Whether you identify as someone who has long been present in the difficult work to advocate for social justice in your communities or whether you are still skeptical about how present-day ill-effects of oppression compromise the livelihoods, dreams, hopes, and successes of millions of Americans, I say: join me on the journey of this book. I promise you will learn something about the participants and, most importantly, I promise you will learn something about yourself.

Note

1 Crew cites from a 1927 Nazi election leaflet distributed to German farmers. The leaflet proclaimed the plight of German farmers was the result of a wider Jewish effort to usurp German wealth.

2 Growing up White and Male
Learning about Diversity in Communities, Schools, and Families

On my campus, the childcare center's playground is right next to the College of Business Administration and across from the library. All of my kids attended the childcare center, and whenever I approached the playground I was struck by feelings many of us have likely had when witnessing a similar scene. When young kids play with one another, they don't seem to discern who among their peers differs by race, ethnicity, gender, social class, or ability. For young kids, each playing companion is simply someone to spend time with, someone to interact with, someone to potentially call a friend. Yet, empirical research suggests kids are not colorblind, they can distinguish racial others, and they can hold biases that are not necessarily equivalent to those of their parents by age three (Aboud, 2008; Hirschfield, 2008; Winkler, 2009).

Exactly how and when do we begin to learn about race, gender, and sexual orientation, and how society treats individuals who have such minoritized identities? When do we learn that we should avoid some kids on the playground and play only with others? Beverly Tatum (2017), African-American psychologist and former President of Spelman College, discussed the phenomenon of intergroup contact in her award-winning book, *Why are all the Black Kids Sitting Together in the Cafeteria?* In elementary school, kids cross racial boundaries relatively freely during play or lunch; however, secondary school lunch rooms find groups seemingly segregated by race or ethnicity, including black students sitting by other black students, and whites by other whites. What was this like in your high school?

Tatum (2017) offered several explanations why this change takes place between childhood and adolescence. During this time, adolescents begin asking questions about identity, including racial and ethnic identity. Questions such as "Who am I?" or "Who am I racially or ethnically?" emerge during this stage of development. Once encounters across race begin for adolescents of color, they may choose to congregate around others whom they believe will understand, commiserate with, or befriend them because they're experiencing similar issues. For students of color, or gay, lesbian, or transgender students, these concerns may be overt oppression they begin to notice in their schools or communities during adolescence.

It's not that white adolescents don't go through a process of asking themselves who they are, but they typically don't experience their development racially. Society does not consider race as saliently for whites as it does for people of color (Tatum, 2017). That is, whites can pass as non-racial beings, a luxury rarely afforded to African, Latinx, or Native Americans. Whites also sit together with other whites in the cafeteria; it's just that we consider that normal behavior, while black kids sitting with one another in an otherwise mostly white cafeteria apparently sticks out as noteworthy (Strayhorn & Johnson, 2014).

The most intimate settings of where we receive, learn, and internalize early information about human difference are communities, neighborhoods, schools, and families (Frey, 2015). All larger social systems, they influence and inculcate our ways of thinking and feeling related to diversity and social justice (Wilkinson & Pickett, 2009). Growing up in an unequal social system affects our beliefs about social relations, human potential, and the ways in which we behave, now and in the future. For example, when we witness discrimination against people of color, individuals with diverse genders and sexualities, or Muslims in the United States, we may sense this is the way it has to be and accept the status quo without challenge.

In such a society, people gravitate toward considering their fellow citizens as primarily self-interested (Goodman, 2011). This has deleterious effects on how humans trust and care for one another; individuals' sense of community and the drive to act on behalf of the common good are seriously weakened. This fend-for-yourself mentality has promoted a system driven by selfishness, money, and the preoccupation with materialism, rather than focusing on morality, responsibility, and community (Goodman, 2011). And when we as humans have given in to the false mentality that there isn't enough for everyone, we become distrustful of others and fear that if others get more, someone must be taking it away from us. Rather than locating the responsibility with the capitalistic, free-market system of rugged individualism and its influencers, many of us blame those we already marginalize.

The Backdrop: A White Man's World

I begin this section with a powerful and perhaps controversial metaphor. Despite slavery officially ending on January 1, 1863, by President Lincoln issuing the Emancipation Proclamation, whites and African Americans remained judicially divided until the enactment of the Civil Rights Act on July 2, 1964. The Black Codes of the late 19th century, *de jure* racial segregation in the American South via Jim Crow laws, ghettoization in the American North of black migrants, and segregated schools are evidence that fly in the face of a socially just racial society. Today, many citizens (most of them white) claim we've arrived in a post-racial society, one hallmarked by the election and eight-year term of the nation's first African-American president, and one in which racism has been reduced to negligible levels

(Feagin, 2013). But have we really overcome all the vestiges of slavery in our 21st century society? Are black Americans and other people of color and whites really equal?

As you think about answering these questions, consider renowned sociologist Patricia Hill Collins's (1993) metaphor of the antebellum plantation to explain dimensions of institutional oppression in society, such as perpetuated by colleges and universities, schools, businesses, work places, and government agencies. On plantations, a clearly demarcated chain of command existed. In control was the white male patriarch, abetted by his affluent white wife who helped with the property and raised his children. Below followed the working-class whites who either were poor and without property, or who helped oversee the slave population (Irvin, 2016). Last came the property, the enslaved workers, who had no legal rights, no education, nor a say over their own personhood.

Is the image of the plantation during slavery still a suitable metaphor to describe today's institutional oppression? To be sure, today's oppression is not as harsh as during slavery, and aside from African Americans, other members of communities of color also face oppression in the United States. However, we can argue that the fundamental relationships between elite whites, working–class whites, and the vast majority of people of color as individual social groups in the United States endure as divided. These relationships built the foundation for the mechanisms of key American social institutions, who to this day are primarily controlled by white affluent men.

Since this book deals with higher education, Collins's (1993) continued analysis of the metaphor of the plantation as indicative of the interlocking form of oppression against race, gender, and class is important here. Consider her image of a predominantly white institution:

> [I]f you are from an American college or university, is your campus a modern plantation? Who controls your university's political economy? Are elite white men over represented among the upper administrators and trustees controlling your university's finances and policies? Are elite white men being joined by growing numbers of white women help-mates? What kinds of people are in your classrooms grooming the next generation who will occupy these and other decision-making positions? Who are the support staff that produce the mass mailings, order the supplies, fix the leaky pipes? Do African-Americans, Hispanics, or other people of color form the majority of the invisible workers who feed you, wash your dishes, and clean up your offices and libraries after everyone else has gone home?
>
> (Collins, 1993, pp. 31–2)

I don't know about you, but Collins's (1993) description fits my place of work well. At my very-white university of nearly 10,000 students (90% of whom are white), few people of color serve the institution in administrative leadership positions. Among the faculty of more than 600 individuals, people of color make up 14%. The most racial and ethnic diversity of any campus personnel is likely found among the custodial staff.

How does your campus do? I bet similarly, if you're attending a predominantly white institution and current national statistics emphasize these disparities. Among university presidents, between 2007 and 2013, 84% were men and 85% were white (Wallace, Budden, Juban, & Budden, 2014). African Americans comprised 10% of public and private college presidents, followed by only 1.7% of Latinx presidents, and less than half a percent of Native-American presidents (Wallace et al., 2014). Thus, university leadership is clearly not representative of the racial diversity of the overall college student population, which, in the fall of 2014, was 58% white, 17% Latinx, 14% African American, 7% Asian or Pacific Islander, and less than 1% of American Indian or Alaska Native (U.S. Department of Education, 2016a). Yet, higher education is not the only social institution in the United States controlled by white affluent men.

U.S. Demographics of Race, Gender, and Class

I want to briefly characterize the U.S. population across gender, racial, and class lines before continuing the discussion of white male dominance. According to the U.S. Census Bureau (2017a), as of July 1, 2016, slightly more than 323 million inhabitants resided in this country. Women-identified residents slightly outnumber men-identified residents by 50.8% to 49.2%. As of July 2015, whites accounted for 62% of the United States' populace, Latinx individuals for nearly 18%, African Americans for 13%, Asian Americans or Pacific Islanders for nearly 6%, and American Indians and Alaska Natives for slightly more than 1% (U.S. Census Bureau, 2017b).

Ostensibly, social class, or socioeconomic status, is a bit harder to measure. Rivera (2015) posited that even among scholars who research social class, disagreement endures about whether class should primarily include a measurement of income, wealth, education, occupation, or a combination of all of the above. Owing mainly to values of individualism and self-determination, class isn't something Americans like to discuss in public. Further, we tend to underestimate our income brackets and class standing in the United States, specifically people who are among the top ten or 5 percent of earners. Thus, it happens that Silicon Valley hi-tech workers raking in a seven-figure salary consider themselves underprivileged because, in their extravagant country clubs or swanky fitness establishments, they rub elbows with folks who bring home eight or nine figures each year (Rivera, 2015).

The middle class, America's bread-and-butter socioeconomic status for nearly 50 years, is shrinking (Pew Research Center, 2015): "in early 2015, 120.8 million adults were in middle-income households, compared with 121.3 million in lower- and upper-income households combined" (para. 1). While the middle class stagnates, the far edges of the income spectrum realize the most growth. Since 1971, the lowest income tier has grown from 16% to 20%, and during the same time span, the upper-income tier has more than doubled from sharing 4% to 9% of the combined U.S. income (Pew Research Center, 2015).

What is middle income though? These are the households that bring in between two-thirds and double of the American median incomes, adjusted by household size. Lower-income households fall below 67% of the median and upper-income households realize incomes more than double the median (Pew Research Center, 2015). In 2015, the U.S. median household income was $55,775, where household refers to the main householder and all people living in the household who are older than 15 (Posey, 2016). So, middle-income households range from $92,500 to $111,500 in 2015, while lower incomes registered at $39,300 or below. Upper incomes were those beyond $111,500. For a check on where you or your family fall in terms of socio-economic status, consult the various calculators online, such as by CNN Money, the Pew Research Center, or Fortune. Where do you fall? Did you accurately figure your place in the income bracket, or did you over- or underestimate yours or your family's spot?

In the pages that follow I will refer to a class of *elite* or affluent white men who disproportionately control American society. But exactly who or what constitutes the elite? Over the last decade, you've likely noticed movements such as Occupy Wall Street who suggested that the elite or upper class make up the top 1% of earners. According to Rivera (2015), given the difficulty in measuring class standing and the reticence of Americans to flaunt their income, the "99% conversation" has stuck, because we can all safely assume that the top 1% of any society constitutes some kind of elite, privileged, or super-rich group of citizens. These folks have enormous power in how they access scarce and valuable resources, have the most opportunities for social mobility, including excellent secondary and post-secondary education, and have attained undergraduate, graduate, or doctoral degrees from some of the top institutions in the country or internationally. Lastly, the elite includes individuals who have the fortune of serving the most desirable firms in the most prestigious positions of employment, including lawyer, engineer, scientist, military officer, or doctor.

The Connection between Race and Class

Before moving to the discourse on the disproportionate overrepresentation of white men in the United States, I want to leave you with an analogy that illustrates the connection between race and class. And it's a funny story, or at least some may find it funny.

I love watching stand-up comedy routines. One of my favorite American comedians is Chris Rock, an Emmy and Grammy-decorated African-American entertainer. Now in his early 50s, Rock rose to stardom as a 1990s cast member of *Saturday Night Live*, movie actor, HBO comedy-specials host, and a two-time host of the Academy Awards. In his 2008 HBO Special *Kill the Messenger*, Rock performed a comedy bit about his neighborhood in Alpine, New Jersey, a swanky New York City suburb across the Hudson River. Here's what he said:

> In my neighborhood, there are four black people. Hundreds of houses, four black people. Who are these black people? Well, there's me, Mary J. Blige, Jay-Z, and Eddie Murphy.... Do you know what the white man that lives next door to me does for a living? He's a fucking dentist. He ain't the best dentist in the world.... He's just a yank-your-tooth-out dentist. See, the black man gotta fly to get something the white man can walk to ... I had to make miracles happen to get that house. I had to host the Oscars to get that house.
>
> (Callner & Rock, 2008)

There are opinions about whether Rock's story is factually accurate, for example about who the black neighbors really are, and whether a white dentist really lived next door. But that's not the point of the story. The point is to emphasize the incredible wealth gap between whites and people of color in the United States, and the resulting inability for most members of American communities of color to ever crack the ceiling that would allow them to buy a house in super-rich ZIP codes. And we don't need comedians to show us this is the case. Recent empirical evidence makes clear that African Americans and Latinx individuals generally need higher incomes than whites to live in affluent neighborhoods (Reardon, Fox, & Townsend, 2015). In fact, the 400 richest Americans, 395 of whom are white, together own more wealth than the entire U.S. African-American population and one-third of the Latino population *combined* (Asante-Muhammed, Collins, Hoxie, & Nieves, 2016). That is, 400 privileged Americans together are richer than 60 million of their racially minoritized fellow citizens. Yes, I gasped too when I read that statistic for the first time. It's clear that income and racial background have been, are, and always will be inextricably linked in the United States. It's up to the millions of Americans in the middle and on the bottom of that spectrum to topple the elite's perched sanctuaries.

White Male Overrepresentation in U.S. Society

Since the founding of the United States of America, this country has been ruled by affluent white men, and being a true democracy with equitable representation of all citizens by government continues to be a gross American illusion. For starters, the U.S. Constitution was passed by 55 white men who represented the upper 2% of inhabitants in economic terms (Feagin, 2013), and ever since powerful white men have run and ruled this country in ways befitting their own interests. People of color or women had no influence in the writing or passing of the Constitution, and they continue to find their social groups trampled on by white men who tell the rest of Americans what to do and how to do it. In their recent book *Elite White Men Ruling: Who, What, When, Where, and How,* Joe Feagin and Kimberley Ducey (2017) coined the concept of the *elite-white-male-dominance system* to convey the over-arching and interlocking systems of sexist, classist, and racist oppression created by white male Americans.

Despite some recent social gains by minoritized groups, today's Americans grow up in a nation as controlled by affluent white men as was the case throughout history. These men disproportionately lead national, state, and community governments, pass legislation, rules, and policies that govern the lives of their constituents, and they control the country's biggest institutions and industries, including politics, banking, healthcare, transportation, the military, and education (Feagin, 2013; Feagin & Ducey, 2017; Feagin & O'Brien, 2003; Kimmel, 2013).

Rich white men reign the United States and its people from atop their sociopolitical and socioeconomic penthouses. In 2011, nearly 75% of all Fortune 500 CEOs were white men (and 100% of Wall Street firms), followed by about 13% of white women (Feagin & Ducey, 2017). In 2016, the percentage of white male CEOs of Fortune 500 companies was up to 95% (Feagin & Ducey, 2017). Despite a push to increase diversity in the business world, the number of people of color among Fortune 500 CEOs has been in sharp decline since 2000 (Zweigenhaft & Domhoff, 2014). In fact, in the post-civil rights era, white male overrepresentation in American managerial positions saw little change, with white men holding 57% of such jobs between 1966 and 2000 (Stainback & Tomaskovic-Devey, 2009).

White male overrepresentation extends into the political sphere as well. Eighty percent of the 114th U.S. Congress were white and 80% were male, while people of color accounted for 16% of the delegates (Manning, 2016). As a sharp but welcome change in direction, the 116th Congress is the most racially diverse in this country's history. Still, the seats gained by people of color and women in both the Senate and the House of Representatives provide a percentage that falls far short of their overall representation in society. And who represents us in our individual states? According to the National Conference of State Legislatures, women hold less than a quarter of all state legislative seats and black legislators are represented at below 8% (Kurtz, 2015). Among state legislators, 75% are white and male, as well as 84% of the mayors of the top 100 American cities (Feagin & Ducey, 2017).

As you may be aware, President Trump and his Republican pals have been trying to sabotage and repeal the Affordable Care Act (ACA), so far in vain. One amendment to the ACA in early 2017 supposed to help pass the repeal dealt with women's reproductive rights, specifically trying to get rid of or drastically reduce access to birth control, maternity care, and abortion (Forster, 2017). A corresponding photo went around the world in March of 2017 showing Vice President Pence speaking to white men in suits and ties sitting and standing around a large table, presumably in the White House.

Only about half of the room is in view and we can make out 25 individuals, but among them doesn't seem to be a single woman or person of color. I can't say for sure whether there was a woman or person of color outside of the purview of the photographer, but I doubt it. Rich white men, most of them likely straight, and most of them likely Christian, have long decided about and controlled the access to health care of millions of Americans, at least half of whom are women, and at least 30% of whom are people of color. *Representative government* in a democratic nation looks differently as far as I'm concerned.

A variety of attempts to circumvent *Roe* v. *Wade* (1973), the Supreme Court precedent that makes abortion legal, have been passed on state levels under certain parameters. Twenty-six states currently regulate the provisions of ultrasounds prior to scheduling a legal abortion, and four states require the provider of the abortion to show and describe the image of the fetus (Guttmacher Institute, 2016). In my own state of Wisconsin, recently ousted Governor Scott Walker, a conservative, affluent, straight, white, Christian male, signed into law Wisconsin Act 37 that, among other things, regulates the possible termination of a pregnancy. As a result, women are forced to either receive a transabdominal or transvaginal ultrasound and must endure a description of the fetus by the medical provider (Kroll, 2013). Ask yourself how you would feel if your daughter or partner, whose right it is to get an abortion, had to subject herself to the invasive procedure of an unnecessary ultrasound.

In an even more maniacal move, eight states have recently passed laws that outlaw abortion and include the potential of charging the mother with a crime. Alabama is the proverbial front runner in this movement, having voted into law the most restrictive abortion law in the country. The Alabama legislation only allows abortions if medical evidence suggests the child can't survive outside the womb; it does not allow for abortion in case of rape or incest (Iati & Paul, 2019). These laws are passed by a majority of male representatives in state legislatures. Women throughout the country are outraged, and men should be as well. In a real democracy, members of one social group should not have the power to continue to curb the freedoms of other citizens or single-handedly decide what the laws should be that govern all people (Feagin, 2013).

Who on the state level enforces these laws? According to a recent study at Vanderbilt University (Wolf, 2016), among state trial and appellate judges, 58% are white men, less than one-third are women, and only 8% are women of color. Among our nation's law enforcement, people of color make up only about 27% of local police forces, and only about 10% of all U.S. police officers are women (Bekiempis, 2015).

In K–12 education we notice similar white male overrepresentation, with one perhaps unsurprising exception. During the 2011–12 school year, whites made up 80% of public primary and secondary school principals and 87% of private schools. The difference compared to the other sectors of society is that women make up a slightly larger proportion of leaders, with 52% of principals at public and 55% at private elementary schools. However, white male public high school principals outpace white female colleagues nearly two-and-a-half to one (Bitterman, Goldring, Gray, & Broughman, 2013). During the same time, only 20% of all public-school principals were people of color (U.S. Department of Education, 2016b).

According to the U.S. Department of Education (2016a), the racial diversity of public-school students in the United States is vastly changing. In 2012, white students represented 51% of the public-school population, 24% were Latinx non-white students, 16% were African Americans, 5% Asian Americans or Pacific Islanders, and 1% were American Indian or Alaskan Natives. By 2025, the Department of Education (2016a) predicts, white students will only make up 46% of all public-school students, while Latinx students will realize the sharpest increase. Perhaps not a startling observation, our teaching force at public schools can't and likely won't match the racial diversity of the student population. In the 2011–12 school year, whites comprised 82% of public-school teachers, while 7% of teachers were black, and 8% Latinx individuals (U.S. Department of Education, 2016b).

We can summarize that the diverse population of individuals of the United States are governed, taught, led, and policed by a vast majority of affluent white people, including a preponderance of white men. This overrepresentation of white men in the United States leads to a hegemonic culture and a white supremacist mindset and perspective. It becomes the backdrop against which socialization in communities and schools takes place.

Learning and Interacting Across Difference in Communities and Schools

One of the most important settings in which Americans are socialized is their community. This is where people grow up, make friends, shop, and where they attend school. The diverse make-up of our neighborhoods helps provide or prevents opportunities for interactions across difference.

Residential and School Segregation

For those of us born or raised in the latter half of the 20th century, the term segregation invokes images of Jim Crow, the doctrine of *separate but equal* (upheld by the Dred Scott decision by the U.S. Supreme Court in 1896), strong separation between white and black people, and black ghettoization in the northern United States (Anderson, 2016). We know that this separation was involuntary for black people who had few resources, as well as little access to employment, education, and public assistance for at least the first 70 years of the 20th century (Frey, 2015).

The Great Migration of black citizens to the industrialized northern U.S. cities from the agrarian South took place in two waves. The first wave occurred between 1910 and 1930, and cities like Chicago, New York, Philadelphia, Detroit, or Cleveland became sought-after destinations for blacks looking for opportunity they didn't have in the South. This migration resulted in the rise of northern black ghettos, because black residents were only allowed to live in certain neighborhoods due to northern whites opposing integration (Frey, 2015). This white obstruction took the form of violence and protests to prevent black families from moving into white parts of town. Black residents were also subject to zoning laws, homeowner association regulations, and city planners who vehemently objected the integration of their all-white enclaves. Many city officials used a special covenant arbitrarily declaring that specific neighborhoods or properties couldn't be rented to or occupied by black citizens, say, for a period of 99 years (Frey, 2015). Such policies were sanctioned by the Supreme Court in the mid-1920s, and not overturned until 1948.

Remember the term *white flight* to northern suburbs from your high school or college history classes? This took place when the population expansion of blacks in cities could no longer be restricted to ghettos because of continued migration and population growth. Less of a voluntary move by white residents and more of an orchestrated strategy by real-estate agents, white flight was abetted by "blockbusting" (Frey, 2015). Real-estate agents would use the first black family on a given block to chase whites out of the neighborhood, to slowly change the neighborhood from white to black, and to reap high profits from black families who moved in. Northern white opinions on black citizens integrating their cities were anything but favorable: "a national survey in 1942 showed that 84 percent of whites agreed that 'there should be separate sections in towns and cities for Negroes to live in'" (Frey, 2015, p. 170).

The second wave of black northern migration followed the post-World War II period, but the dispositions of whites to accept black neighbors hadn't changed. Fraudulent zoning, selling, and rental policies were the law of the land to continue to keep African Americans away from white neighborhoods. The practice of "redlining" boomed in American cities in the 1960s, entailing banks that refused to lend mortgages or to lease apartments to residents (mostly blacks) of a specific area (mostly inner-city neighborhoods) demarcated by a line drawn on a map. The availability of post-war loans, given almost exclusively to whites, ensured a suburban housing boom to which blacks had no access. During the 1960s and '70s, black residents were often relocated to large, urban, and government-aided housing complexes, also frequently referred to as housing projects, or simply "projects." The separation of African American or other citizens of color by whites has been commonly referred to as segregation.

Demographers measure segregation by the *dissimilarity index*, which "ranges from a value of 0 (complete integration), where blacks and whites are distributed similarly across neighborhoods, to 100 (complete segregation), where blacks and whites live in completely different neighborhoods" (Frey, 2015, p. 169). In other words, the value depicts the percentage of people of color who would have to move from theirs to another neighborhood to become more integrated with whites. Indexes of 60 (i.e., 60% of people of color would have to move to become fully integrated) or above are considered high values of segregation, while indexes of 30 or below are considered low. In the 1970s, when most of the parents of today's college students were in secondary school, the average American black–white dissimilarity index, or segregation level, was well above 70. According to Frey (2015), however, the index was much higher in large U.S. metropolitan areas like Chicago, Detroit, or Los Angeles, that pushed levels at or above 90. During the same time, southern cities like Atlanta, Dallas, or Miami showed indexes of greater than 80 (Frey, 2015).

Today's college students likely think differently about the term segregation, although, for most of their young lives, segregation of whites and people of color has continued to divide and isolate Americans (Feagin, 2013; Frey, 2015). In most large metropolitan areas, the dissimilarity indexes have witnessed a steady decline since 1970. However, in 2010, segregation remained between indices of 68 and 78 in cities like Los Angeles, Philadelphia, St. Louis, Cleveland, Detroit, Chicago, and New York. The most segregated city, it shames me to say, is Milwaukee, the largest metropolitan area of Wisconsin, my current state of residence. In Milwaukee, 82% of African-American residents would have to move from their current neighborhood to fully integrate with whites (Frey, 2015).

But segregation of African Americans isn't the only type of separation of people of color from whites. Average Asian and Latinx segregation levels are considerably more than half that of black segregation rates (between 38 and 44 from 1990 to 2010 in the 100 largest metro areas), but they also fluctuate much more than black segregation. Compared to black segregation levels dropping steadily over the past four decades, segregation rates of Asians and Latinx citizens have either grown or held steady (Frey, 2015). Reasons for this is continued immigration from residents with Asian and Hispanic cultural or national heritage, self-selection into specific neighborhoods or communities because of common language use, and lower upward mobility due to schooling and language deficits (Frey, 2015).

The American neighborhood of the future will likely be more racially diverse. We also know that nearly all future population growth will come from non-white Americans, and America is gearing up for a majority–minority society by the middle of the 21st century (Lichter, 2013). The more recent movement of members of communities of color nearly everywhere, and black migration southward and westward, has led to more dispersion of residents and decreases in segregation (Iceland, Sharp, & Timberlake, 2013).

Despite some easing of the color lines, by 2010, a year during which most of my research participants would have been in high school, the average white resident lived in neighborhoods with far less racial diversity than residents of color from any group (Iceland & Sharp, 2013). We also find that whites, more than people of color, prefer to live in neighborhoods that include fewer blacks or Latinx individuals (Lewis, Emerson, & Klineberg, 2011), so voluntary or willful separation of whites into nearly exclusive white neighborhoods may continue to persist.

Although residential segregation endures, whites live in more integrated neighborhoods today than they did 20 or 30 years ago (Frey, 2015). The average person of color lives in neighborhoods that are nearly one-third white, and, in the case of Asian Americans, one-half white (Frey, 2015). According to Frey, the trend to more integrated living continues, which makes us look confidently into a future in which segregation will likely diminish. This is perhaps one of the reasons scholars like Frey (2015) are optimistic that demography may be the panacea to reduce our anxieties around living in a more racially diverse nation. He suggests that "in many communities, a broad spectrum of racial groups already is accepted by all, particularly among the highly diverse youth population" (Frey, 2015, p. 2). Plenty of evidence exists that supports Frey's assumptions about the favorable dispositions of young Americans toward diversity or multiculturalism (Blau, 1977; Smith, McPherson, & Smith-Lovin, 2014; Munniksma & Juvonen, 2012); however, as an educator I want to make sure we supplement the growth of an increasingly diverse population with effective primary, secondary, and post-secondary education to explore issues of diversity, equity, and inclusion. Simply relying on chance and demography doesn't have a precedent in the United States; that is, we live in the kind of polarized society in which leaving problems alone only heightens separation and segregation (Orfield, 2015).

The polarization of Americans is also evident in our nation's schools, which continue to be highly segregated. About 10 years ago, less than one-third of all school children attended high schools classified as multiracial, and more than one-third of white students attended a high school that was 90% to 100% white (Park & Chang, 2015). Since the tipping point for African-American desegregation of schools in the 1980s, a reversal has taken place (Orfield, 2015). Latinx students have experienced an increase in their school segregation ever since the late 1960s. In some metropolitan areas, the orders to desegregate public schools after the landmark *Brown* v. *Board of Education* (1954) decision seem vestiges of times gone by, as New York City, for example, is home to one million highly segregated school children (Orfield, 2015).

Suggesting segregation by race or ethnicity is the only kind of separation of diverse school children doesn't tell the whole story. Double and triple segregation by a combination of race or ethnicity, poverty, and language is the case in many school districts (Orfield, 2015). Blacks and Latinx students are often segregated in these schools, in impoverished neighborhoods and towns, and suffer from lack of knowledge about college or lack of opportunities for college prep coursework. Many of these schools don't even appear on the lists of college admissions counselors to visit because most students tend to lack college entrance capabilities (Orfield, 2015). These kinds of national inequities privileged members of society need to become aware of and challenge.

To underscore the effects of present-day segregation, let's turn to some of my study's participants. Todd, a student at Midwest University, grew up in a metropolitan area 90 miles east of Chicago: "My middle school had just over 800 kids in it and there were probably about three black kids in the entire school and no Latinos, a couple of Asians and everyone else was white." Growing up in a city in which only 60% of residents are white, systemic segregation may have affected the way in which Todd, and his white male peers, interacted across racial difference. Paul, at Southern State University, grew up in a large metropolitan area in northern Florida and experienced segregation in a stunning fashion:

> I went to a private school all the way to 10th grade … I transferred my final two years to a brand new [public] high school. I played football and [became] really good friends with someone who is African American and he live[d] downtown. He didn't have a ride so I would drive him home every day. It's almost scary how the world is completely different down there. Like, once you cross over the water. It was just kind of an eye-opening experience. What I was surrounded by growing up was only a small part of what's really going on around the world.

The effects of segregation in this city come alive through Paul's usage of words like "almost scary," "down there," or "once you cross over the water." However, these words also "other" the experience of people of color who live in neighborhoods like this. In such a place, spheres of whites and people of color likely rarely overlap, and Paul witnessed this separation firsthand. We're also not sure if Paul and his African-American teammate ever connected much beyond the drive home.

Kipp, a student at Southern State, grew up in a suburb of Paul's hometown. He noticed how African-American peers in high school "really lived different[ly] than I do as far as middle class and lower class." Seeing how members of communities of color live, or have to live, had important effects on Paul and Kipp. Educators must engage white college men in discussing their potential experiences across difference and what lessons they may draw to potentially develop more empathy and identification with under-represented peers. Asking Paul or Kipp in a class to explain their encounters and what they learned could have helped other white men with similar experiences and to advance knowledge of American social issues.

Cliff, a student at Mountain State University, who grew up in a suburb of a large metropolitan area in Colorado, discussed segregation by color of skin and socioeconomic class (i.e., double segregation) in his possible school choices:

> The reason I chose the [second school] was because there was a little more diversity and they had a better academic program. The [first]

school, which my sister went to, was basically 80–90% white people who come from very rich … families. So, I made that conscious choice because I recognized that I didn't fit into that group of people. I kind of just wanted to fit in with a group that would accept me.

Denver, as a metropolitan area, is about 52% white, 32% Latinx, and 10% black, but Cliff's suburb was nearly 90% white. It's clear from Cliff's statement that socioeconomic and racial segregation went hand in hand at the high school he didn't choose.

Tony, a Lucas College student, described racial diversity and the apparent segregation in his high school in the Minneapolis-St. Paul metropolitan area in this comment:

> [My high school] was very cliquey in a way where a lot of the black population would stay more within their inner circle and then we'd talk about the white kids that want to be black kids, "ghetto kids" you could say. There was [sic] a few white kids that fit in with the black groups but it wasn't much more. I'm trying to think of the word but segregated just keeps coming to mind. It was much more segregated than I would have liked.

One final account of perceived segregation in high school comes from Trent, a white male Callahan College student who grew up in the Baltimore suburbs.

> TRENT: Compared to my high school, Callahan is very diverse. In my high school in my graduation class we were probably 97% white.
> JÖRG: *[surprised]* Even in a city like Baltimore?
> TRENT: Well, I went to a private school. I went to the school closer to Annapolis. And I was one of maybe three kids who were from the north side of school. It was basically a lot of rich white people.

Annapolis as a metropolitan area is 60% white, while Baltimore's residents are nearly two-thirds African American. These demographic statistics provide additional data to substantiate the level of segregation at Trent's private high school.

Social Contact Across Difference in Communities and Schools

Gordon Allport, renowned American psychologist of the mid-20th century, was one of the first theorists to study *intergroup contact*, the contact between members of different racial or ethnic groups. In Allport's (1954) now classic work, *The Nature of Prejudice*, he asserted the *contact hypothesis*: that interpersonal contact between diverse groups had the potential to reduce racial or ethnic prejudice under the presence of important conditions:

> Prejudice (unless deeply rooted in the character structure of the individual) may be reduced by equal status contact between majority and minority groups in the pursuit of common goals. The effect is greatly enhanced if this contact is sanctioned by institutional supports (i.e., by law, custom or local atmosphere), and provided it is of a sort that leads to the perception of common interests and common humanity between members of the two groups.
>
> (Allport, 1954, p. 281)

These lines are of a trailblazing nature, given Allport penned them during the heyday of Jim Crow laws in the American South and widespread racial segregation and discrimination. However, we also need to view them in their historical context to interpret their value to our work with racial or ethnic diversity today.

The probability that whites and blacks had equal status in any social, economic, or political endeavor in the 1950s was low. Today, we can see how adolescent high schoolers or college students from different racial groups could have even status in a classroom; however, even that example leaves out important effects of privilege and oppression. Striving for common goals may occur as teammates on the same sports team or co-workers in the same firm; however, in the 1950s that would have been nearly impossible to realize. Laws or customs were almost never on the side of oppressed racial groups of the 1950s, especially not while interacting with whites. Even today we can make the argument that, legally, whites and blacks do not play on a level field. Finally, the notion of common humanity and interests is vital because it hints at the idea of achieving a socially just society. However, we're more than 60 years removed from Allport's theory and still haven't eradicated prejudice and oppression, nor have we achieved a socially just society.

Perhaps Frey (2015) has reason to be optimistic about the positive effects of racial integration and continued desegregation of American communities, especially in metropolitan areas. However, that optimism likely fades a bit when we consider that access and exposure to difference don't automatically mean deepened experiences of interactions across difference. Many of the participants of the current research study, especially those from metropolitan areas, discussed their exposure to racial diversity. Milton, a student at Callahan College, a small liberal arts college in the Upper Midwest, grew up in close proximity to New York City: "Being close to a major city, I felt I wasn't restricted to suburbia so I gained access in [school] and also living where I do, I'd say to great diversity." Milton seemed to at least have access to diversity; however, we don't learn about how deep or meaningful his interactions across diversity were. Andrew, a student at Midwest University, grew up in southern Florida and discussed his exposure to a wider variety of diversity: "I went to high school in a predominantly Jewish town ... I'm half Jewish as well. I was friends with black males ... with kids from all different denominations and religions, kids with different ethnic backgrounds, [and] mixed families." Andrew uses the term "friends" here to describe his contacts across ethnic or racial lines, but we're not sure about how deep these friendships were. Ivan, a student at Southern State University, who grew up in northern Florida, discussed more in depth the level of friendship he experienced:

> I had a couple of black friends; that's mostly who I hung out with in middle school. Actually, I have seen them all pretty recently, so from sixth grade [on] we were always really good friends. There's still this one kid, Gerald McNicholl [name changed], who I have a handshake with that we still do to this day ... I still get to see him, still get to talk to him ... and what's been going on in our lives.

Cale, at Lucas College, grew up in the Chicago suburbs and had a similar experience as Ivan: "My best friend is African American from my hometown, so I've had someone with a different race in my life since I was in fifth grade, so I was more accustomed to change at a younger age." Ivan and Cale are the only two participants of more than 90 who described friendships with peers of color in more depth than the others, but only Ivan discussed still being in touch with a close friend of color he's known since sixth grade. If my analysis is accurate, 98% of my participants did not have deep friendships or interactions with someone from a different race while growing up. If these findings are at all transferrable to other white male students in other settings, we have more work to do than simply relying on demographic changes and the resulting increases in desegregation.

Aside from the opportunity for connection across difference in metropolitan communities, several of the white men in the study shared how participating in sports or activities allowed them to interact across racial difference. Evan and Martin, both students at Southern State University and participants in the same focus group, shared stories from their upbringing in a Southern metropolitan area:

> EVAN: I grew up in a black neighborhood, right on the outskirts. My street was the nice street and beyond that was what they called Sin City, so my closest neighborhood friends were black and usually I was accepted because I could play basketball.... So that's why my closest friends in the neighborhood were black.
>
> MARTIN: Like [Evan], I grew up in a black neighborhood, too. We were on the nice street, same thing. I ended up moving, but there's like that common ground, especially with kids, there's always that common ground.

Evan and Martin seemed to experience equal-status relationships with peers of color; however, it's also clear that many of their acquaintances from the basketball court were not of equal status in the neighborhood, considering they lived off the "nice street." Ron, also at Southern State, had a similar experience with interactions across race with fellow basketball teammates:

> I pretty much was the only white kid on my high school team four years in a row. In AAU [Amateur Athletic Union] as well. I played out of Miami and never [played with] another white kid. Never had a white coach [either]."

Aaron, a student at Mountain State University, grew up in Memphis, and shared a story about his relationship with a black peer football player in high school:

> I remember I was like, "Dion, can I call you the N-word?" And he was like, "Yeah, but you got to go through N-word training." And I was like, "Okay, let's do some training." And he said, "Okay, I'll see you in the locker room." We were getting ready for football and Dion and two of his henchmen turn the corner and [he] is like, "Alright, training time." And he pinned me against the locker and punched me in the ribs a lot [*Aaron laughs*] but then I got to call any black kid at our academy the N-word. For a little while, and then Dion came up and said, "Okay, time for reinstatement." And I said, "No, thank you. It was a great ride." But Dion and I are pretty good buddies.

This peculiar account is difficult to interpret. Aaron and his African-American friend seemed to have an interpersonal connection, which may explain the willingness by Dion to be called the most inappropriate derogatory term for black people, or to allow Aaron to call all African-American students at his school the N-word. But perhaps Dion was also enraged by the request, which is why he and two other friends initiated Aaron in what sounds like a hazing incident. Despite Aaron's comment that he and Dion were or are buddies, I didn't deduce a deep ongoing relationship.

In Trent's experience in Baltimore, connecting across cultural or racial lines took place by playing chess:

> At home I made a lot of friends playing chess because that's what I did. And in Maryland most of the scholastic chess players were not white. It's a game that a lot of Asian Americans play at that level and half of the white people are from Russia or the Ukraine anyway. A lot of my best friends were from Japan, China, or India, someplace in Asia, or they were Asian American.

Trent was the only student in the sample who connected more deeply with individuals from Asian or Asian-American communities during his secondary school experience; however, he didn't mention how deep the contact was or whether or not he was still "best friends" with the peers he mentioned.

Activities or sports worked as venues that connected our participants, at times, as equal-status participants across race, ethnicity, or culture. Because these young white men experienced this contact, their potential for prejudice or stereotyping likely was strongly diminished, confirming research by Brown, Brown, Jackson, Sellers, and Manuel (2003), who found that whites who had African-American teammates showed more positive regard for blacks than whites who did not compete in team sports. However, whether or not the contact continued beyond high school does not seem likely for the majority of our participants.

Social Distance in Communities and Schools

We've seen that some participants had contact to peers who were racially, ethnically, or culturally different from them. But how deep was this contact? Of 92 straight white male participants, only Ivan discussed still being in touch with his best friend from sixth grade. This finding generally corroborates existing research on interracial friendships, such as Feagin and O'Brien (2003), who found that most of their affluent adult white male participants did not have significant or lasting interactions or friendships with individuals with diverse racial identities.

Think back to your own high school years, or, if you're in high school right now, reflect on your current experiences. How much or how often did you, or do you, interact with people who differ from you in race, class, sexual orientation, or ability? An interaction in this case is not a head nod or a high five in a hallway, or a "What's up?" in the cafeteria, but an extensive, meaningful encounter that probes deeper, and one that reoccurs. The result of these reoccurring experiences is a friendship that likely lasts for a while, even years. You know something intimate about the person with whom you're interacting, and they have similar knowledge about you. You may also discuss issues of oppression they face in society. Maybe you've experienced that oppression while hanging out with them in town or in school? In any event, your connection takes place on a level that includes feelings and emotions, and it is reciprocal; that is, you share freely with and support one another. So, can you picture the individuals you're thinking of? How many friends of yours does my description fit, and with how many of them do you remain good friends to this day?

Despite persistent segregation in schools across the United States, cross-difference contacts, or intergroup contact, among primary and secondary school students from different races, ethnicities, genders, religions, sexual orientation or ability identities have increased in the last few decades due to demographic change (Blau, 1977; Frey, 2015; Munniksma & Juvonen, 2012; Smith et al., 2014). Larger representation of ethnic and racial difference in schools and classrooms also contribute to students of color feeling safer, less lonely, and becoming the victim of peer bullying less frequently (Munniksma & Juvonen, 2012). Contact across racial and ethnic lines also strongly relates to reduced prejudice among all students (Hallinan & Williams, 1989; Moody, 2001; Munniksma & Juvonen, 2012). Intergroup contact during childhood may positively affect racial or ethnic attitudes in adolescence and adulthood, and children who have deep interracial friendships may acquire better social skills, have higher rates of sociability, and create more diverse social networks than peers who are not friends with anyone from a different racial background (Pica-Smith, 2009).

Theoretically, white students nowadays have more opportunity to establish friendships across lines of human difference, but research has unequivocally found that especially cross-racial friendships are rare (Smith et al., 2014). Even in ethnically and racially diverse schools, students prefer friends from the same racial or ethnic background, rather than cross-difference friends (Moody, 2001; Munniksma & Juvonen, 2012). An extensive interview study in the late 1980s using the High School and Beyond Survey identified only a few hundred interracial friendships among nearly a million pairs of cross-racial high school peers; that is, the likelihood that students would choose an inter-racial friend versus a same-race friend was only 17% (Hallinan & Williams, 1989). A similar study using data from the General Social Surveys from 1985 and 2004 suggests that whom we consider close personal confidants has not changed much over the last three decades, especially across racial lines (Smith et al., 2014). Racial *homophily*, or the degree to which individuals tend to associate with and befriend individuals with the same racial background, remained relatively unchanged between 1985 and 2004. Given this point, researchers consider homophily a social fact, one which "simultaneously reflects and reproduces the social order" (Smith et al., 2014, p. 452). This serves as an explanation why interracial friendships for today's white men in high school (and later in college) seem to be the clear exception, not the norm. We can only hope that in the years since 2004 interracial friendships have increased in our nation's high schools.

Let's turn to my participants to examine this intergroup separation in schools from the perspective of Eli, a student at Lakeside State University in the Midwest:

> I come from a suburb school that's like 50% minorities. And I have lots of friends who are black or Hispanic, or Asian. Everybody seemingly gets along fairly well. [But] I always noticed one thing that was really strange, um, that is every time you walk into that lunch room, it was amazing how segregated it was … I think in terms of diversity, I'm naturally, you know, potentially more biased [to] identify with white people.

Eli struggled to express his thoughts as evident by his frequent pauses and "ums." Perhaps Eli struggled because he thought he may express something inappropriate or that he would offend me as the researcher or his fellow white male peers sitting around the table. Turns out, Eli is correct, based on the research cited above, about the formation of these subgroups and why they form. His understanding of these issues means educators should engage him and others to delve deeper into issues of spatial segregation in schools and how to possibly counter it.

Ken, at Midwest University, addressed a similar issue of student separation at his high school in a large metropolitan area in the Midwest:

> My high school was predominately black and Mexican – well I guess, I don't want to say that, but there were a lot of Hispanic and black [kids]. And a lot of Hispanic kids always got together, spoke in Spanish, and tried to separate themselves from everyone else. I became friends with some of the ones that were in the honors classes.

Ken's statement may invoke several responses. First, it's interesting to see his own correction of the term *Mexican* to *Hispanic*, almost as if he perceived Mexican may be too vague a term to describe the ethnic diversity Latinx students represent, or because it might be considered offensive. Second, the research on why school students may separate likely also explains the perceived self-segregation of Latinx students who share a common language and culture. Third, Ken seems to only interface with Latinx students who were also in honors classes. Finally, we didn't delve deeper into how strong his contacts with Latinx students were. However, we get the sense that Ken's interaction with African–American peers was minimal due to his peripheral treatment of them in his statement. This type of white male experience with racial and ethnic difference in high school is a suitable point of departure for any deeper investigation led by educators of the topics of segregation, racial differences, and how these experiences affect the consciousness and propensity for building solidarity with others in white male college students. College or high school classrooms are perfect venues for such discourse.

Race and ethnicity weren't the only topics of conversation on how the participants interacted across difference. Greg, a student at Lucas College, discussed his interactions with high school peers who identified as gay.

> In high school we had a Pride group but it was very small. I actually had one friend who was gay but he identified as bi-sexual, but it never really came up in conversation with him. It's not like [he] had a boyfriend or brought us to the meeting so it was kind of just something we didn't talk about. It was there, it's not like we shunned him, we all knew it but it wasn't something we discussed or discriminated him for.

In this story, the social distance between the white male student and the student who is considered diverse is palpable. Greg, we infer, had a friend who was gay, but this friendship doesn't appear to be one that explored sexual orientation at a deeper level. We may wonder how invisible sexual orientation felt for the gay student whose identity was never a topic of conversation.

Learning About Difference through Socialization by Parents

Communities, neighborhoods, and schools are no doubt powerful socialization agents of children and adolescents. But what happens in families relative to learning about and interacting across difference is also extremely important. Allport (1954) asserted that the home is the most pernicious source for ethnic bias in children who adopt their parents' views because they seek parent's affection and approval. Prejudiced parents may transfer their attitudes to their children, moderated by the level to which the children identify with their parents (Sinclair, Dunn, & Lowery, 2005). That is, children who strongly identify with their parents should become more prejudiced than children who don't. However, research on adolescents and masculinity shows differences between how boys connect to their parents compared to girls (Farkas & Leaper, 2016). By adolescence, boys may have begun emotionally withdrawing from their parents and tend to show less closeness to parents than girls. That withdrawal may work in favor of male adolescents whose parents display racial or ethnic prejudice in the home; however, the reverse may also be true, that boys may distance themselves from their parents' egalitarian notions about race and ethnicity.

Research finds that white parents' attitudes toward race or ethnicity have an effect on how white adolescents perceive or enter intergroup relationships (Edmonds & Killen, 2009; Tran, Mintert, & Jew, 2016), especially if children highly identify with their parents (Sinclair et al., 2005). We also know that some white parents exhibit greater opposition to a variety of diversity-related issues than parents who are members of communities of color, including rejection of cross-racial friendships or interfaith marriage across racial lines (Perry, 2014; Sahl & Batson, 2011).

Sociological research adhering to a systems perspective of a racialized society suggests that white adults don't often or openly discuss race (Bonilla-Silva, 2014) or even acknowledge that they are part of a specific race (Hagerman, 2017). White parents who don't actively talk to their children may assume their children don't notice race, or that race doesn't matter to their children. This colorblind approach of not discussing race still communicates influential messages to white adolescents (Hagerman, 2017). Conversely, white parents who believed in the importance of racial or ethnic socialization were more than three times as likely to talk to their children about racial oppression than parents who did not consider this type of socialization as significant (Priest et al., 2014).

Turning to my participants, I'll discuss their experiences with parental influence in terms of exploring or understanding racial, ethnic, or sexual diversity. Abe, a Callahan College student who grew up in a suburb of Washington, D.C., reminded me of my own upbringing in a nation's capital:

> One thing I noticed growing up, at least through school, my best friend
> was always a different race than I was and was from a different country

and spoke a different language ... I sort of wondered if I gravitated toward people like that because I grew up around it. My parents were [journalists] living in Mexico when I was born.... So, I grew up bilingual and I always wondered if I had this draw to people who represented two cultures and spoke two languages.

We don't actually know from Abe's story whether or not his parents actively discussed issues of diversity with him; however, they seemed to lay the foundation for his penchant toward cultural or lingual difference by living in Mexico during his childhood.

Ivan, who already shared that his best friend growing up was African American, likely adopted his views from his parents:

My parents definitely had a lot to do [with my outlook on diversity]. [They're] both from up north but my dad most certainly was, for lack of a better word, abandoned as a child and was actually raised by a black woman for several years so.... My best friend as a kid was black and he slept over all the time. [I learned] from my parents and what they've done and ... how they took care of people.

Opening their house to children from different racial backgrounds perhaps had a significant effect on Ivan's development.

Not all participants grew up with parents who were open to racial or ethnic differences, nor potential interactions across difference for their sons. Matt, a student at Southern State, shared an interaction with his parents about race that does not reach back to his adolescence; however, it's instructive about the subtle but apparent hints of prejudice:

My parents, they don't have a problem with it, but they ask me, "Who are you hanging out with?" "Benjamin." "Where's Benjamin from?" "He's from [here] but he went to Lewis [High School]." "Is he Black?" "Yes." It doesn't bother them but since I came to college, I've had a lot more [friends] from different races ... I think college does help you to become more diverse because you're put in a situation where you have to interact with other people with no pressure from someone like your parents around.

I think that despite's Matt's attempts to assuage us of the contrary, his parents seem interested in whom he befriends as they surmised Matt's friend's high school was predominantly black (it is). And in the last sentence of Matt's statement we get the sense that he may have received some pressure from his parents in the past about whom he was calling a friend. These underlying parental messages of prejudice likely didn't preclude Matt from connecting with black students in college. Yet, they affected him in some way as they were important enough to mention during the focus group.

Ron, whom we met earlier, was always surrounded by African-American basketball teammates and coaches. Here he and I talked about his mother's thoughts about his friendships:

> RON: [Where I'm from] it's always diverse, it's just a big melting pot down there. I've never had a problem with it. Right now I have two black roommates. Most of my friends are actually black and I've always [got] a thing from my mom, "Where's all your white friends?"
>
> JÖRG: What do you say to your mom when she says, "Where are all your white friends?"
>
> RON: I say, "Why does it matter?" She just gives me a dirty look. She was raised differently, she was raised in the 1950s, 1960s, and 1970s.

Ron's mother seemed to struggle with the fact that most of his acquaintances were African Americans and communicated this to him in an indirect but powerful question about his white friends. Her questioning also seems to happen somewhat frequently. His mother's views didn't affect Ron not to interact with friends from other races; however, this story was salient enough for Ron to remember.

Derek, a student at St. Margaret University, faced a more specifically racist upbringing. Growing up in suburban Kansas City, he shared his experiences with his parents and how he observed differences between college and his home relative to accepting diversity:

> My dad … was mugged by some black kids when he was younger. I did this immersion trip and was [telling my dad] about how me and [my friend] Darnell were going to go and hang out. And he was like, "Be careful." I was like, "Why?" "Well you just have to be careful … with people like that because they will eventually take your money." That kind of battle. And … my dad, he uses the N-word, and my mom just yelled at him one day … about how one of my best friends was black and how that affects me. So yeah … I didn't know which side was the right side.

This is a very powerful account by a student who seems caught between the values of his father and the values espoused by his university, the most racially diverse institution in my study. The father's racist messages have clearly affected Derek as we consider his use of the term "battle," and his mother has recognized the detriment of racism in the way she confronted his father. Emerging from this racist home as a college student who advocates for diversity seems surprising, and I wonder if Derek's identification with his father has diminished since coming to St. Margaret. Nevertheless, you get the sense of the enormous difficulty of navigating this kind of upbringing with attending a diverse institution.

Dennis, a student at Lucas College, shared an experience similar to Derek's; however, in this case one parent spread homophobic messages:

I was home schooled and I grew up in a really strict, conservative Christian home. My mom would be like, "Oh, gay people, they're weird, I don't understand that." And so, I got this preconceived notion of [homosexuality]. [When] I went to public school, I met a guy and I got to know him really well … and it wasn't until like two or three months later that he [came out as] gay. I was like, "That doesn't change my opinion of him at all." … So, in that way, I kind of grew out from underneath my parents' notions of society and had a really great learning experience.

Before entering public school, Dennis may have adopted his parents' view on homosexuality, but through the experience with a gay male student he changed his views on what being gay meant. It still appears as if he tries to justify that being friends with someone who's gay is indeed appropriate, noticeable in him mentioning character and personality. We don't know whether Dennis continued to be friends with the gay student; however, the learning experience seemed to have a strong effect on him. Dennis's experience is what Jack Mezirow (1991), late famous American sociologist, called a *disorienting dilemma*, the first step in transformative learning. Dennis transformed his original preconceived notion about homosexuality transmitted by his parents through an experience with befriending a gay man. He changed his ways of knowing despite the potential discomfort with or backlash from his parents about his new perspective.

We see that the experiences of the participants varied in terms of the messages they received from parents about diversity, whether those messages were prejudiced or open minded, and how strongly the messages affected the students. Despite components of a colorblind ideology in some participants, or despite justifications of parental or own viewpoints, the participants, by and large, seemed largely unaffected by negative messages and positively affected by a more discerning or open-minded parental approach. Some interacted with peers from different social groups despite their parents' prejudiced notions. In the case parents passed on the importance of diversity and open-mindedness to their sons, the participants absorbed their parents' notions of egalitarianism or social justice.

White Habitus, White Racial Frame, and Gender Intensification

Despite some gains in desegregation compared to the generation of their parents, and despite open-mindedness on the part of our participants about intergroup contact, the vast majority of them didn't engage in deep, personal contact with peers from different racial or ethnic backgrounds while growing up. This held true even for participants who grew up in more racially or ethnically diverse regions, such as metropolitan areas of the East, the South or the Midwest. Among all 92 participants, only two seemed to have been best friends with a peer from a different race during high school, and only one appeared to remain in touch with this individual. These findings confirm research on interracial friendship that suggests that typically fewer than 10% of whites have black friends (Bonilla-Silva, 2014) and that white high school students may not be interacting meaningfully across racial differences (Park & Chang, 2015). Why is this the case?

To explain the experiences of the participants, we have to consult the concepts of *white habitus* (Bonilla-Silva, 2014) and *white racial frame* (Feagin, 2013), as well as masculinity and *gender intensification* during adolescence (Smiler & Heasley, 2016).

White Habitus and White Racial Frame

If you've grown up in the United States, chances are you have been socialized in a system that has been dominated by the viewpoints and framing of the affluent, straight, white, and male population (Bonilla-Silva, 2014; Feagin, 2013). Exploring these frames is essential to figuring out why white adolescent men may not engage in frequent or deep interpersonal contact with peers from different racial or ethnic backgrounds.

White Habitus

Bonilla-Silva (2014, p. 152) defines the concept of *white habitus* (i.e., habit, behavior, conduct) as a "racialized, uninterrupted socialization process that *conditions* and *creates* [author's original emphasis] whites' racial taste, perceptions, feelings, and emotions and their views on racial matters." The white habitus is the result of decades, even centuries, of white spatial and residential segregation from people of color in the United States. Traditionally a concept used to explain the separate experiences of communities of color, racial segregation can also be viewed from a white perspective. Considering this viewpoint, we can argue that whites in the United States are actually the most isolated racial group of all (Bonilla-Silva, 2014). A primary result of this segregation, the white habitus, creates commonality among whites (Bonilla-Silva, 2014) and a culture of pejorative views of racial others, mostly African Americans and Latinx individuals.

Whites typically express approval of an interracial lifestyle when asked on surveys or public opinion polls. Whites are also proponents of integration of schools and residential desegregation, and most seem committed to interracial friendships or even marriage (Bonilla-Silva, 2014). However, in practice, whites' behavior looks much different. Few of Bonilla-Silva's (2014) white participants interacted across race and admitted that none of their closest friends were people of color, nor that they ever had a romantic relationship with a person of color. findings match those of my research. Most of the participants in Bonilla-Silva's (2014) study didn't interact with cross-racial peers, even when living in racially or ethnically diverse neighborhoods.

Similarly, in my study, only the men who lived in mixed neighborhoods or who engaged in activities with teammates of color seemed to have enduring exposure to people of color. Whether this exposure resulted in meaningful connections or even friendships is unclear for most of the participants.

Does segregation, or even hypersegregation, as in the case of most affluent whites in the United States (Frey, 2015), alone explain the lack of deep personal interaction among white adolescents and their cross-racial peers? Bonilla-Silva (2014, p. 156) poses the following question to help us explore: "[I]f whites had the demographic chance of interacting with blacks of similar status, would they do so?" The answer is "no," at least for the vast majority of Bonilla-Silva's (2014) nearly 1,000 research participants. We have to examine the school experiences of American youths to understand this predicament.

At the majority of desegregated high schools, the cross-racial interaction among whites and their peers of color is not deep enough to create long-lasting relationships. Additionally, tracking often results in white adolescents experiencing a nearly all-white classroom experience even in integrated schools. Ken mentioned this in his comment about some Latinx peers in his honors classes. Had they not been in his honors classes, would Ken have interacted with them? A final reason for the lack of strong personal relationship across racial or ethnic background may be the fact that whites typically don't attend integrated schools until high school (as with a few of my participants who attended private or religiously affiliated elementary or middle schools which were predominantly white). By that time, many whites have forged white-only social and support groups, have learned pejorative views about people of color, and have absorbed how to successfully evade or navigate a few cross-racial encounters (Bonilla-Silva, 2014). This kind of racial isolation that began in school typically continues for whites throughout college and their careers, despite the opportunities to interact with a larger number of people of color during later life stages (Bonilla-Silva, 2014). In fact, a 2013 poll by the Public Religion Research Institute (Jones, 2014) surveyed Americans to identify as many as seven individuals with whom they had engaged in conversations about matters important to them in a six-month time span. The poll aimed to explore the closest social networks of respondents and revealed that white Americans' closest friends were 91% white. What's more, three-quarters of white respondents to the survey had entirely white social networks without the presence of any people or color (Jones, 2014).

White Racial Frame

Feagin (2013) coined the concept of the *white racial frame* as a viewpoint, perspective, or worldview that is innate, unconscious, and automatic for whites in the United States. As a result, the frame is "imbedded in individual minds (brains), as well as in collective memories and histories, and helps people make sense out of everyday situations" (Feagin, 2013, p. 9). If the term *frame* is a difficult concept to grasp, think of the terms *frame of mind* or *frame of reference* to help you think about the nature in which many whites in the United States view and act toward racial others. It becomes a dominant way of looking at the world, it gets passed on over generations, it asserts the perspective that white people are good, virtuous, moral, and superior, and it promotes views and actions that are disparaging of people of color. Since slavery began in the American Colonies in the early 17th century, whites have perpetuated this frame, and over centuries the frame has come to include several parts we as whites use to make sense of our lives. It combines beliefs, cognitive components, visual and auditory aspects, emotions, and the disposition for action.

Much like in the white habitus, whites do not reflect on the nature of the white racial frame. In general, we have a difficult time to describe ourselves or identify as racial beings or in racial terms. Race for whites becomes a negligible issue, and one that isn't questioned or explored. For the majority of whites, racial segregation in residence and schools is "just the way it is." We don't realize that our way of life is dominated or regulated by a racialized frame of mind, or that we "routinely operate from some version of this dominant frame" (Feagin, 2013, p. 199). Because of the acceptance of this normal state, whites have tended not to be radical proponents of desegregation of all American institutions, or of the aggressive enforcement of socially just laws and policies.

Similarly, whites have not questioned their lack of deep personal contact or interaction with colleagues or friends of color. It's no surprise that white male adolescents or, later in life, white college men won't experience friendships across racial or ethnic lines, or wouldn't think to interrogate their lack of contact or friendship with peers of color (Feagin, Vera, & Imani, 1996; Park & Chang, 2015; Picca & Feagin, 2007). According to Feagin (2013, p. 222), because of the widespread racial isolation in the United States, whites "have no really deep and sustained equal-status relationships with Americans of color."

The white racial frame can have significant effects on whites who haven't engaged in successful interactions with people of color. These whites cannot make up their own mind about what contact across racial lines should look like; hence, they rely on information propagated by the media, by parents, or by white peers. This is often fraught with racial and ethnic stereotypes and becomes a substitute for genuine interactions with people of color. Fostering these interracial or interethnic interactions, thus, is of key importance, both in successfully disrupting white racial framing and in moving toward a more democratic and socially just society. From such a disruption Americans of color would benefit due to the possible decrease in oppression. We as whites would benefit because our isolated worldview would expand and we'd be able to embrace the historical, cultural, and human riches we've been missing because of the severe lack of in-depth interactions across racial difference.

The perhaps most challenging subframe of the white racial frame is the idea that white people are always virtuous, hard-working, ethical, and not implicated in the oppression and plight of Americans of color (as well as Americans with other minoritized identities). This central subframe includes the insistence of many whites that the United States are a fair, tolerant, and egalitarian society in which people succeed if they want to (claims of America as a post-racial society due to Obama's two elections as President underline this thinking). People who fail to make it, according to the white virtuousness subframe, typically do so because of their own mistakes or wrongdoing. The subframe includes views of white superiority (e.g., intelligence, work ethic, morality, attractiveness) and manifestations of strong personal entitlement to what whites have. Nowadays, whites refer to this sense of virtuousness when we emphasize that we've worked hard and earned what's ours (Feagin, 2013). Our inability as whites to realize we're using this subframe is one of the main reasons why racial oppression continues to exist so fervently in the United States.

Gender Intensification

Explanations for why young white men may struggle to interact meaningfully across ethnic or racial lines also emerge from the literatures on masculinity, gender role socialization, and psychology (Wong & Wester, 2016). Specifically, during adolescence or early adulthood, men's relationships begin to include trust and emotional sharing and cease to be defined by proximity and shared activities (Smiler & Heasley, 2016). During adolescence, male friendships also are marked by *gender intensification*, a concept Smiler and Heasley (2016) define as a greater adherence to masculine gender roles. Traditional American masculinity norms have emphasized independence or self-reliance and emotional stoicism, which often results in young men showing restricted affectionate behavior toward others, particularly other men. Boys or young men who were raised to be independent and to resist emotional expression may feel they are encouraged to disconnect from others who may be otherwise well-suited for friendship. And because relationships with other young men, specifically across racial lines, require interdependence, trust, and an emotional connection, young white men may show difficulty engaging in meaningful contact with peers of color.

Additionally, white male adolescents who do engage in cross-racial contact and who form relationships with peers of color may be monitored and evaluated by white peers who function as a sort of gender or race police. Some young white high school men may disapprove of their white male peers engaging in interracial contact – unless in sanctioned spaces like the gym or the playing field – and they may shun or insult their friends who don't adhere to these norms. Facing being fired from the male peer group, young white men may think twice about whether to engage in interracial contact not sanctioned by their friends (Kimmel, 2008).

Evidence shows that the vast majority of young men can navigate this intricate system of masculine norms during adolescence and report they have at least one good male friend (Smiler & Heasley, 2016); however, we also know that the vast majority of whites cannot report having at least one good friend of color. This suggests that while same-race relationships are possible for the majority of young white men, interracial friendships are much more difficult to develop and sustain because they undergo more scrutiny from other male peers and from society at large.

Summary

Much adversely affects young American white men who want to learn about diversity or forge meaningful, deep, and lasting relationships with individuals from different backgrounds, specifically peers of color. Most of the straight white men in my study, and, according to research, many young white men in the U.S., grow up in racial isolation and away from people of diverse racial or ethnic backgrounds. We as whites don't question this segregated way of life and our racial and gender privilege tells us, "this is just the way it is." Even the participants who grew up in racially diverse neighborhoods rarely crossed paths in meaningful ways across racial background. Only two participants reported having best friends who were peers of color during middle or high school.

The extant research, some of it going back more than a half a century, suggests clear and unambiguous outcomes: if people from different racial or ethnic backgrounds but of similar standing (e.g., high school students, teammates, college students, colleagues) find ways to interact with one another or work toward similar goals, prejudice and stereotyping will be reduced, especially for whites. We should not rest on the fact that interactions across racial difference are hard, but do whatever we can, especially as educators, to provide avenues for this interaction to take place in secondary and post-secondary institutions, communities, on athletic teams, or in after-school or co-curricular activities in college. Here we must go beyond the shallow depths of superficial interaction, but let men know what we aim to accomplish, instruct them of the obstacles, and help guide them and their peers along the way to develop deep, long-lasting interactions.

I want to close this chapter with the words of a participant you heard about earlier. Jonathan, at Southern State, got what my study aimed to do: to help straight white college men see that branching out, learning about diversity, and interacting more profoundly across difference can enrich their lives. He also understood what socialized him to maintain his way of life: the forces of segregation, isolation, a normative peer group, and a conservative and male-dominated upbringing:

> In Catholic school, we had black kids, we had kids of other races, but I never hung out with them, never tried to befriend them or anything like

that. I think part of that is me, the upbringing I had. I grew up in a very conservative white male dominant environment, [like] I grew up hunting and fishing. I would say that even into college now, I've made little effort to befriend anyone that I find super diverse [from] me. I always look for someone who is very similar to me in many aspects.

Just because interaction across difference is difficult doesn't mean that white high school or college men couldn't be engaged in deeper contact. It seems to me Jonathan wouldn't turn down any additional discussion on diversity or social justice, or block any assistance in helping him discover new ways of connecting meaningfully with others. Especially white educators owe it to Jonathan and similar straight white college men to guide and mentor them in this way.

3 What's in it for Me? Defining, Experiencing, and Considering Engaging in Diversity in College

I'm sitting in the Dean's Office conference room at Southern State University. Gazing through the enormous windows I see a portion of the lush green campus, the student union, where people congregate to eat, chat, or simply sit in the sun. I also notice the vast pond, lined by exotic plants and palm trees, in which ducks and egrets search for edibles. It's a gorgeous, sunny, and warm November day. I've come here to conduct focus groups, and my dear friend Anne, a professor in a sport-related undergraduate program, has recruited 22 straight white college men in her courses to participate. Even though I've conducted many focus groups with college students over my career, I'm a bit anxious, not knowing what to expect or whom I'll meet. The campus of Southern State University is one of the first stops of my research project, and I'm still feeling my way around the process and the questions. What will these men think of me? How will they answer my questions? They know the research is about diversity. I hope they will engage.

It's two o'clock in the afternoon and I'm expecting six men to join me for this first of four focus groups I will conduct here over the next couple of days. Anne assured me all who signed up will show because they seemed eager to participate. A little before 2 p.m., one by one, they file into the conference room. They don't seem to be jumping with excitement, but they're very polite as I shake everyone's hand, smile, introduce myself, and ask their name. As they find chairs around the opulent conference table, I make nervous small talk about the weather. "Gorgeous day, today, huh?" I mutter. "I'm from Wisconsin. It's in the 30s there today with light snow." The guys laugh sheepishly, as if to express sympathy or as if they wondered why I found today especially gorgeous. Most days here are like this. "It's in the mid-80s here," one of the guys says with a smirk as he plops down in one of the high-back, executive-style leather chairs.

As we continue the small talk, I find out that most of the participants are from the South and that they are between 19 and 28 years old. Jude, the oldest participant, declares with a grin, "I've been going to this school for a while." Chuckling ensues from the others. All men are either in their second, third, or fourth year in school.

After sensing it may be time to start the focus group I say, "Are you OK if we begin?" Nodding around the table. I give the typical pre-focus group spiel I always give: how the study is about straight white college men and what they think about diversity initiatives on campus, and topics like race, gender, sexual orientation. Some of them look skeptical, perhaps even a bit anxious. I share the latter feeling but don't let them know.

"Has any of you ever participated in a focus group or other qualitative research?" I ask. No one says yes. "It'll be fun," I respond nervously. I take a deep breath and begin the questions.

We start by exploring their definitions of the term diversity. I inquire about their experiences with people different from them in high school and college, and I probe what it's like for them to be a straight white man at Southern State University. The participants answer my questions willingly and all of them contribute to the conversation. When I get to the question that explores their perceptions about why white college men tend to disengage from college diversity initiatives more than other students, the tone slightly changes.

Bill, a tall, clean-cut, bigger guy, sits exactly across from me. His eyes are stern and his voice deep. He's kind of intimidating. Bill grew up in the city in which the university is located, a metropolitan area of 1.5 million. He's 23, a senior, and responds to my question assertively.

> I've got other things on my plate that I feel like I need to attend to or want to [do.] Even if I get a day off [from] classes, the first thing I'm thinking is, "All right, I'm going to go fish."

Bill's statement reaps smiles and nodding from his comrades around the table. He continues, "If I saw a flier today [about an event] about Chinese culture, I'd be like, 'Well, that was four seconds of reading that I didn't need to do.'"

Sitting next to Bill is Ron, a 22-year-old senior, from the southern part of the same state. His hometown is located in a metro area of about five million residents. Ron is thin, has dark hair, and is wearing a polo shirt. Equally critically, he responds, "Yes, that does not appeal. I've got other things to do. Especially when the university tries to [put on cultural events] like that, it's just really contrived. Nobody wants to be there." More nodding from the others. "For me," Ron continues, "it feels like they're trying to shove it down my throat. Maybe that sounds stupid or whatever. I don't care."

Following the conversation about the lack of engagement of white college men in campus diversity efforts, Bill chimes back in a few minutes later. "[I'm] a 23-year-old college kid. Why do I need to have all this diversity knowledge? If I was a CEO of a company, I might need it, but right now, it's of no value to me." His face looks even more serious now. "Honestly, what's of value to me [right now] is [that] I don't know what time I'm going to leave for [the western part of the state] tomorrow to watch the [football] game." He concludes, "Just like I said, there's not a ton of value to [diversity], to me, as of right now."

Bill's and Ron's statements make painstakingly clear the issue many of the other participants confirmed: diversity on campus or in society may be entirely irrelevant to large swaths of straight white men in college. I get why raising awareness, gaining knowledge, building skills, and figuring out how to stand up for what's right is important to us educators. I wouldn't conduct research on this topic or write this book if I didn't. On the other hand, I also get the young straight white men who feel this way, because I was one of them once. I likely wasn't any younger or any less mature than the Bills or Rons or some of the other 90 participants. Can you identify with them as you read their statements, at least when you were of similar age?

In the previous chapter I addressed the socialization of straight white men in families, schools, and communities. Very few of the participants had deep or meaningful interactions with people of different racial or ethnic backgrounds, and many of the participants lived and attended school in racial isolation. This chapter reports how the participants defined, experienced, and considered participating in diversity discussions, initiatives, or coursework at their college or university.

Diversity Defined

Picture a TV station conference room in the 1970s. Colorful suits and shirts, big lapels, and large, horn-rimmed glasses. Only men sit around the table, other men stand around the table, and only four woman-identified individuals seem to be present in the scene. The women play no role in this meeting, and neither do many of the men. All people in the scene appear to be white. When the station director enters the room to make announcements, the main news anchor is asleep in his chair, with his head tilted back, while the others gab about a wild party they attended last night. The director greets the crowd and proceeds to announce what news stories needed to be chased that day. When he's finished talking about the potentially biggest news story of the summer, he reveals, "In addition, a lot of you have been hearing the affiliates complaining about a lack of diversity on the news team." One of the men seated at the table sneers, "What in the hell's diversity?" The anchor, now semi-awoken from his on-the-job snooze, replies, "Well, I could be wrong, but I believe diversity is an old, old wooden ship that was used during the Civil War era." The guy next to the anchor nods his head in affirmation. "I would be surprised if the affiliates were concerned about an old, old wooden ship, but nice try," the director retorts. "Diversity means that times are changing," he adds, and introduces the new female co-anchor, who just entered the room: a young blond woman who announces she looks forward to contributing to the team.

Many readers will likely recognize this scene. It's from *Anchorman* (McKay, 2004), a well-known American comedy, starring Christina Applegate as Veronica Corningstone, the new co-anchor, Will Ferrell as the enigmatically notorious Ron Burgundy, the previous sole anchor, and Fred Willard as the producer of fictional KVWN Channel 4 in San Diego, California. The movie deals with male chauvinism, sexism, and misogyny. The male colleagues prey on women, treat them as sex symbols, and despise Corningstone for becoming more successful than Burgundy. In the end, Corningstone and Burgundy reconcile and become co-anchors at a CNN-like news outfit together.

Sure, the scene is funny, in a way, but the underlying message is that a hegemonic culture of white men prevents women from being successful and that it considers women as objects of male desire. Especially noteworthy for this section of this book is the men's indifference to and mockery of the term *diversity.* Yes, *Anchorman* is a comedy, takes place in the 1970s, makes light of difficult social topics, and, in a way, calls attention to sexism and misogyny. But *Anchorman* is also a reminder of how male hegemony continues to work to suppress individuals from groups it minoritizes, for sure 40 years ago, but also today.

To examine how institutions of higher education typically define diversity, we notice two specific components (Umbach & Kuh, 2006). *Structural diversity* refers to the representation of human difference; that is, how many members of a specific racial, ethnic, or religious group are part of an institution at a given time, or to the inequalities that exist between privileged and marginalized social groups in a given society (Andersen & Collins, 2010a). If the numbers of students, staff, or faculty from diverse backgrounds and identities are relatively low, the likelihood of interactions and learning across such difference is equally low. Most predominantly white institutions have understood they should raise the level of structural diversity to enhance student learning.

Second, institutions typically offer *diversity initiatives*, including but not limited to required or elective courses with diversity-related content, diversity workshops or training, speakers, or events. Initiatives also include cultural centers, student organizations, and resource offices (e.g., advising or mentoring) that typically benefit students and staff of color, women, or students with diverse genders and sexual orientations (Umbach & Kuh, 2006). The creation of these efforts usually serves at least two purposes. One, they provide spaces and advocacy for traditionally minoritized student, staff, and faculty populations, and two, they often serve as educators of the campus on issues of privilege, oppression, inclusion, equity, and social justice.

Institutional Missions of Diversity

The mission ... is to educate the citizens and citizen-leaders for our society. We do this through our commitment to the transformative power of a liberal arts and sciences education.

Beginning in the classroom with exposure to new ideas, new ways of understanding, and new ways of knowing, students embark on a journey of intellectual transformation. Through a diverse living environment, where students live with people who are studying different topics, who come from different walks of life and have evolving identities, intellectual transformation is deepened and conditions for social transformation are created.

The above words are taken from one of the mission statements of the oldest and most recognizable institution of higher education in the United States, Harvard University (Harvard College, 2017). To be more precise, the excerpt is part of the mission of Harvard College, the undergraduate arm of the university. As you can surmise, the mission uses the word "diverse" to describe the living environment, the differences in areas studied, the distinctive walks of life from which students hail, and their developing identities. This mission lets us suspect that Harvard's educators pledge to uphold the diversity it heralds as important, but we don't know for sure. How does the mission instill a sense of challenge, accountability, or responsibility in the administrators, faculty, staff, and students to actually institutionalize diversity in the way they pledge?

Harvard's mission does not distinguish that establishing or discussing the connection between diversity, inclusion, equity, and justice ought to be important for students and staff. I interpret the last part of the mission to mean that Harvard's focus on diversity has the potential to transform the lives of students, both in an intellectual and social nature. This is certainly a noble pursuit, and if this were to take place Harvard College graduates could say their alma mater kept the promises it made. It's easy to include such goals in an institutional mission statement, but it's far more difficult to realize this mission in the lived institutional experiences of students, faculty, and staff, many of whom, at Harvard for sure, identify across a wide variety of privileged and oppressed social groups.

Most, if not all, colleges and universities include diversity as a staple in their institutional mission (Banks, 2009; Roper, 2004). Diversity initiatives in college typically engage learners in ways that foster the understanding, appreciation, and even celebration of human differences (Goodman, 2011). These efforts aim to raise individual and group consciousness to explore and more fully develop awareness of self and others (Ortiz & Patton, 2012). Examples include required or elective diversity courses or co-curricular activities or programs (e.g., speakers, culture weeks, teach-ins, movie discussions, ethnic foods events, festivals, or college-community fora on specific issues) that span a wide range of disciplines and explore important topics, such as race, ethnicity, gender, sexual orientation, socioeconomic status, age, ability, national origin, religion, or veteran status. College faculty and staff are trained (some better than others) on issues of diversity, to raise their level of consciousness, build skills or expertise in a specific area, or to teach, advise, and support diverse students.

Diversity has certainly long been a buzzword in educational institutions, including in secondary schools and post-secondary colleges and universities, so much so that some students from privileged social groups (like Ron whom

I mentioned previously) have the visceral "you're cramming this stuff down our throats" reaction when they hear the word (Johnson et al., 2008). In my study, I used the term "diversity" in our focus group questions to center the participants' conceptualizations of a term with which they were familiar, and about which they probably had an opinion.

Veiled in disguises of inclusive excellence, social justice, inclusion, or equity, diversity also has become a rhetorical piece in the speeches, visions, and strategies of most American college and university leaders. I would go as far as to say that most predominantly white institutions of higher education have long considered diversity as a box to tick on annual reports, in reaccreditation portfolios, or during institutional research efforts. Talking about diversity, celebrating diversity on special days or during specific months, and making constituents think that diversity is of prime institutional importance is one thing. It's another to live and commit to diversity as a daily reminder of American social and economic inequities that institutions should promise to help fix rather than simply talk about.

According to D-L Stewart (2017), professor and scholar of social justice issues in higher education, college administrators typically engage in the politics of appeasement of their liberal as well as conservative critics. First, they focus on the lingo of understanding and appreciating human differences as diversity work, and subsequently on the attempts to raise awareness toward social justice and equity. As Stewart (2017) asserts, the goals of student activists from the 1960s through the 1980s were not to engage campuses in more celebration of human difference, but to call needed attention to and to hope for institutional transformation in generating a critical mass of individuals of color on campuses. Over the past 50 years, colleges and universities have upped their attempts to celebrate human difference and have aimed to become more diverse, inclusive, equitable, and socially just. We've tried to recruit more staff and faculty from underrepresented groups, have instituted diversity offices overseen by senior diversity officers, have attempted to train instructors on how to deal effectively with diversity issues that may arise in classrooms, and have put more money into student financial aid and diversity programming.

What hasn't changed at predominantly white institutions, or not nearly to the amount we announced it would, are the levels of attrition for students from underserved backgrounds, the rates of perpetration of oppressive behavior and microaggressions on college campuses, and the enormous shortcomings to retain faculty from underrepresented identities. The problem isn't the well-conceived efforts in which we have engaged, or the students and staff of color who leave, but the lack of systemic change, as well as the glaring misses in institutional and individual transformation. This issue rests squarely on the shoulders of white male administrators and faculty who must interrogate why racial, ethnic, gender, and sexual oppression, stereotype threat, and microaggressions have been daily occurrences on our nation's campuses for decades and who must help lead the way to stop this oppression from occurring

(D'Augelli, 1992; Harris & Ray, 2014; Porter, 2013; Rankin, 2004, 2005; Steele, 2011; Solórzano, Ceja, & Yosso, 2000; Stotzer, 2010; Sue, 2010; Van Dyke & Tester, 2014).

Don't get me wrong. Appreciating human differences is not an unworthy pursuit; however, our most important effort as educators should be to explore how human differences relate to the structural nature of privilege, power, and oppression (Andersen & Collins, 2010a). This must include challenging white male faculty, staff, and students to interrogate their own privileges, and inspiring them to act in solidarity with their peers from minoritized backgrounds to disrupt systemic institutional oppression. Once predominantly white institutions are competent in identifying and arresting how they perpetuate systems of oppression, we can focus on celebrating human differences. Should we continue to fail to commit to equity and social justice, we will not only preserve our white institutions as oppressive bulwarks for minoritized individuals, but also not realize any improvement of campus climates as environments in which all students and staff can thrive (Bondi, 2012). Celebrating diversity, or acting as if, alone won't help.

Straight White Men Defining Diversity

Let's now turn to the data from the Straight White College Men Project to consider how our participants conceptualized diversity.

Physical and Invisible Characteristics

First, the participants defined diversity as what's visible when looking at other individuals. It's important to note, however, that the participants included invisible characteristics more often than physical ones in their definitions. Trent, at Callahan College, made this representative statement:

> OK, I guess a lot of things come to mind when I think of diversity. First, things that are visible, so looking at people thinking different skin color, gender, or ethnicity. Then things that are not visible, like different opinions, differing views on things, whether it's about religion, politics, or some part of identity that is not visible like sexual orientation or anything like that.

Race or physical appearance seemed to be defining characteristics of diversity to some of the participants:

> When I hear [diversity], I think of just race right off the bat.
>
> (Jude, Southern State University)

> I guess I would think just more racial diversity. You can see it immediately. You can walk past a gay guy and have no idea, you know?
>
> (Alex, Riverside State University)

I think [the] knee-jerk reaction [to] diversity, when you think of it, you
think of different cultures and races.

(Jacob, St. Margaret University)

Jake at Southern State understood that changing one's physical appearance
may be relatively easy; however, changing one's color of skin was impossible: "You [*addressing the researcher*] said [your] beard, for instance, you
could shave tomorrow. That's something you could change in five
minutes; whereas, you're not going to change your skin color." Max at
Riverside State also addressed the salience of race or ethnicity in diversity
definitions:

I don't think people are going to be able to see past physical traits.
Because you can look at anyone, you don't have to talk to them. I can
be walking to school, or walking to class and see 400 different kids, and
never say a word to them, and I could be like, "Oh, he gets bad grades,
oh, she must be really smart."

Even in the definitions of the term diversity, the automatic or innate framing
(Bonilla-Silva, 2014; Feagin, 2013) we do as whites was evident:

I think often that the media has a big influence. You turn on the news
and you rarely hear about African-American males who got like a citizenship award. You're more likely to hear an African-American male
who was murdered somewhere.

(Nick, Lucas College)

Nick's comment signals that media has a strong effect on how Americans
view or define diversity, and what, specifically, white Americans think about
it. Theo at Lucas College underscored this point:

To speak on whether it's a good or a bad thing, I would say that the idea
of [diversity] being a system of differentiation based on differences doesn't
have to be bad. But the way it often gets looked at or gets addressed by
people in society makes it become bad.

In Theo's mind, the way society has defined diversity has become a detriment. White men in college, or whites in general, have fallen prey to the
differentiation of white, black, and brown, or good and bad, and have not
spent time thinking or been challenged to think about their own definitions
of diversity and how that definition leads to power differentials and inequities
among fellow citizens.

The majority of the participants defined diversity as featuring hidden or
invisible characteristics or traits. Consider this statement by Cliff at Mountain
State University: "Diversity is the identities that people carry. So, their sexual

orientation, their nationality, how they identify in terms of gender." To Ivan at Southern State, diversity simply implied human differences: "I think of different people from different places, people that are raised differently ... I just think of many just different people, different aspects, and different thoughts, different temperaments, different talents, different everything." For Zane at Lakeside State University, diversity implied the following: "I mean, I see diversity as kind of where you come from ... like nationality, financial background, your interests, like if you're into, say, sports, as opposed to video games, or if you like to read." During a focus group at Mason College, two participants discussed their definitions of diversity:

> JOSHUA: [We need to] not just focus on what groups are represented within a larger community but also what experiences, what attributes, what skills are present within individuals. What they've been exposed to, what they've been born with, what they've been taught.
> CHRIS: Um, and that to get at the heart of [diversity], you need to talk about, like, you need to go into like stories, lived experiences.

Toward the end of the discussion at Mason College on what diversity is and how its definitions should change in the future, Chris made this impassioned plea:

> I feel like we do need to change our definition of diversity. We label certain differences as, "this is diversity, but this isn't." Um, for example, we talk about racism and homophobia, and sexism, but issues such as ageism, you hear about a lot less. And one of the reasons that many people of color in the American school system often feel like museum exhibits is that our contemporary definition of diversity often leads people to feel like they should go out and pursue people of color to learn more about them.

I wonder why the conversations about the definitions of diversity during the focus groups with straight white college men focused primarily on visible and invisible characteristics. Are social or institutional definitions or media depictions of diversity so much about race that participants noticed the visible characteristics first? Most institutional diversity statements encompass a large variety of identity characteristics in their definitions; however, history and society have taught us that diversity is primarily about racial and ethnic differences. Perhaps that's why the participants offered so many definitions of diversity that incorporated invisible identity traits. Notice they mentioned hobbies, ideologies, upbringing, and ways of learning more often than sexual orientation, class, religion, or learning disability, all of which are also invisible identities. I interpret the participants' broad conceptualizations of diversity to mean that, deep down, they would like to belong or be part of generally agreed-upon definitions of diversity. The fact that straight white men may be confused about whether they officially *count* as part of diversity in their institutional context is evident in the following two themes.

"It's Not About Me"

In every focus group we asked participants to reflect on their own definitions of diversity: "How do you as straight white men fit the definition of diversity you just provided?" One of the most consistent themes of the entire study featured participants' thoughts and feelings about how diversity is *not* about straight white men. Consider the following comments by participants at different institutions:

> I think diversity means everything that's not a white male, that's what I think of. This is the separation. You've got white males and then everything else is diversity.
>
> (Bill, Southern State University)

> It's all about other diversity, besides the white males.
>
> (Alex, Riverside State University)

> I never even thought that I was thinking like that, but I don't know. It feels like I don't add to diversity. Whereas, someone who's [a] minority can feel like they add to diversity.
>
> (Cliff, Mountain State University)

> My knee-jerk reaction when I hear diversity is just instantly anything non-white because that's kind of how it's driven home, specifically on this campus.
>
> (Mel, St. Margaret University)

Several participants on different campuses discussed how they are overlooked when it comes to diversity or how they have nothing to contribute to diversity. Consider Max's statement during his Riverside State focus group on this point:

> It just seems like we are overlooked when it comes to diversity. Kind of that whole topic is how do we make less of [white] guys. So, you just feel odd about it, because like, I don't know, it's almost like we're an issue, like we're causing a problem and we need to fix this with more diversity.

Max had difficulties expressing what he may have thought sounded offensive to me or to his fellow focus group participants. However, his perceptions of straight white men not being included or made part of diversity efforts seemed to sit deeply.

Stuart at St. Margaret delivered a humorous soundbite about white men not being unique in the context of diversity:

> We don't really have a cultural identity. You joke about it with your friends like, "Oh, I had a sandwich, the food of my people." [*laughter*] I'm a white guy and I like video games and sports. Our cultural identity is very vague. It's just weird how that has never really been a huge part of me growing up, like, "Oh, this is what our people do."

I hadn't heard the sandwich joke (it's kind of funny) but it's indicative of the invisibility of whiteness in society. In this case, Stuart thought of white people in terms of an undifferentiated group of European Americans. Had he thought of the vast diversity of white ethnic groups, he likely could have come up with different ethnic foods, and vastly distinctive histories and experiences.

During a focus group at Riverside State University, Leo addressed the lack of uniqueness he perceived about himself as a heterosexual white male: "Everybody else looks just like us, you don't really stand out in a crowd, which is fine. But, I feel like, like I'm not really unique, I'm just kind of run of the mill, like everybody else." I wonder whether Leo indeed thinks that not standing out in a crowd is fine. To me he sounds disappointed that he may not be unique in the context of diversity, especially when compared to other white men who seem, at least at the surface, very similar.

Having nothing to contribute to diversity or to discussions about diversity pertains to the perceived privilege with which we as straight white men have grown up. Consider Mitch's comment from his focus group at St. Margaret University: "It's like, if we try to jump into the conversation and talk about issues, people are like, 'Oh, you don't understand, you've never had to go through anything like that.'" In the same focus group, Derek responded a while later: "When I say anything about feminist issues, racial issues, anything basically that is on the other side of the privileges I have, I'm not perceived as credible … It's the end of the conversation, it's not something that's valued."

The reason straight white men may feel apart from the definitions of diversity or efforts to engender more diversity is because of how they have been taught what diversity is and has become. Consider the following quote from Chris at Mason College:

> Commodity is probably the best word for it. We have commodified diversity. Diversity is now a selling point. There are so many things that you can learn from somebody who seems so very similar to you. I mean, there are probably great differences between us [here] even though, by the contemporary definition of diversity, it wouldn't seem like it because we are all white, straight college student males in the same age range.

The irritation and dejection of the participants is clearly visible in the preceding comments. Much like the majority of them would define diversity to include non-visible characteristics that would make them diverse as straight white men, they feel frustrated about the fact that what is valued about diversity by colleges and universities seems to be about the identities of traditionally minoritized people. I not only interpret the "diversity is not about me" theme as a sign of resistance to, in my participants' minds, outdated definitions of diversity; part of me also thinks they want new definitions because they want to belong to a concept which they believe hasn't included them.

That some participants couldn't see the need for diversity definitions at all is evident in the next theme.

"We're all the Same"

The final theme among the definitions of diversity included perceptions of why diversity was necessary at all because "we're all the same." These conceptualizations of a colorblind ideology are widespread among white college students (Bergo & Nicholls, 2015), and Bonilla-Silva (2014) has coined *white colorblindness* as a new form of racism in America.

According to Nathan, a student at Lakeside State University, diversity should not matter because of its misplaced focus on race:

> Personally, I've always had, like, a problem with the phrase diversity, because everyone thinks that, "Oh, [to] look diverse, it requires black, Asian, very mixed people," when in a school setting you shouldn't be looking at, "OK, how many black students do we have? How many white students do we have?" You should be looking at what is the intellect of our student body. I'm not going to go to this school because [it is] diverse.

I can understand Nathan's attitude toward diversity because at one point during my undergraduate college career I shared it. However, as long as minoritized identities of individuals prevent them from being treated equitably in society and in higher education, efforts to make colleges and universities more equitable must remain.

Being united by the same institution was what Andrew at Midwest University had in mind when he said:

> We came to [this] university and we chose to be here and at the end of the day we're all [Owls] and that's what I feel like the most important thing is. I'm not wearing any [Midwest University] stuff right now, but when walking around campus you realize you're the same. When you go to class you realize you're going through the same thing everyone else is going through. We all share the basketball team; we all share the football team.

The notion that students on a particular college campus are connected by an institutional ethos or culture that equalizes identities is not misdirected. I'm sure many college students, whether their salient identities are mostly privileged or oppressed, identify in some way with their institution, its mascot, its sports, its faculty and staff, or with other activities. However, identifying as an Owl or Crane, a Wildcat or Panther, a Husky or Greyhound, will not make a student feel better or safer when they're the target of blatant racism, sexism, or homophobia.

At Lucas College, Myles shared: "I just don't feel any different from people. I feel like we're all the same and we're doing what we have to do. When I'm walking around and I see a minority, nothing goes through my head about that." Justin, whose stepfather is African American, added: "Same with me. I never even thought twice. My stepdad is black, so there is no difference in my opinion. I don't see color. I also know it's there but it doesn't mean anything to me." When white men say, "I don't see color" (I've said it myself), many of us likely mean that we're cool with people having different colors of skin, and that we won't discriminate against them because of what they look like. What we should think about before we make such statements is that we acknowledge differences in race and ethnicity (and all other identities that are the cause for discrimination), that we support friends, colleagues, and family members who are marginalized because of their racial differences, and that we will stand in solidarity with them in the fight to end this system of oppression. If that's what we mean by "I don't see color," we should say it. If we say "I don't see color" in the frontstage (in public), but actually mean the opposite or actively discriminate against people of color in the backstage (among friends), we must reflect on the underlying reasons for our oppressive behavior and change our hearts and minds. And white male educators must help with this important work.

Jude, at Southern State University, pointed out that he was not judgmental about the identities of others:

> I feel like I am a very diverse person, I really don't judge until I know them personally. I don't judge somebody on the color of their skin, the beliefs they have, with religion, and like their financial background. For me it doesn't matter how, like what your background is, at all. It just matters how we treat one another.

Jude's point is well made. In the end, how we treat one another is an important prosocial quality and goal. However, we can aim to generate these qualities while also recognizing that not all our peers are treated equitably. As I mentioned earlier, the celebration of human differences, or treating each other well in spite of our diversity, can be an accomplishment after we've understood how systems of oppression minoritize some of us and privilege others.

During another discussion at Southern State, Clay shared this about our identity as human beings:

I don't see color. We're the same. I also had friends that were gay, bisexual, lesbian, I didn't care. I have a friend now that goes here and she's a lesbian. I have no problem going out to dinner with her, in public going out with her. She's the sweetest girl you'll ever meet. I feel like we're all the same, it doesn't matter like what your sexual orientation is, what the color of our skin is, we're all human beings in the end of it.

Again, the key phrase is "we're all the same" and that it doesn't matter to Clay to have friends who identify in ways that are often subjugated in society. Notice though how he discusses going out, in public, with his lesbian friend in college, as if it weren't typical or common to be seen in public with someone who identifies with a different sexual orientation. Embedded in Clay's comments may be the white virtuousness concept Feagin (2013) discusses. When whites are good – in terms of Clay's points whites may be good when they're not actively discriminating against others or see all diverse others as "the same" – we shouldn't have to worry about issues of racism, sexism, or homophobia. As I have shown in this book, regarding our society as having somehow arrived at a post-racial, post-gender, or post-sexual orientation state is a mistake.

The last statement in this section comes from Micah during another focus group at Southern State University:

People of different color, to me that doesn't make a difference. I just treat them like they're a person, like they have a soul. I'm a Christian. And I believe people perceive that in a way that [we're] bigots and people perceive that [we] hate gays and they go to hell and stuff like that. And I'm here trying to say, "Hey, no, we love them still. They're still people with souls." I treat them with love the best way I can.

I can see how some readers may struggle with Micah's points. Referring to peers with different sexual orientations as individuals who are *still* loved or who are *still* people may indicate his struggles with truly accepting them. His attempt to befriend and treat diverse others with love and respect is likely good natured. However, educators could help him realize that differences in sexual orientation (or color of skin) are actually the cause of gaping inequities in this country and that he should reflect on his role in helping undo these wrongs. Again, the virtuousness of a straight white male identity perspective is visible in Micah's quote.

The next section transitions from defining diversity to providing a glimpse into the participants' actual experiences with diversity on their respective campus.

Experiencing Diversity in College

As we saw in the preceding chapter, the vast majority of our participants did not interact deeply or meaningfully with peers from different racial or ethnic groups while growing up and throughout their secondary schools. This was partially due to residential and educational segregation and isolation of the white participants and their families. Not interacting more frequently and at deeper levels across difference stemmed from growing up in a racialized social system that taught young straight white men to primarily spend time with individuals who were like them. How the participants fared when they went to college, I will discuss next.

In the demographic data for this research project, we gathered that the average hours of contact across difference was 5.52, defined as the total number of hours per week participants estimated they spent in close personal interaction (longer than 30 minutes) with someone different than them (e.g., race, sexual orientation, ethnicity, religion). Had we asked how many hours a week they spent with individuals who identified along the same characteristics of race, gender, and sexual orientation, would that number have been higher?

A few men addressed how they noticed aspects of diversity more than they did before coming to college. Owen shared this experience from his first day at Southern State University:

> I walked in and there [were] two girls making out in front of a group of people and nobody even looked at them. That was my first day on campus. I went and said to my wife, "Do you know what these kids are doing on campus? This is on campus, this isn't at night at parties, this is on campus during the day. It's sunny out." [*laughing*] But it's just normal. I looked at other people that weren't even paying attention and I just kept going.

Owen's comment indicates his surprise that the kissing women weren't hiding their affection toward one another, as he may have expected they would based on his upbringing or experiences with sexual orientation. Telling his partner, noticing the reaction of other students walking by, and just passing without judgment, at least during the focus group, to me indicates this experience was important to Owen's learning.

Drew, a student at Riverside State University, told this story about an experience across racial difference that he described as a highlight of his college career up to that point:

> I have a friend who's Asian and I've been friends with him for a couple years now. We were both freshmen in the dorms. Just within the last couple months, I didn't even realize that he was Hmong and then we had a long discussion about it. I was comfortable enough around him … to ask him questions. I wouldn't have to worry about him getting offended.… That was the best experience I had here so far.

It seems as if college was a place for some of the participants where they were able to engage more deeply across difference.

Three men in the sample discussed interactions with diverse fraternity mates or roommates as a way to establish deeper or more meaningful interactions across difference. At Southern State University, Ivan chose a fraternity based on his perceptions of how the brothers were dealing with and welcoming diversity:

> Well, the best experience I can think about when it comes to [diversity] is the fraternity I'm in…. During rush week, when I went around to all the different fraternity tables, one of the things that I definitely noticed was the diversity among the Sigma Chi fraternity…. That was great to see because I didn't see that at other fraternities…. And now I am a brother [and] … that [diversity] is still alive in our fraternity.

As you may recall from the previous chapter, Ivan was one of two participants among 92 whose best friend growing up was African American, and they remained in touch throughout their college careers. Although Ivan didn't share in this comment whether he engages in deep or meaningful contact with his fraternity brothers with different racial or ethnic backgrounds, I assume he is amenable to those interactions because the diversity of the group was a factor for him to choose the fraternity in the first place.

During his focus group at St. Margaret University, Jacob told this story about profound interactions with his roommates:

> My older brother is my roommate and then we have another guy in the apartment who is also gay, he's black. We've kind of touched on some topics where we talk about [diversity], especially my black roommate. We had a really long discussion about the whole situation in Ferguson [Missouri], and I've heard him talk with his sister and his mom…. It's just the passion he has for it and his interest in the topic is something I just don't understand. Not that it doesn't appeal to me but [I think about] how important that issue is for him. And it's the same thing with my brother. We talk about sexual orientation and he said that if he could make the choice of being either gay or straight, he'd rather be straight because being gay you have so much more that you deal with that I will never really comprehend … I feel like I can empathize more with them.

This is one of the most essential quotes of the entire book because Jacob addresses several issues on which readers and straight white college men should reflect. Because his roommates matter to him, their issues facing discrimination or oppression are important to him. He still struggles to understand but doesn't resist thinking about his roommates' difficulties or refuse to engage in conversations about the oppression they experience. Because they matter to him, he can create or feel empathy for their concerns. He may not ever experience concerns like they do, but he can identify with his roommates and friends as they face discrimination. And although he declares he lacks the skills to comfort people, he attempts to find comforting words.

This episode is of non-trivial importance to educators at all levels who work with young white men before or during college. Men are not incapable of identifying with others who are hurt by discrimination or oppression. It may be easier for them to identify with the concerns of people they love, yet they should also learn to develop empathy for individuals not close to them but who are oppressed just the same. Men like Jacob may already feel empathic toward issues of oppression, and can learn skills to not only comfort but also advocate for equity in society for people who are minoritized and oppressed. We as educators have to do better at engaging straight white men in this way. I'd hate to think our focus group was Jacob's only educational outlet at St. Margaret where he shared this story and engaged with other straight white men on what the experience meant.

Reviewing the participants' interactions across diversity in college and comparing them to their experience across difference in their hometowns or high schools, I draw the following conclusions. Given the demographic data, and the small number of participants who discussed learning from engaging with diverse peers in college, I posit that for the vast majority of straight white men in my study, interactions across racial, ethnic, or sexual orientation diversity did not drastically increase during college. Were that the case, I would have more data to share speaking to these interactions. We know that all institutions are predominantly white colleges and universities, but all of them also enroll students of color, students from different ethnic or national origins, and those who openly identify as students with diverse genders or sexual orientations. Considering the participants' age and point in their collegiate careers (71% juniors or older), as well as the institutional diversity that surrounds them, it's not that they couldn't have developed deeper connections across difference but that they didn't.

Second, the participants who did engage in interactions across difference during college indicated something they hadn't necessarily done during school: making the diverse identity, and corresponding issues of oppression, a topic of discussion with their peers. This kind of engagement seemed to be altogether missing during high school, or at least it wasn't part of the men's recollection of their high school friendships. That these types of interactions are meaningful for white men lends great credence to the extant research asserting that interactions across diversity in college are instrumental, as the next section shows.

What White Men Learn from Diversity

The vast body of research on the effects of college student engagement with diversity makes an unequivocal assertion: interacting across human difference, completing diversity courses, and attending co-curricular programs all strongly influence positive student outcomes (Chang, 2002; Parker, Barnhart, Pascarella,

& McCowin, 2016; Nelson Laird, Engberg, & Hurtado, 2005). A growing subset of research suggests that white male college students also learn from their engagement in diversity initiatives (Hu & Kuh, 2003; Hurtado, 2005; Spanierman et al., 2008), perhaps even more so than women or students of color (Engberg, 2004; Sax, 2009). However, white college men are also the most ardent resisters of diversity education in college than their counterparts (Heinze, 2008; Schueths, Gladney, Crawford, Bass, & Moore, 2013; Vaccaro, 2010). White college men frequently say they feel excluded from or frustrated by diversity efforts, suggest diversity is not about them, and wonder whether they have anything to contribute to the discussion on diversity (Banks, 2009; Roper, 2004). The previous discussion of the data from my study confirm these research findings.

How does diversity affect college men specifically? Linda Sax's (2008) research on the gender gap in college suggests that men show more problematic academic behaviors than women, such as skipping or coming late to class, not completing homework, or reporting being bored by the content. Yet Sax (2009) asserts that men achieve higher learning gains from studying, doing assignments, or prepping for class than women. Men who spend more time and energy on their studies may become more interested in larger political and cultural contexts, which does not hold for women in the same way (Sax, 2009). Specifically relative to diversity in college, men may consider formal and informal diversity experiences more liberalizing, motivating, and awakening than women (Sax, 2009). Compared to women, men were more committed to improving race relations and being more progressive toward gender roles when they engaged in diversity workshops and coursework.

Turning back to my study, by asking participants the question, "What do straight white men gain from diversity initiatives on campus, such as courses and programs?" the following themes emerged.

Personal Growth and Open Minds

Confirming empirical research findings on the positive effects of diversity on the learning and development of college students, the participants shared that interactions and experiences with diversity would increase their personal growth if they engaged in them. Greg at Lucas College shared:

> I know that the first time I *really* talked with somebody who was different from me, I probably said terrible things and asked terrible questions. But luckily those people were my friends and they were comfortable with me … where they could tell me, "Hey, that's bad to say and here's why." … I think diversity and race and sexual orientation becomes something you can't talk about if you're not comfortable.

Greg's statement is indicative of his willingness to learn and his relief that he learned more about diversity by interacting with friends who helped to set him on the current path. I also appreciate Greg addressing how learning about and growing from diversity is important for the rest of his life. The concept of comfort is extremely important here. No comfort means no discussion and no learning. College educators who work with students like Greg should point out that their white male desire for comfort is a bonus only individuals with traditionally privileged identities get to experience. Peers with different genders or sexual orientations, but specifically students with racially minoritized identities, typically won't have time to get comfortable with their identities first. Homophobes and racists will not offer that luxury.

During a focus group at Riverside State University, Anthony shared growing into a more tolerant person because of diversity:

> I have more acceptance of, or respect of others that are of different, uh, race and background. Before, I didn't really, I'm trying to look for what to say. Just going into education, you have to respect everyone's backgrounds and I'm a lot more tolerant, like humble about [those] types of things. Like before I would make jokes and like everyone else, growing up, but now looking back, like, I just thought that was stupid.

Anthony's learning, development, and progress over time is clearly visible here. The fact that straight white college men learn from diversity is undisputed. What we as educators have to do is to appropriately challenge them to engage in this content.

Closely related to personal growth is opening minds, the next theme that emerged from the data in response to the question what white men learn from diversity on campus. Listening to peers who faced oppression on campus was instrumental for Brad at Lakeside State University:

> Hearing testimony from people who have [had] hard experiences or racist jokes or something like that, I think that can be very beneficial, just to kind of bring it home. 'Cause we live in northern [name of state], we are very white, and I think that a lot of [us] haven't interacted with that before, and I think that to see that in front of your face with a peer, right there, I think would be very beneficial.

Brad's point is well made. However, educators also have to be aware of the fact that already minoritized students shouldn't have to do the labor to teach white men what they need to know. Educators, especially those of us who are white, must strike a balance and challenge white men to engage in their own reflection, while also centering and raising the voices of students with minoritized identities.

Anthony at Lucas College learned to increase his sensitivity by engaging in diversity initiatives in college: "I would say it's made me a bit more sensitive to other people, being in public, just watching what you say, and just have a lot more respect. It's kind of the whole practice what you preach thing."

During his focus group at Lakeside State University, George also suggested diversity initiatives helped him become more sensitive about the potential oppression of others:

> We can learn more about [other] cultures, beliefs, and stuff, so you can kind of see why they think stuff is offensive, see where they are coming from. So it'll help you not cross any boundaries that would be offensive.

Ivan at Southern State University felt that interacting with and learning from diversity during coursework had the potential to open one's mind:

> IVAN: Just to carry on from just being open, I think it's just about, it's not necessarily just learning information that is put in front of you, but changing your mindset.
> JÖRG: One of the reasons we are doing this study.
> IVAN: Exactly. I think that people need to learn to be more open and I think that's one of the things [diversity] could teach them.

During another Southern State focus group, Alfred noted that diversity can open minds, especially considering one's future:

> It teaches us to be more open-minded, like Professor Evans talks about in classes. The majority of organizations run right now are run by a bunch of old white guys, that's how she'll put it. So, it's like our generation coming up, we're going to be the old white guys running something, so if we grow up and kind of learn to be open-minded about things, we'll bring in the best possible candidate for a certain situation.

Alfred's comment harkens back to the first chapter of this book where I addressed the vast overrepresentation of white men in all American institutions. Straight white men in college who have not learned how to interact with or open their minds to human difference may be ill equipped to help lead diverse organizations.

Aside from the more abstract and altruistic benefits of personal growth and open minds, the participants also discussed a more utilitarian benefit to learning from diversity, as the next section will show.

Jobs and Careers

The top priority for the vast majority of American college students is to get a job after college, a good job, and one that pays well. Most college students perhaps don't foresee the importance of diversity when they enter college, but companies certainly do. According to an employer survey conducted by Hart Research Associates (2015) on behalf of the American Association of Colleges and Universities, more than 90% of employers deem critical thinking, communication, and problem-solving skills more important than the applicants' undergraduate major. Relative to the importance of diversity in a career, a whopping 96% of employers agree that all students should have experiences in college that impart collaborative problem-solving skills with individuals who hold different identities, views, and values. Finally, more than 75% of employers confirm that all students should be competent in intercultural skills and that they should understand cultures and societies beyond the United States (Hart Research Associates, 2015). Aside from the fact that educators need to do better communicating these desires of employers to students, learning across diversity in college is absolutely indispensable for those who want to be competitive in a future job market.

Turning to our data, we see that some students would be more interested in learning about diversity if the connection diversity–career were made more explicit by educators and institutions. Jude, a student at Southern State University, said:

> I think if [diversity] was marketed that way, if we were told that that would really help [in a job] … I'm not going to think of that on my own. I might think of what an employer might want, but I also think when we go to school a major that is going to get us a job, we think that that's teaching us what we need to know to get that job.

Two important issues surface in Jude's comment. First, we notice his reticence in taking responsibility to learn about offerings that could be beneficial beyond what is already required or presented to students. Second, as I mentioned previously, Jude is unaware that employers expect more knowledge than what students learn in the classrooms of specific major fields of study.

Alex at Riverside State University made the connection between a potential career and diversity during interviews for internships:

> So, both interviews were pretty short, [they] maybe asked six questions. But one of them was, "Do you have any experience with diverse populations?" and I said "No" both times because I haven't. And I guess that's just a direct benefit [of diversity initiatives on campus], especially if I want to get into criminal justice where you are dealing with all sorts of populations.

This is a crucial statement, not simply for the link between diversity and employment, but for the entire study. Alex had not thought about how diversity and his future life may connect, he didn't have anything to share about potential experiences across difference, yet he got both internships. Not only is this a privileged position to be in, but the lack of reflection on diversity in white men's lives appears over and over. I'm glad that Alex was honest in the interviews for the internships, but the lack of experience across diversity mirrors the experience of so many young white men in America.

Educators must do better to make diversity relevant for white men at a younger age. If a job interview is the first time a white male applicant is prompted to reflect on experiences with diversity, secondary and higher-education educators are failing their role as teachers and mentors, as well as challengers of the experience of our most privileged students.

Nate, a student at Southern State, also thought about how having engaged in diversity initiatives could work in his favor during a future job search and potential interview:

> We're all juniors and seniors [in this focus group], and we're in the final stages of graduating in a highly competitive field.... All these opportunities, I would love to network with more people, I would love to meet more people, I would love to expand more of my thoughts. "What is it like to be a white male on this campus?" We all fumbled that question [you asked us].

Nate added that if he faced this or similar questions in a job interview, he would like to be able to provide a more insightful answer. White college men who are in the ultimate stages of their collegiate careers and who realize they may have missed opportunities to interact or network across difference are typically not lost in the job market. Their privileges likely will bestow on many of them a fairly certain future in a chosen profession. Yet institutions of higher education need to ask the critical question whether they failed to engage students who may have yearned for such opportunities earlier in college but were unable to express it.

Jonathan, another student at Southern State, would likely approve if his institution offered diversity initiatives to help with students' employment opportunities: "You go to college to learn, because a lot of our classes are related to the things we're actually going to do. So [Southern should add] something along the lines of [diversity], because it's an employability skill." Ron responded: "If [diversity] is something that employers have a vested interest in and that they want, then it should be the university that puts an impetus on [diversity initiatives] because they want people to come here." It seems as if Ron wanted his institution to recruit students with career prospects in mind (I'm sure most institutions already do this); however, perhaps diversity has a place in recruitment if students knew interacting across difference and gaining important skills were key employment outcomes.

Our participants' statements about how diversity initiatives connect to their future world of employment imply the following conclusions. Some of the men understood that interactions across difference and resulting skills may be important in a job search. They evaluated how engagement in diversity initiatives might benefit or profit them. This utilitarian approach to learning about diversity speaks of the social privileges these men enjoy relative to their race, gender, and sexual orientation. They have the luxury of evaluating whether diversity is something in which they choose to engage, for potential future value. Their peers from traditionally marginalized identities aren't afforded the same advantage. The white men aren't necessarily speaking of intrinsic benefits to the study of diversity, but of the extrinsic and marketable benefits of having engaged across difference in college. Their institution plays an important part in how it challenges white college men to reflect on diversity more frequently than just during a job or internship search. And they need to show more responsibility in seeking out these experiences. If connecting employability to diversity gets white men's butts in seats, so be it; but, educators, especially straight white male educators, must instill in their students a deeper sense of interrogating privilege, power, and oppression, and raising their consciousness and responsibility for social change.

The perfect arena for the connection between diversity and the world of work is college coursework, and how our participants experienced their courses relative to diversity is the next theme that emerged from the data.

Experiencing Diversity in College Coursework

Enrollment or engagement in curricular activities engenders positive change in college students (Harper & Yeung, 2013). Specifically, completing diversity-related coursework positively affects students' moral development and reasoning (Hurtado, Mayhew, & Engberg, 2012; Parker et al., 2016), and raises students' racial awareness (Cole, Case, Rios, & Curtin, 2011; Soble, Spanierman, & Liao, 2011), civic-mindedness (Cole & Zhou, 2014; Denson & Bowman, 2013), engagement in social action (Nelson Laird et al., 2005), and development of white empathy (Spanierman et al., 2008).

Most institutions may now require their students to enroll in such coursework, at least in general education programs. Some studies have examined the how required college diversity courses affect student outcomes; yet, few report the what students thought about being required to take the course (Littleford, Ong, Tseng, Milliken, & Humy, 2010). Generally, those students who completed required diversity courses showed better attitudes toward human difference than those students who didn't engage in such coursework (Chang, 2002). Of the nearly two-thirds of institutions who had established diversity coursework, nearly 70% required their students to take at least one course in this area (Perry, Moore, Edwards, Acosta, & Frey, 2009).

Studies exploring the effects of diversity efforts on students also indicate positive outcomes for white collegians. Their engagement in diversity initiatives results in increased openness and appreciation of human differences, raised awareness of racial privilege, and reduction of a colorblind ideology (Harper & Yeung, 2013; Hurtado, 2005; Neville, Poteat, Lewis, & Spanierman, 2014; Spanierman et al., 2008). And white students who were involved in more in depth diversity initiatives, such as intergroup dialogue, increased their development as social justice advocates (Alimo, 2012; Reason, Roosa Millar, & Scales, 2005). It may be important for college diversity educators to communicate these benefits to white students, specifically to white men, because many will not be keen on participating in diversity coursework, may find it unchallenging, or may ardently resist it.

Lack of Depth in Required Diversity Courses

Despite the positive outcomes men may realize from engaging in diversity courses or programs, white college men often either feel left out of or frustrated by diversity initiatives (Plaut, Garnett, Buffardi, & Sanchez-Burks, 2011; Roper, 2004). They do not regularly engage in diversity initiatives willingly (Vaccaro, 2010), actively resist explorations of diversity and social justice inside or outside of the classroom (Bondi, 2012; Heinze, 2008; Johnson et al., 2008), or suggest they do not contribute much to diversity on campus (Banks, 2009).

Recall the demographic data in Chapter 1 of this book which suggested that over their entire college career each participant, on average, enrolled in fewer than one diversity elective course beyond the institutional requirement. For our participants this means that required courses were the only formal instruction on issues of diversity they received. According to DiAngelo (2011), this one required course, or a one-off required cultural competency training in a future workplace, may be the only time in their educational or professional careers that white men face a direct challenge to their understanding of diversity, inclusion equity, or social justice. Additionally, not all institutions required diversity coursework from their students and, as we will see from the participant comments, the content that fit under the general definition of "diversity course" was dubious at some of our research sites.

Turning now to the data, we will observe how the participants perceived their institution's diversity courses. In the case of Lucas College, a new diversity requirement was usually broad enough that "you could get all of your general education requirements without having to take something that would deal strictly with social justice and diversity" (Dan). The following conversation underscores the perceived lack of diversity requirements at Callahan College, a highly selective national liberal arts college,:

JÖRG: So, you don't actually have a diversity requirement in terms of the curriculum on this campus?

MITCH: Nope.

TRENT: Not at all.

JÖRG: Not in general requirements?

TRENT: Nope.

MITCH: Well, we have lots of things like interdisciplinary psych, humanistic inquiry … [where] you will address diversity, but no class completely devoted to it. I actually think that's a good thing.

TRENT: The classes I used to fulfill those requirements, I took a lot of Russian. We don't talk about diversity in those classes, we talk about another culture.

This interaction hints at a problem in the way predominantly white universities "teach diversity." Foreign language courses should not substitute for U.S.-based diversity or social justice content. A white male student who learns how to speak Russian fluently may have learned valuable skills, no doubt. However, he won't gain basic awareness of power, privilege, and oppression in an American context by taking a foreign language.

The participants also shared thoughts about the lack of challenge and depth in diversity coursework. Andrew, a student at Midwest University, stated: "We [have] to take world culture classes. So, I guess in that way you are exposed to other ideas. But I also feel like that's pretty minimal, how much you really interact with [diverse] people." Zane suggested diversity requirements at Lakeside State University vary in quality and challenge: "In all honesty you don't learn much, it's not really worth your money, you're not really challenged ... I know someone who skipped like half the days and they still passed." Institutions of higher education can ill afford communicating the importance of diversity in a way that shows students that power, privilege, and oppression deserve little time and effort, minimal course credit, and negligible engagement by students and faculty. This tangential treatment of diversity silences the experiences of minoritized members of the campus community and promotes the adherence to a white hegemonic culture.

Along with the lack of focus on or depth in diversity at some of the research sites, participants shared their perceptions about the instructors teaching such courses, explored in the next section.

Instructor Skills in Teaching Diversity Coursework

Studies have suggested for decades that college professors are crucial in the socialization and development of students (Astin, 1993; Kuh, Nelson Laird, & Umbach, 2004; Pascarella & Terenzini, 2005). Effective instructors who create environments that are both challenging for privileged and validating for underserved learners are indispensable for valuable diversity coursework (Brayboy, 2003; Charbeneau, 2015; Heinze, 2008; Larke & Larke, 2009).

In my study, only Kellen at Lakeside State University directly addressed his positive impressions of a professor teaching a diversity course:

> The experienced professors can get around pretty quickly among students. If you know that someone is very well qualified for a certain class, you might actually take that one. I took Native American History ... and it covered a lot of ... issues ... and I thought it was a really good course ... I definitely recommend it to somebody else because the professor was pretty solid.

White students typically examine instructors of diversity courses or diversity requirements more critically than faculty in their own field of study (Schueths et al., 2013). Jude at Southern State indicated, "The teacher gets to the class and realizes, in general, that people don't want to be there. It's not something they have a genuine interest in pursuing with their life so [she] makes the class easier." A course he perceived was a waste of time, Nathan at Lakeside State University shared this experience with a diversity course instructor:

> I just took a diversity class, and I have to say it was the biggest waste-of-time class ever. My teacher was over in England, and out of the 15 weeks we met 7 times, because she couldn't get internet.... If they're going to have diversity courses, they better have somebody who actually knows what they are talking about.

Some participants perceived faculty of diversity courses as having low skills or not being committed to the course or the topic. Ron, at Southern State University, took a required diversity course focusing on "Native American Indians because I heard the professor was really easy." Speaking with Jake at Lakeside State University, I inquired whether students considered the apparent quality of the professor teaching the required course as important. Jake said, "Exactly, and that's why if we do make that course a 3-credit course you can't have the head football, [or] the head softball coach [teaching it], who are just here to coach those sports." Certainly, undergraduate students may be unaware of the specifics that go into how departments staff faculty for courses and it's possible, if asked, that faculty or administrators at the research sites would differ with the students. However, our institutions must be strategic and transparent about who teaches diversity courses. Letting instructors who may not be entirely qualified teach critical content sends the message that diversity may not be an institutional value.

Further, the literature indicates that students may assess faculty in diversity courses, most often women or people of color, more harshly than white or male professors (Littleford et al., 2010; Schueths et al., 2013). Students who are members of privileged social groups also challenge, sometimes strongly, the expertise of professors who discuss race, privilege, and oppression in diversity courses (McGee & Kazembe, 2015). White students may also not appreciate course content that challenges their beliefs of their own nonracist identity or in a meritocratic system (Boatright-Howowitz & Soeung, 2009; Littleford et al., 2010; Perry et al., 2009).

Some white students may think that instructors teach with a biased or self-interested perspective (Czopp & Monteith, 2003) or that they aren't trained or knowledgeable in matters of diversity (Lim, Johnson, & Eliason, 2015). For example, white students may posit that African-American instructors who discuss racism do so principally because they want to highlight the experiences of their own cultural ancestors (Littleford et al., 2010).

Examining literature on white and male-identified professors, we find that men don't include diversity content in their courses as often as woman-identified instructors or faculty of color (Nelson Laird, 2011). Faculty with mostly privileged identities may actively resist multicultural education altogether (Ukpokodu, 2007). Such instructors may practice what Schueths and colleagues (2013) have termed *ducking diversity*; that is, white faculty purposefully sidestep diversity content in their courses. Yet many of their students do not assess this willful exclusion of content poorly and some white faculty may simply get away with not teaching about diversity.

In my study, several participants took issue with faculty whom they perceived as biased or opinionated. This criticism stemmed from students who may have disagreed with the instructor's apparent political or ideological disposition. Derek at St. Margaret was upset at one of his political science professors:

> When my Presidency [course] teacher says, like, "Bush only won because bible thumpers showed up and ... they don't know that voting for the Democrats would actually help them more." I just get turned off. I'm like, "You realize there's bible thumpers in [my home state], we don't all just worship the word of God all day long, we actually have rational thoughts occasionally?"

During his focus group at Lakeside State University, Nathan shared an experience about how faculty who share their opinions may not be fit to teach: "Teachers need to be better. In my opinion, they are not properly trained. They're all opinionated. They're supposed to be the ones teaching us to learn how to be more diverse with our thoughts, with our actions."

At this current point in the U.S., college students are inculcated specifically by right-leaning religious and political groups that a college education must always be neutral. On the one hand, the critics deride the need for trigger warnings or safe classroom environments for college students who may suffer from post-traumatic stress disorder (PTSD) or other mental health conditions. On the other hand, they squirm when college faculty discuss a specific perspective, which, under the standards of academic freedom, is permissible if the content relates to the topics central to the course.

Some of our participants perceived their faculty in diversity courses did more than just teach poorly, as the next theme shows.

White Male Shaming by Professors

At four of the research sites conversations took place about instructor-generated behavior the participants considered "white male shaming." Despite the low occurrence of this data category, the discussions were deep enough to report the participants' thoughts here. Myles at Riverside State University pointed out:

> I guess I would say that, especially when you're learning about the history, [professors should] emphasize that it is history. It happened in the

past. We, today as white males, are not responsible for the slave trade that happened two hundred years ago. Same thing with the Holocaust. A German kid who is born today shouldn't be held accountable for something that happened 50 years before he was born.

The idea that today's straight white male college students do not feel responsible for historic tragedies and the resulting sense of discomfort surfaced in most focus groups. I addressed this in the first chapter to this book and by telling my grandfather's story; educators need to instill a sense of responsibility in white men to engage in discussions about historical and present-day oppression emanating from people who look like us. Today's white men in college may not have been responsible for the social wrongs of history, but they continue to live in a society that oppresses minoritized people, and young white men benefit from that system of oppression. That ought to be discussed in college courses.

During a conversation with participants at Riverside State University, Ryan shared an experience which garnered agreement from his peers:

Well, I don't know about your classes, but mine was definitely a lot of white bashing to a point where instead of talking, it was a lot of blaming white individuals for racism. Or blaming you for discriminating against women, blaming males. I feel like that kind of talk shouldn't be used. It should be more of a unification of the two sexes or different races instead of just blaming one for something.

In the same focus group, Ben added a comment about an in-classroom encounter with a women's studies professor:

When you have a teacher who's bashing white people, it becomes offensive … [My] teacher legitimately just hated men, or at least that was the impression I got. It made it unpleasant to go to class and [I] didn't want to learn.

Jamie, a student at Lakeside State University, shared a similar experience with a female professor in a required social stratification course: "[On] the first day, [the professor] basically just pointed out how if you are white, male, and middle class, you're a horrible person, because of all these different reasons." Jamie felt "kneecapped right from the beginning."

College educators, especially those among us who identify along privileged identities, have to challenge straight white men on issues of privilege and oppression, and we have to do it in a way that doesn't let them retreat or withdraw from the classroom or learning. Our social privileges allow us not to engage in discussions that make us uncomfortable. In such an environment, no learning occurs. When no learning occurs, white college men exit the classroom without having developed skills they need to assist with social change; in effect, they leave college with the same low level of awareness with which they entered. Derek at St. Margaret University underscores the point of men wanting to go unnoticed in classrooms and how speaking out during diversity initiatives may backfire:

> I guess, typically in a classroom or in a large setting, I just kind of want to blend into the crowd and not stand out. Like at the [diversity program], you really watch what you say and whenever you go against it, you're the worst thing there.

What Derek describes I have called the white male students' way of hiding in the corner with a blanket over our head. We want to blend in, not say anything wrong, but we also don't want to be shamed. Educators need to draw white college men out from under the blanket, appropriately challenge their thinking, and help them engage more critically in all types of diversity work. We also have to help them grow much thicker skins than what they may be used to. Discomfort is a necessary factor in learning, and we as educators need to stop avoiding discomfort in students from traditionally privileged identities.

We've known for decades that college students not only learn critical content in their courses of study, curricula in their major, or inside of classrooms, but also while engaging in co-curricular offerings including but not limited to student organizations, athletics, Greek Life, working on campus, living in residence halls, or simply engaging with and experiencing college with their peers. These settings can transmit important knowledge about how to function in a diverse world, how to build solidarity with others, and how to begin advocating for social change. In the next section I discuss under what circumstances the participants considered engaging in out-of-class diversity initiatives at their institution.

Considering Engagement in Co-Curricular Diversity Initiatives

If you are a current college student, or if you're a college graduate, think for a moment how many co-curricular diversity initiatives you attended over your career at your alma mater. These could be events, speakers, educational programs, festivals, movie screenings followed by discussions, presentations, or workshops outside of class. What were the deciding factors for you to participate in such a diversity initiative? Intrinsic interest? Incentives, such as food or extra credit? Encouragement by an instructor, a staff member, or a friend? Thinking about my own undergraduate experiences, I tended to frequent events relative to diversity if they were organized by and for international students, or if a friend asked me to go with them. However, to say that I engaged in these types of out-of-class experiences frequently would be an overstatement. Can you relate?

"I'm Not Here for This"

As I've shown previously, no other social group of college students engages less frequently in diversity initiatives than white men. This includes conversing with college peers who differ in key identities, such as race, ethnicity, sexual orientation, or ability, attending co-curricular programs or speakers, or selecting and enrolling in courses beyond the requirements. What's more, the trend for interactions across difference for white college students actually stagnates between first and senior years, while the rates of interactions across difference increase for all other social groups. That is, white student seniors interact across difference at the same rates as they did as first-year students (National Survey of Student Engagement, 2017). In the present study, participants attended an average of fewer than two diversity-related events during a given year at their institution.

How did the participants explain the obvious lack of engagement of straight white male collegians in co-curricular diversity initiatives? During all focus groups, we asked the question, "If some heterosexual white college men struggle with involvement in diversity initiatives, such as programming or elective courses, what would have to happen differently to get them to engage?" The answers participants supplied furnished the data reported in this section.

A consistent data category exemplified the participant's reticence to engage in co-curricular diversity initiatives because they either weren't interested, because they said they didn't have time, or because they had other priorities. In responding to the above question, Bill, whom we met at the outset of this chapter, said:

> Diversity programs often seem like it's for that group. "Pilipino Day" or whatever. It seems like it's a chance for people of that group to get together. To me it doesn't feel like something I am supposed to go to.

In a focus group at Riverside State, Max asserted, "It just doesn't seem enjoyable to me. Like, I'd rather sit at home and watch *Duck Dynasty*. It's not that I don't care, it's just that I'm not necessarily interested in it." Dustin at Danbury College explained, "I mean, if it's interesting, I'd go. But if it's a stupid topic, then why? Why do we have to go? What am I getting out of this?" During a later focus group at Danbury, Gabriel stated, "The racial course, or whatever, doesn't really interest me. I know that there's [sic] diverse [or] different people. Different cultures. Things like that, but I'm here to get my pilot's license." As we've seen in the opening anecdote to this chapter where Bill's priorities were fishing and football, and diversity-related initiatives seemed like wasted time, the comments here by other participants speak again to the idea that white college men may find diversity irrelevant and not essential enough to spend any time or energy on. Derek, a student at St. Margaret, provided the most detailed account for why he or other white men may not be interested in attending or resist participating in co-curricular diversity initiatives:

> [So] we went to Chinatown to the [local] Science Center, and right next door is the African-American Museum. We let the group choose and everyone [went] to the Science Center and [only] two staff members went to the African-American History Museum. They were kind of disappointed that no one went with them. But I think it's just that the people didn't have ... an affinity for learning that stuff or wanting to embrace that history. It's harder for me to sit through things like that.

This anecdote is very important for this book. Earlier, I discussed the concept of identification and how it may be difficult for straight white men to identify with the history, oppression, or cultures of minoritized social groups in the United States. Derek is honest about his lack of identification with and affinity for African-American culture and history.

Students who announced they didn't have time to attend diversity events usually mentioned other priorities to which they felt they needed to commit. At Lucas College, Tony shared: "I've got other things going on. Do I really want to dedicate all this time to [attending diversity events]? As bad as that sounds, it's a factor."

White Guys Welcome!

Several of the participants indicated they would like to be explicitly invited or made to feel welcome to diversity initiatives on their campus. Brian, at Lucas College, commented: "[These events are] put on by the Diversity Center ... I feel like, 'Oh, I shouldn't participate in it because it's the Diversity Center.' There needs to be that push to be like, 'Yes, white people you're invited too.'" During the same focus group, Theo suggested: "The first thing is definitely what was mentioned earlier, making it feel accessible for a white guy to go to a diversity thing, that's the first thing." Lucas College seemed to be a source of important student discussions about who was invited to diversity events, as Shaun indicates:

> I was part of the Connect for Success hosted by the Diversity Center, and they are really determined to try and make things more diverse, I guess. The funny thing is that they say that the Diversity Center is an okay place for people to go to and they also have to mention that, "White people, it's okay for you too."

It is encouraging that Lucas students seemed to have been talking about diversity events, the office responsible for this kind of out-of-class programming, and how white students may fit into these events. Shaun's comment, though, is indicative of what I addressed at the beginning of this chapter:

many straight white college men may not even listen when someone says "diversity" because they perceive they're not part of the definition or the target group for diversity-related co-curricular events.

Zane at Lakeside State talked about making white men feel welcome in terms of courses; however, the link to out-of-class initiatives is easy to see:

> When [students] take a diversity class … they don't want to potentially be the only [white student] there because you'll feel really out of place. So, you have to make people feel, like, welcomed in any sort of class like that and maybe not focus entirely on diversity … I don't know how the diversity classes are taught, I've never taken one.

This is an eye-opening statement for many reasons. Zane wants the comfort of not being the only white man in specific course, he suggests white men should be made to feel welcome, he has never taken a diversity class in college (he was a sophomore at the time of data collection), but he has specific conditions under which he may consider one.

The notion of inviting straight white men to participate in diversity initiatives, to make them more comfortable attending co-curricular events, or to redevise event marketing so that white men would be more apt to attend was evident in these statements. Once again, the overall theme of white male comfort emerges from these data; comfort they need to feel to consider engaging in diversity efforts on their college campus, or ease they want to sense to enroll in courses or to consider attending events.

White College Men's Identities, Resistance, and Fragility

The data highlighted in this chapter suggest a major dilemma for many straight white college men, the institutions they attend, and the educators who instruct, guide, and mentor them. On their campus, white men want to count in the context of diversity. When institutions broadcast their missions for diversity, white men want to implicitly and explicitly belong. Yet many straight white college guys say diversity is not about them, or that diversity shouldn't matter because all students are the same. The participants knew they can realize important gains from diversity initiatives in college and take away key outcomes in personal and professional growth. Yet many of them do little to interact with diverse peers, to enroll in elective diversity courses, or to attend co-curricular events. The majority of the participants say they're not in college to engage in diversity, that courses have low depth, and that some faculty are unskilled. Some participants even feel shamed by their institutions and instructors for being white men. To even consider enrolling in courses, or to ponder attending programs or events, many white male collegians want to be invited, incentivized, or made to feel welcome.

What explains the participants' perceptions and how can college educators help solve this dilemma? In this final section of the chapter, I compare the findings of the present study to the existing empirical and theoretical literature on the topics presented to make sense of the experience of our straight white male participants.

White Male Diversity and Intersecting Identities

While I was in the beginning stages of writing this book, I remember posting a question on Facebook in a group of college and university administrators from around the country (nearly 27,000 members). My question dealt with whether the members of this group would be interested in reading a book like this one, and if they were, how they would use the information presented therein. Next to a number of "Likes," my post received several comments. Some said they wouldn't read another book on white college men because it would only perpetuate white men's superiority. I anticipated those answers and respect the professionals who provided them. Other comments referred to the potential for such a book to inform current college teaching or administration, and how faculty or advisors may engage straight white men more effectively on their campus. Those comments I also expected and I'm hopeful this book meets that goal.

What I didn't expect was a post from a colleague who didn't consider the question whether to read a book on this topic; rather, they took issue with my use of the term *white men*. This colleague seemed alarmed that I was taking the second-largest group of college attenders (only white women boast higher rates of enrollment than white men) and reduced them to two words: white men. It turns out, my colleague had a good point. Reducing this diverse mix of distinct identities, characteristics, traits, personalities, ideologies, trains of thought, or worldviews to two words may indeed seem a bit too general.

My colleague insisted that a possible book on straight white men needs to handle them as a diverse group of people. Their plea harkened that of Renn and Reason (2013) who caution to identify college students only as part of single-identity groups; in this case, by their racial identity. However, in this book, I go beyond the single identity of race. I center the identities of race, gender, and sexual orientation because I'm after a structural understanding of how heterosexual white men interrogate or perpetuate privilege and oppression on their college campus (Bonilla-Silva, 2014; Feagin, 2013). Race, gender, and sexual orientation are the identities that bestow straight white men a host of social, political, and economic privileges. They are also the identities for which women, people of color, and people with diverse genders and sexual orientations face daily oppression in this country, and have for centuries. A recent tweet – pinned by Twitter and retweeted more than 110,000 times – by "austin," a Brazilian and California-based artist, makes this point: "Dear white people: no one is saying your life can't be hard if you're white but it's not hard because you're white." If Twitter provided the option to bold or italicize font, personally I would have highlighted the word *if* to emphasize the identities for which white people may be marginalized, such as age, class, ability, national origin, religious affiliation, or others. Likewise, I would have emphasized the word *because*, since white people are not oppressed *because* of their race. Add to that, men are not oppressed *because* of their gender, and straight folk are not oppressed *because* of their sexual orientation.

I want to briefly return to my colleague's concern about treating white men as only having two identities. Are straight white men diverse? Yes. Absolutely. They identify across different ethnicities, abilities, socio-economic statuses, and national and geographic origins; they have different ages, cultures, and speak different languages. Many of them have served in the military, and they have a variety of different political ideologies, professions, religious affiliations, and pastimes. Not calling them – as a group – "diverse" would be to give in to the same obstructive viewpoints that make social groups other than straight white men different, exotic, or deviant (Andersen & Collins, 2010b). White is a race, male is a sex, and heterosexuality is a sexual orientation. In a TED Talk (2012), Jackson Katz, American educator and author on gender, race, and violence prevention, made a similar point:

> When we hear the word race, a lot of people think that means African American, Latino, Asian American, Native American … when they hear the word sexual orientation, they think it means gay, lesbian, bisexual. And … when they hear the term gender, they think it means women. In each case, the dominant group doesn't get paid attention to…. As if white people don't have some sort of racial identity … as if heterosexual people don't have a sexual orientation, as if men don't have a gender. This is one of the ways that dominant systems maintain and reproduce themselves, which is to say the dominant group is rarely challenged to even think about its dominance, because that's one of the key characteristics of power and privilege.

Think, for a moment, how you identify. What's most important to you *about you*? And which of your identities matter most to others, to either point out commonalities or differences? All members of a social system recognize they're made up of a variety of identities, also called intersecting identities (Crenshaw, 1989, 1991). For example, if you're in school, I'd say being a student is an important part of who you are. If your peers or family matter to you, I'd say you care about being a friend, a daughter, a sister, or a niece. These identities are context and time specific. Once we're not college students anymore, our identities as students likely cease to be prominent or vanish completely. At that time other identities may become more important, including employee, co-worker, or supervisor.

Next, let's think about our most *salient* identities. I'm referring to social identities (those constructed by a social system) that may be central to our core as individuals, such as race, gender, sexual orientation, religion, or social class status. One or more of these identities may become more or less salient depending on situation. For instance, a low-income college student may be forced to think about the salience of social class if they and their family struggle to come up with enough money for college, while observing other students for whom paying the bill isn't an issue (Jones & Abes, 2013). If you attend an institution where most other students don't have the color of your skin, where most students don't believe in your God, or where most don't identify as gay, bi, trans, or pansexual, your salient identities of race or ethnicity, religion, gender or sexual identity may matter a great deal, often more than you may choose. Thus, salience is not only determined by the value or importance an individual ascribes to a certain identity, but by the context in which the identity occurs or appears salient to others (Jones & Abes, 2013). Which would you say are your most salient identities, and how would you react if the salience of your identities were the reason others oppressed you at school, on campus, at work, or even in your own family?

Socially constructed identities, like race, gender, or sexual orientation, are often the most important identities for people from oppressed social groups, because living in the United States constantly confronts them with the salience of these identities. Andersen and Collins (2010a, p. 1) emphasize this by suggesting, "Race, class ... gender [and sexual orientation] matter because they remain the foundations for systems of power and inequality that, despite our nation's diversity, continue to be among the most significant facts of people's lives." White people in general, and white college men specifically, may not readily recognize this dilemma and may need deeper engagement with salient identities and how they depend on social context. Instructors, advisors, teachers, or parents should also ask white men to frequently explore and articulate their own salient identities, and how these intersect with privilege and oppression.

Yet despite intentions by researchers to foreground the experiences of individuals with traditionally oppressed identities, Andersen and Collins (2010a) also assert that focusing too much on the experiences of people in poverty, people of color, and women can prevent us from seeing class, race, and gender as important identities to everyone, including individuals with multiple privileged identities. This point warrants the study of how a social system of power benefits some and oppresses others across intersecting identities, and what privileged individuals can do to help undo identity-based oppression. It also means that it's possible for straight white college men to name their own oppressed identities, or mention reasons for why they perceive possible disadvantages.

To come back to our participants, many straight white college men may feel excluded from the definition of diversity because for their entire life they've assumed, or they've been taught, that "diverse" means non-white, non-male, and non-straight. Because they feel outside of this definition, but because they want to belong, they attempt to widen the gaze on diversity and are keen to include invisible characteristics, which they have and which they sense make them diverse. These provide straight white men with a connection to the topic and a potential sense of belonging, at least in the context of diversity on campus.

The key for educators is not necessarily to extend the definitions of diversity, but to observe how diversity functions vis-à-vis power, privilege, and oppression. Should straight white men be "counted" as diverse beings who have a race, a gender, a sexual orientation, and a host of other privileged and maybe even marginalized intersecting identities? Absolutely! It may be more critical, however, to engage them in conversations about how their need to be included in definitions of diversity relates to the wider discussion of understanding privilege and oppression. For instance, whites don't tend to give people of color the option of going by who one is and not how one looks. Someone who is using a wheelchair to move about doesn't have that luxury either. The salience of the oppressed identity looms so large that it's the only thing privileged individuals notice.

I want to return, one final time, to my colleague who cautioned me to write a book about white men and not treat them as diverse beings with a host of intersecting identities. I can't help but see reflected in this comment the desires of my participants to belong or to be counted among America's diverse people. If we didn't include straight white college guys in the ways we as institutions defined diversity, what would happen to them? Would they go away, be forced to leave campus, or suffer academic difficulty? Likely not, at least not in the same way racial, gender, or sexual oppression hinders the daily existence of traditionally oppressed students on American campuses. The plea to count straight white men equally as diverse as their peers with oppressed racial, sexual, or gender identities seems a bit like white resistance and white fragility, two concepts I will discuss next.

White Male Resistance to Diversity Initiatives

When Shannon Gibney, Professor of English and African Diaspora Studies at Minneapolis Community and Technical College (MCTC), entered her Introduction to Mass Communications classroom one day in the fall of 2013, she may not have dreamed that a discussion on structural racism would result in a formal reprimand from her employer, and her encounter going viral on the internet. While Gibney was teaching, a white male student interrupted her and, with a defensive demeanor, asked why racism had to be a topic in every class. Another white male student followed suit, questioning why all white men are always the bad guys and why Gibney had to mention this in class. After Gibney explained that structural racism is alive and well in 21st century America, she added that students, if they so choose, could file a complaint with college officials. They did. This landed Gibney a formal demerit from her Vice President of Academic Affairs, who wrote in a letter:

Shannon, I find it troubling that the manner in which you led a discussion on the very important topic of structural racism alienated two students who may have been most in need of learning about this subject. While I believe it was your intention to discuss structural racism generally, it was inappropriate for you to single out white male students in class. Your actions in [targeting] select students based on their race and gender caused them embarrassment and created a hostile learning environment.

(Aran, 2013, para. 5)

Alienating, singling out, embarrassment, and hostile learning environment. It's problematic that institutions of higher education, and their disproportionate white male leadership, continue to cater to the white majority, to the loud voices of white students and parents who don't think college should challenge their perspective or ideology, and to white boosters who want their alma mater to refrain from seemingly indoctrinating students with leftist views. Think, for a second, how Gibney's case would have turned out had she been Shane Gibney, a white male professor teaching about white nationalism and the objectors had been two black male students who didn't want to hear another word about the KKK. Would the white male Gibney have received a reprimand? I would sure hope so but I wouldn't hold my breath.

Strong empirical evidence asserts that white college students, and white male students in particular, frequently and often ardently (as seen in the case of MCTC) resist instruction on issues of diversity, power, privilege, and oppression inside and outside of the classroom (Brown, 2004; Heinze, 2008; Johnson et al., 2008; Martin, 2010; Pittman, 2010; Pleasants, 2011; Rich, Utley, Janke, & Moldoveanu, 2010; Robbins & Jones, 2016; Vaccaro, 2010). What's more, their institutions of higher education often back students with traditionally privileged identities, an act that perpetuates white supremacy and the college or university as a system of oppression for minoritized individuals (Bondi, 2012).

Resistance to diversity content often manifests in students' failure to sufficiently prepare for class, including purposefully missing homework or reading, in not participating during class discussions and activities, and in eschewing class assignments that request students to engage in cross-cultural interactions (Brown, 2004). A vast majority of male participants in a study on voluntary or mandatory sexual assault awareness programs for college men revealed strong feelings of anger as resistance (Rich et al., 2010). Men perceived they were unfairly targeted as potential offenders of rape or sexual assault and stated the intended educational initiative didn't relate to them. My good colleague and higher education scholar, Annemarie Vaccaro (2010), found an alarming level of white male resistance to diversity efforts in her campus climate study. Respondents refused to have deep dialogue about diversity, found diversity efforts unnecessary or discussed too frequently on campus, or threatened to withdraw financial support as alums if the institution continued to foster diversity (Vaccaro, 2010). At my institution, we've had similar results in our most recent campus climate study. More than three-quarters of undergraduate male participants declared the institution was doing enough or too much for diversity on campus. Among male staff and faculty that value was about 58%.

Participants of the present study confirm the extant research findings on white male student resistance to course content related to privilege and oppression, as well as to professors teaching these courses. Some of our participants implicitly resisted learning about topics or power, privilege, and oppression. This was evident in their lamentations about the quality of most of their faculty teaching diversity courses and in their perceptions of being shamed when white. The participants desired faculty who can present information in an unbiased, professional manner, without getting the sense the professor is shaming them for the sins of their cultural ancestors. This confirms research on student resistance in classrooms where privilege and oppression are topics because students do not want their own nonracist identities questioned (Brown, 2004; Ehrke, Berthold, & Steffens, 2014; Martin, 2010; Walters & Sylaska, 2012). To be certain, professional faculty behavior is necessary in college classrooms, and arbitrarily targeting or downgrading white male students must be avoided. However, faculty with traditionally marginalized identities often feel targeted or triggered by white male resistance in classrooms (Boatright-Horowitz & Soeung, 2009; Johnson et al., 2008; McGee & Kazembe, 2015) and no faculty member, regardless of salient identity, should guarantee student comfort in diversity courses. The importance of discomfort, cognitive dissonance, or disorienting dilemmas (Mezirow, 1991) in learning new content needs to be communicated by faculty at the onset and throughout every course that interrogates power, privilege, and oppression.

Despite the active levels of resistance emerging from the attitudes and behaviors of white college men about content related to privilege and oppression in and out of the classroom, some scholars posit that resistance is likely a better sign of participation and learning than complete disengagement from the content, dropping the course, or leaving a lecture on oppression (Heinze, 2008; Pleasants, 2011).

White Fragility: The Need for Racial Comfort

Not in all cases will whites eagerly resist diversity initiatives and education. They may instead claim they don't need additional training on issues of power, privilege, and oppression because they perceive themselves as progressive and anti-racist. *White fragility*, or the lack of resilience for racial issues, is an attitude we may consider as a form of white resistance to topics of power, privilege, and oppression (DiAngelo, 2011). Whites typically approach racism or other forms of social oppression with dualistic or binary thinking. They assert racism is immoral and bad, and they consider themselves to be moral and good people. Ergo, good whites can't be racist, and good whites don't perform heinous racist acts. The fact that whites typically view racism only as a performance, an action, or a behavior is, according to DiAngelo (as cited in Adler-Bell, 2015), "one of the most effective [white] adaptations of racism over time" (para. 17). And we as whites defend our perceived morality and goodness against anything and anyone who questions our good intentions.

One of the ways in which white, male, or straight fragility manifests is through the perceived lack of comfort in a situation in which race, gender, or sexual orientation are topics of discussion. White supremacy, the white habitus, and the white racial frame have bestowed upon us whites a sense of entitlement to constant comfort around issues of privilege and oppression (Shih, 2015). When they engage in diversity coursework many white students may expect the same kind of racial comfort they are afforded in society, comfort that obscures engaging in critical content on issues of privilege and oppression. When not provided this comfort in daily interactions, whites become stressed. Moreover, whites respond to small amounts of race-based stress with annoyance, impatience, guilt, aggression, fearfulness, argumentative behaviors, or retreat (Shih, 2015; Wigg-Stevenson, 2016). And white fragility isn't the only response of privileged individuals. In men, able-bodied, or heterosexual individuals, male fragility, able-bodied fragility, or hetero fragility show up as hurtful actions or self-protective reactions toward people from minoritized backgrounds.

Rather than building more racial stamina, humility, or resilience toward possibly being called racist – incidentally the worst insult you can hurl at a white person – we white people, and the white men in our study, call for the need for comfort or safety. In a recent interview, DiAngelo discussed how we as whites conceive the ways in which we would like to receive feedback about racism:

> In my workshops, one of the things I like to ask white people is, "What are the rules for how people of color should give us feedback about our racism? What are the rules, where did you get them, and whom do they serve?" Usually those questions alone make the point. It's like if you're standing on my head and I say, "Get off my head," and you respond, "Well, you need to tell me nicely." I'd be like, "No. Fuck you. Get off my fucking head."
>
> (cited in Adler-Bell, 2015, para. 30–1)

We educators must engage in discussions around white college men's perceived need for comfort about privilege and oppression. Perceived need for comfort around college professors who have different opinions, about attending a diversity-related event on campus, or about wanting to be invited to diversity initiatives should provide ample fodder for training and building white racial resilience. This racial resilience is what we as whites so often suggest people of color lack when they rail against centuries of racial oppression. Actually, we as whites must understand that we're in fact the social group that is most deficient of resilience around issues of race. A thicker skin, humility, and empathy are needed, not a desire for more comfort, in a corner, with our blanket.

Summary

Diversity is not about me.
I'm not in college for this.
I've got better things to do.

As you can see, many of our participants think primarily in terms of their own self, rather than as part of a collective society, culture of college students, or group of young Americans. They say if institutional or societal definitions of diversity don't include *me*, why should *I* engage in learning more about it during college? If diversity is not about *me* as a straight white guy, then why should *I* care about it? How is it relevant to *me*? What do *I* get out of it?

As we've seen in this chapter, the participants define diversity to primarily include visible characteristics that include race and ethnicity. However, they were also keen to include generally invisible aspects of identity in their definitions of diversity so they could be included in the definition, or allowed to become part of how we conceive of diversity on college campuses. In defining diversity, some of our participants expressed colorblind points of view. Color of skin, sexual orientation, or other typically minoritized identities didn't matter to them, as if to say, they don't discriminate against people who appear to be different from them.

Considering interactions across difference in college, we continue to notice some isolation from racial, ethnic, or sexual orientation difference in our white male students. What began before and during high school continues in college for them. On the other hand, the few participants who shared that they experienced increased interactions across difference in college indicated that these discussions had probed more deeply about issues of oppression. Many of the participants also asserted that personal growth, an opening of minds, and job or career skills may be important takeaways from interactions across difference.

However, the participants also decried how lackluster the diversity courses they took seemed or lamented the apparent low level of skill of their instructors. Some of them were further reticent to engage in out-of-class diversity initiatives for a variety of reasons, including perceiving these efforts to be a waste of time or irrelevant. To even consider attending, the participants wanted to be invited, encouraged, or explicitly welcomed. Resistance and need for comfort were significant themes among the data furnishing this chapter.

When we interpret the myriad ways in which the sum of my participants conceptualized diversity, their interactions across difference, their potential learning gains, their perceptions of courses, instructors, and of the effect of out-of-class diversity initiatives, we can't help but notice a gaping continuum of development of understanding diversity. It's nearly impossible to typecast our participants in stages of development because they're virtually all over the board in how they approach the topic of diversity. An individual participant may define diversity in well-thought-out ways, may say he learns a great deal from diversity initiatives, may interact more across difference than he did in high school, but then feel shamed by an instructor, or criticize well-intentioned diversity programming. Diversity and how the participants fit into this concept is not a linear kind of development.

The findings imply that we as educators, both before and during college, must instill in straight white men a practice of reflection about how they conceive of themselves in the context of diversity, what they take away from their engagement with diversity, and how they commit to working with diverse others in an increasingly pluralistic world. Helping men build solidarity and activating their responsibility for social change are predicated upon this reflective exploration and understanding not who *I am myself* in terms of diversity, but who *we are together*.

One of my biggest realizations of more than 20 years as an educator, and supported by my own experiences as a younger man, is that many straight white men in college will likely not engage in diversity-related content on their own. To whet their appetite for these topics may be the responsibility of teachers in schools or colleges and more straight white male educators must commit to this work. If we continue to fail to engage white men more critically during college in learning about diversity, we stand the chance of losing them forever. That is, once they leave college we lose the chance to guide or mentor them the way we could during the four to six years they were with us on our campus. At that point, it might simply be too late to engage straight white men in a cause for which they saw little relevance during college.

4   White is Norm
Acknowledging Privilege, Power, and Oppression on Campus

It's nice. I don't wake up and think, "Oh, I'm a straight white male."
(Stuart, St. Margaret University)

Well, you're definitely not in any minority, so whatever benefits come along with being the majority – being a straight, white, male – [you] get it here.
(Jack, Riverside State University)

I think a black kid going into a class of 50 white kids might not feel as comfortable as the 49 white kids there.
(Ron, Southern State University)

Privilege, Power, and Oppression in Contemporary America

It's been a while since the 2016 Presidential election in the United States, but I wonder if you remember some of Trump's political platforms. Aside from the typical Republican mantras of free-market enterprise, economy and job growth, cutting taxes and spending, and bolstering the military, he went on the offensive, declaring most of his running-mates and Republican primary opponents (only one of whom was a woman) as inept. He did so with brash language, hurling personal insults at Jeb Bush, Carly Fiorina, Scott Walker, Mike Huckabee, Ted Cruz, and Marco Rubio.

But what Trump did to Senator Hillary Clinton was worse. He painted her as a criminal as she ostensibly obfuscated justice by sending classified e-mails from a personal server. Trump also campaigned relentlessly against the policies of President Obama, whom he accused of obstruction. As if this weren't enough, Trump also insulted millions of American citizens and international allies by publicly deriding and admonishing people of color, women, members of the LGBTQ+ community, citizens with disabilities, Americans and international individuals with non-Christian religious beliefs, citizens of different countries, veterans, journalists, and the media. Despite all this, he was elected, not by winning the popular vote, but by winning the Electoral College. At the time of writing, with three-quarters of his first term done,

Trump has not let up from being the most disgraceful political bully the United States has ever seen. What's even more disconcerting is that he may well be guilty of all the behaviors for which he insulted his Republican and Democrat colleagues on the campaign trail. He has not disclosed his tax returns, he discussed classified information over a $200,000-per-plate dinner at his hotel in Florida, his personal lawyer paid off a former porn actress to remain silent about Trump's potential adulterous affair with her, and he may have been deeply involved with Russian leaders who meddled in the 2016 national election. And he gets away with all of it. Still.

This chapter deals with privilege, power, and oppression as perceived by our participants. Donald Trump is the incarnation of privilege (race, gender, sexual orientation, and class), power (among the two or three most powerful politicians on the planet), and oppression (where to start?). The empirical effects of privilege, power, and oppression have long been misunderstood, downplayed, or attacked by Americans who believe in the adage of the American Dream or the myth of meritocracy: that only hard work, blood, sweat, and tears are the reasons for individual success. Further, many Americans falsely claim that the absence of such personal virtues results in their apparent economic and social plights of members of disadvantaged, minoritized, or impoverished communities. It's dishonorable that one of the richest countries on earth continues to desecrate those who have the least as those who are at fault for everything that apparently plights our nation. Spurred by an incessant White House motor of polemics, newly emboldened whites live out their hatred against people of color, immigrants, Muslims, transgender, gay, and lesbian people on a daily basis and for all to see on social media. This treatment of people is absolutely disgusting, and it is high time that straight white men, as a group, interfere and help end the disgrace.

But you might say, "Not all whites are privileged." It's true, as I discussed in the previous chapter, that some whites may be at a disadvantage because of their socioeconomic standing, their impoverished upbringing or current life situation, their differing levels of abilities or health, or their lack of wealth or social capital. Indeed, some whites in this country are minoritized based on their life circumstances or their poverty. But we as whites have to begin to understand that those who keep us stuck to our rung of the social ladder are not people of color, women, or people with diverse genders or sexual orientations. The folks who step on our hands or kick our heads as we try to climb upward are other whites: the rich, white, male demagogue politicians, financiers, legislators, CEO-types, or men-made-by-others (as opposed to self-made men), many of whom are progenies of incredible financial capital for which they didn't have to move one finger. These great white manipulators will make you believe that the fellow citizens who also yearn for a bit more in their lives, and who stand next to you or below you on the ladder, are to blame for your bruised hands and bleeding heads. And the elite white male schemers and plotters have succeeded for generations in baiting us with their propaganda of the racial, ethnic, religious, gender-queer, gay, lesbian, bisexual, or female "other," who only gets ahead when we stay in place. Regular white folk in this country must begin to resist the zero-sum game palaver, and, together with our brothers, sisters, friends, and colleagues with multiple minoritized identities, reach up and proverbially pull the top-rung sitters off the ladder.

Definitions of Race, Gender, and Sexual Orientation Privilege

When scholars define or explain privilege, they typically speak of groups of individuals reaping unearned benefits based on social group membership (DiAngelo & Sensoy, 2014; Edwards, 2006). These benefits tend to include social, professional, education, or economic opportunities, such as getting a better job, being accepted by an elite college or university, or receiving a promotion with a salary increase. In the United States, identity characteristics that bestow privilege include gender, race, ethnicity, sexual orientation, religion, ability, social class/socioeconomic status, national origin, and age. However, we must also take into account the intersections of these identities. For example, an able-bodied, Christian, female African-American college professor may consider herself privileged in her identities as an able-bodied Christian professor. Her race and gender identities are traditionally oppressed identities, and the treatment she faces as a black woman in society is likely primarily because of her racial identity. A straight white male high school student with a learning disability growing up in foster care in an impoverished rural community may seem privileged, considering his visible identities don't seem to include any historically subordinated characteristics. However, his oppressed identities of socioeconomic status and ability may tell another story about how much access he actually has to educational, career, or housing opportunities.

For the purposes of this book, we need to differentiate between gender, race, and sexual orientation privileges, even though there are many others, typically one for each intersecting identity we call salient or important. Regarding gender privilege, educators who engage college learners in activities about personal safety may soon realize that it's harder for men to articulate daily strategies to staying safe on campus (Goodman, 2011). Women-identified individuals tend to list such behaviors more quickly.

Considering racial privilege, whites typically gain advantages over people of color, or people from different ethnic groups with darker skin, including identifying a role model in an elevated position, gaining employment without people thinking affirmative action was responsible, not being the only person of the specific race in the room, not being followed in a store, not being stopped and frisked, and not being threatened of being hurt or shot. White privilege (much like gender privilege) allows whites to be oblivious to, take for granted, or not interrogate the benefits that come with being white because being white is the normative and dominant social identity in the United States (Sue, 2010). In his book, *White Guys on Campus: Racism, White*

Immunity, and the Myth of "Post-Racial" Higher Education, Nolan Cabrera (2019), race and masculinity scholar at the University of Arizona, aptly uses the term *white immunity* instead of white privilege. He argues it more accurately describes the inoculation whites experience from systemic racism, and that privilege falsely individualizes benefits that are more systemic in nature. Because of this immunity, whites can likely come up with at least a few items describing how people of color are disadvantaged in this society, but will struggle to identify the ways in which white people benefit from racial discrimination (McIntosh, 2004).

Even though *Obergefell* v. *Hodges* (2015), the recent Supreme Court decision guaranteeing the universal right to same-sex marriage in the U.S., was a major triumph for social justice, heterosexual privilege continues to exist. It typically allows straight couples to freely show their affection, hold hands in public, speak openly about their partner or bring them to an event, not worry about losing their job because of their sexual orientation (which is not a protected "class" in each state or each institution under the constitution), or not fear whether their partner will be accepted as family under hospital policies or inheritance laws (Goodman, 2011).

During a focus group at Southern State, Bill and I had this fascinating exchange about privilege:

> BILL: At the risk of sounding extremely racist or bigoted maybe, when I look at it, I think of [privilege as] how good I've got it. I had to take a Black Studies [class] at [the local community college], [and] when I sat down and you hear about all the things that different cultures have been through … I just sit back and say, "Man, I've got it good."
>
> JÖRG: But is that a learning moment? Is that an, "I need to do more?"
>
> BILL: I guess, a learning thing. I guess … I've always thought I've had it good, but then you realized how much better you've had it than [others]. And it just kind of … instills more, I don't know, pride in being a white heterosexual male.
>
> JÖRG: Does it motivate to say, "Man, other people have it like shit, we need to do something more for them?"
>
> BILL: To me it doesn't.

I must have read this excerpt 100 times. In fact, I can see Bill in front of me, I hear his voice saying these lines, and I can remember the setting in the Dean's conference room I described at the outset of Chapter 2. It's difficult for me to interpret what's going on here, I admit. One the one hand, I applaud Bill for taking a class – despite "having to," as he says – in an area that may have been, at first glance, uncomfortable for him. And throughout the course, he seemed to learn about issues of privilege, oppression, and perhaps racism. All of that probably left something in him: an indelible mark of privilege, that he has it better than many others in his hometown, state, or this country. So as an educator who wants to help white college men raise their awareness, I rejoice. But I also struggle because what Bill appears to take away from this learning opportunity is not the kind of advocacy or activism I would hope this learning instilled. Rather, it seemed to instill a growing sense of pride in being straight, white, and male; not the impetus or motivation to help, be in solidarity with, or lend a hand to those he (now) knows have it worse than he does. At least not yet.

Empirical Effects of Race Privilege

In the 2017 true-crime documentary, *Strong Island* (Ford, Barnes, & Ford, 2017), director Yance Ford chronicles the violent death of her brother William in 1992 when he was shot and killed by a white car mechanic. The all-white jury in the case failed to indict William's murderer, who claimed he was defending himself against the unarmed William. Over the course of the history of this country, there are literally many thousands of Williams: Americans of minoritized racial backgrounds who were hurt or killed at the hands of white men who got off scot-free, simply because they had race privilege. In *Strong Island*, William's mother, Barbara Dunmore Ford, speaks about her noticing this privilege while growing up in Charleston, South Carolina, during the late 1940s and early '50s:

> All of the years that we were growing up, if we went through a section, or pass a section [of town] that was predominantly white, you ran. That's when I started to realize the economic difference, okay. So these people weren't wealthy, but their wealth was that they were white.
>
> (in Ford, Barnes, & Ford, 2017)

This quote is an apt reminder that not all white people benefit the same from social privileges. Poor whites, in any area of the country, probably don't have economic, political, health, or advanced education privileges. They may not feel privileged by any means, but compared to Americans of color they do have their white skin as an indicator of power over people of color in a system created by whites for the benefit of other whites.

One of the earliest and most influential pieces of writing on white privilege was a 1987 essay by Peggy McIntosh (2004) in which she uses the analogy of white privilege as an invisible knapsack (backpack) that white people get to carry around. The knapsack provides the maps, tools, codes, passports and visas, clothes, emergency gear, and money to succeed in a white-dominated society. Following her argument, a society normed by whiteness doesn't give out such knapsacks to people of color.

We can extrapolate from McIntosh's arguments that, beyond racial privilege, straight men carry additional utensils that women or people with diverse genders or sexual orientations are not afforded. While the invisible knapsack is a useful metaphor to help us think about what privilege is, it doesn't provide concrete data or factual evidence of the dire effects of such privilege.

And this is where privilege, specifically racial privilege, is often misunderstood or criticized. The lack of racial privilege directly translates to deleterious effects for people of color as they interact with law enforcement, as they enter education or a job, and as they apply for housing (Kimmel & Ferber, 2014). The data provided in the following paragraphs are but a sliver of the vast evidence that exist on the disparities between racial and ethnic groups in the United States.

Taking a look at the context of American law enforcement, young black men are disproportionately more apt to be killed by police during arrests than white men, according to data from the FBI's 2012 supplementary homicide report (Lind, 2014). "Driving while black" may be somewhat of a term of slang; however, data by the Department of Justice from more than 10 years ago showed that black drivers were three times more likely to be searched during routine traffic stops, twice as likely to be arrested, and four times as likely to experience the threat or use of force than white motorists (American Civil Liberties Union, 2007). Under the controversial NYPD "stop and frisk" policy, the vast majority of citizens stopped and searched have been people of color. For instance, in the first quarter of 2017, 57% of those stopped were black, 32% were Latinx individuals, and 9% were white (New York Civil Liberties Union, 2017). These numbers have been remarkably constant for the last 15 years, according to reports completed by New York City police officers. What's more, nearly 90% of those individuals stopped were innocent.

In the context of the American prison system, we also see stark contrasts between whites and people of color. Americans of color make up about one-third of the population of the U.S.; yet people of color account for nearly two-thirds of the prison population. About 1 in every 15 African-American men over the age of 18 find themselves in prison, compared to 1 in every 36 Latinx men, and only 1 in 106 white men (American Civil Liberties Union, 2011). In their lifetime, 1 in 3 black men may expect to end up behind bars (Lyons & Pettit, 2011). Our nation's law enforcement has fought its infamous war on drugs disproportionately in communities of color, and people of color have been arrested at higher rates than whites, as well as received disproportionately higher sentences (Human Rights Watch, 2009). Data suggest that in a near 30-year span starting in 1980, about one-third of all adults arrested related to drugs were black, despite blacks making up only about 12% of all Americans during the same timeframe. Of these 12%, only 60% were of adult age.

Similar disparities between people of color and whites exist in education. According to a study conducted by the Organization for Economic Cooperation and Development (OECD; 2013), the U.S. is one of only three developed countries that invests less in disadvantaged students than in their more privileged counterparts. Disproportionately, disadvantaged secondary school students largely stem from communities of color or low-income households. According to data from the U.S. Department of Education

(Lewin, 2012), black students, especially young men, are more often the perceived culprits of trouble in school than members of any other student group. The Civil Rights Data Collection's 2009–10 statistics from more than 70,000 schools (Lewin, 2012) revealed that black students made up less than one-fifth of the students sampled. Yet they represented more than a third of the students suspended once, 46% of those suspended more than once, and 39% of all student expulsions.

Once in college, completion rates vary sharply by race and ethnicity. Overall, about 55% of all college students who enter a specific institution graduate from that institution within six years; however, 62% of white and 63.2% of Asian-American students complete their degrees from their initial institutions, compared to 46% and 38% of Latinx and black students (National Student Clearinghouse Research Center, 2017). The same report indicated that African-American men have the lowest rate of four-year degree attainment of any college student group.

In the job market, the disparities among members of different racial or ethnic backgrounds are as pervasive as racial discrimination itself. A groundbreaking and widely cited study by Princeton and Harvard sociologists revealed that white, black, and Latinx job applicants in a low-wage labor market had inequitable chances to gain employment (Pager, Western, & Bonikowski, 2009). The researchers matched the participants on characteristics and skills and provided equally qualified resumes. Results revealed that black applicants received a recall or were offered the job only half as often as white applicants. Astonishingly, white applicants with faked prison sentences did just as well in securing employment as black and Latinx job seekers with apparent squeaky-clean backgrounds.

Finally, people of color may continue to face severe discrimination in attempting to secure housing in their lifetime. After the stock market crashed in 2008 due to pernicious and predatory loan practices, then Federal Reserve chairman, Ben Bernanke, suggested that the housing crisis disproportionately affected people of color because of policies like redlining (see Chapter 2) and pricing discrimination. Banks pushed people of color to sign up for more volatile and costly subprime loans even when they could have received lower-interest prime mortgages (Kurtz, 2012). Such malice led to nearly one-third of Latinx people and 42% of African Americans receiving subprime loans, compared to only 18% of whites (Waldron, 2012).

If you're still not convinced that white privilege is a thing, consider the vast body of literature on Implicit Association Tests (IATs) (Banaji & Greenwald, 2016). IATs are sorting activities used in psychological research that measure the strength of associations of concepts, evaluations, and stereotypes between mental representations of objects in memory. IATs are scored based on how quickly respondents sort concepts and associations, like European Americans or black Americans, along with words that are pleasant or unpleasant. The *Race IAT* has predicted and shown that white Americans have an automatic preference for other whites, to the tune of 75% of whites who have taken the IAT. Second, the IAT predicts discriminatory behaviors of whites toward people of color, even if they commit to egalitarian values (Banaji & Greenwald, 2016). And in the last decade alone, hundreds of studies have been published that show similar results of white stereotyping and preference along with predicting discriminatory behavior. The Race IAT evidences what the theories of the white racial frame (Feagin, 2013) and the white habitus (Bonilla-Silva, 2014) have conceptualized.

Beyond raising awareness of how privilege manifests among different social groups in the United States, we also need to study how privilege may lead individuals to have power over others in social, economic, and political contexts.

Defining Power

Simply put, power decides who in a social structure gets more or less of whatever is desirable (Lemert, 2007). Access to food, health care, housing, education, income, transportation, and other staples of life differ by where in a society individuals stand. Children who grow up in lower socioeconomic conditions have fewer options for housing, food, or schooling, and poor people tend to remain poor (Rivera, 2015), not just for a time, but typically for their entire life (Lemert, 2007). Upward mobility, for the vast majority of Americans who live in poverty, is as much of a myth as meritocracy and the American Dream (Rivera, 2015). Power is the mechanism that controls this inequitable sorting of human beings into their rung of the social ladder (Lemert, 2007).

Power and race (or gender or sexual orientation) are inexorably linked. When members of traditionally privileged groups vehemently assert today that all people can be racist (white on black, black on white, Latinx on Asian), they're likely adhering to a definition of racism based on individual or ideological prejudice, and one that doesn't take into account that power is the main variable of racial oppression. In leaning on David Wellman's (1977) early definition, racism functions as a system of advantages based on race. That is, racism isn't simply a personal ideology based on learned prejudice, or an individual pathology (Bonilla-Silva, 2014). Rather, racism is a larger social structure that combines systemic or institutional messages, policies, mores, and traditions with the beliefs, attitudes, and actions of individual citizens. According to Tatum (2004), many diversity educators typically use the definition that *racism equals power plus prejudice*. In this sense, power and access to resources combined with prejudice engender the creation of racist policies and practices. These policies and practices can be seen in inequitable access to housing, jobs, or education for American people of color. In such a system of dominance and power based on social categories, it's simply not enough to say, "I'm not racist (or sexist or heterosexist) as an individual, and I don't have or want any power over anyone else," but to do whatever is possible to disrupt the actual systemic cogs and wheels that motor the machine of power and oppression.

An undeniable and inextricable linkage also exists between power and masculinity. According to Kimmel (2010, p. 28), "manhood is equated with power – over women, over other men." Kimmel explains that masculinity may be defined as an effort to avoid emasculation; that is, we as men exert power and dominance over others and dispense harsh social sanctions to those not considered fully manly, including women, gay men, men of color, or immigrant men. This power is ubiquitous in all U.S. institutions and results in an overrepresentation of men, like the one I addressed in the introduction to this book (Feagin & Ducey, 2017; Feagin & O'Brien, 2003).

According to Raewyn Connell (2003, 2014), distinguished Australian sociologist and the originator of the concept of *hegemonic masculinity* (more recently also referred to as *toxic masculinity*), masculinity and power are interrelated. In this sense, hegemonic masculinity legitimizes patriarchy, which guarantees men the dominant position over subordinated women and individuals with other gender identities. As famed German philosopher Hannah Arendt (as cited in Kimmel, 2010) pointed out, power is not property of an individual, but of a group that bestows power on the individual. Take elected politicians, for instance. As long as their constituents elect them into office, their power is widespread. Once no longer in office, they may still have influence based on their privilege, but their political power may wane.

Although I don't side with scholars who make assertions about men as preys or victims of gender relations (Synnott, 2009), I'm convinced that despite having power as a result of male privilege, many men, especially young white men in college, may not feel powerful. Much has been written about this *paradox of masculinity*, especially by sociologists and psychologists. Kimmel (2010) explains that feminists have suggested that masculinity is about the drive for domination, for power, and for conquest, because women experience masculinity in this way. Women also feel not in power, afraid, and vulnerable. And they have assumed that men, as individuals, must feel powerful. However, that's not the experience of most men who don't see or investigate the disconnect between how sociologically they are in power as a group and the psychological perception, that as individuals, they feel powerless (Kimmel, 2010). You can find this paradox of masculinity in statements men make about "everyone bossing them around," or in their feeling disempowered, constrained, or fenced in.

Many men may feel powerless because the rules that govern manhood have instructed them to be independent, strong, daring, aggressive, and self-reliant, and to strongly reject any inclination they may not be straight (Dowd, 2010). The vast majority of men will fail to meet these restrictive expectations, experience shame as a result, and fear expulsion from their circle of male friends. To hide their shame, men may discriminate against or exclude less-dominant individuals to prove that they are indeed manly. This, according to Kimmel (2010, p. 30), manifests as "the manhood of racism, of sexism, of homophobia."

During a discussion about power at Lucas College, Scott and Brian shared:

SCOTT: I'd say, maybe just personally, it's not really a priority to me to get rid of my power. It's not something I go, "Man, I'm privileged, I'm going to knock that down." I don't intentionally go out of my way to do that very often.

BRIAN: I don't think very many people do.

SCOTT: Yeah.

The fact that Scott acknowledged that he held a certain amount of power compared to others is a step in the direction of advocating for social change and building solidarity with those less powerful. His temporary or ongoing inability to more critically interrogate this power and how some of it could be transferred to historically marginalized peers is an important next step in the education of straight white college men. Whether they have a change of heart to actively pursue advocacy for those without relative power in our society, educators should frequently challenge white men like Scott ought to continue to develop their thoughts about what it would look like to actually "knock power down," as he says.

Defining Oppression

For oppression to occur, social power must be uneven so that one group can gain access to resources and goods, rewards, and punishments to acquire the means necessary to influence or subjugate another group (Goodman, 2011). Johnson (2010) states that for every privileged social category, one or more other categories in relation are oppressed: "Just as privilege tends to open doors of opportunity, oppression tends to slam them shut" (Johnson, 2010, p. 20). Sociologists typically use the term *oppression* compared to discrimination, bias, or bigotry to indicate the structural and pervasive nature of social inequalities. These inequalities are part of the stained fabric of social institutions, and they are also implanted in individual framing and consciousness (Bell, 2007). The systemic nature of oppression is visible when the dominant culture, in this country represented primarily by European, masculine, and straight worldviews, pushes itself, overtly or covertly, on citizens with minoritized racial, gender, and sexual identities (Sue, 2010). Once the ruling class of privileged individuals create policy, procedures, or a culture that keep marginalized people without power, as well as control resources or constrain opportunities for minoritized individuals, we speak of systemic oppression, or a system of oppression (Goodman, 2011). This system is alive and well in the United States in every sector and every institution of public life.

To experience oppression means identifying with a group, category, or salient identity that can be oppressed. A group needs power to oppress another, so, for instance, men can't be oppressed as men, whites can't be oppressed as whites, and people who identify as straight won't be oppressed because they're heterosexual (Johnson, 2010). It is possible for straight white men to feel oppression but they have to identify with at least one marginalized category, such as religion, social class, ability, or age.

The most pervasive forms of oppression include racism, sexism, heterosexism, and classism. Ageism and ableism are also prevalent oppressive forces, but they are not part of the scope of this book. Young (2010) conceptualizes the five dominant faces of oppression as exploitation, marginalization, powerlessness, cultural imperialism, and violence.

Exploitation occurs when the benefits of the labor of the oppressed group transfer to the group in power. A simple example would be agricultural production in the United States. The pickers do the hard labor for a fraction of the income the grower makes when selling the products. An added layer in this example is that gender and race play as factors: most laborers who pick vegetables, fruit, or cotton in the United States are people of color or women.

Marginalization is perhaps the most insidious form of oppression, and it targets the people a system of labor cannot or refuses to use (Young, 2010). Marginalization is pervasive in the sense that it does not only target people of different racial, ethnic, or national backgrounds; it also affects older citizens who need work but won't be considered for a job, younger job seekers who can't find work or are in a state of flux between employment or unemployment, and especially African-American and Latinx young adults who can't find a first or a second job (Young, 2010). Marginalization also affects single mothers and their children, people suffering from mental or physical disabilities, and most Native Americans, especially those living on reservations. Given that marginalization pervasively transcends racial and ethnic lines, it is possible for straight white men to be marginalized in this society. But they won't be marginalized for their racial, gender, or sexual orientation identity.

Powerlessness is a form of oppression from which people suffer who work in non-professional positions. These workers rarely have authority to make decisions, while plenty of decisions that affect them are made by others. Powerless workers also have limited opportunity for additional development, training, or the exercising of new skills. They don't have the power to give orders and don't have the luxury of not accepting them from supervisors. But the powerless do not only suffer from their low status at work as this form of oppression permeates their lives. People who are powerless are generally segregated from those who are powerful, they can't afford the same amenities of life, such as cars, vacations, or clothing, and often have special health and educational needs (Young, 2010).

While exploitation, marginalization, and powerlessness all relate to one another and to the social division of labor in a society, *cultural imperialism* refers to the oppression that occurs when the dominant culture, traditions, or meanings of life render the oppressed group's culture invisible and marks it as "the other" (Young, 2010). This type of oppression projects the experience of the dominant culture onto all subordinated groups. In the United States, straight white men can be seen as those whose cultural expressions have become the norm, while all other social groups become the remarkable, the deviant, or the inferior. Subordinated groups are stereotyped and the dominant group doesn't contest the stereotypes: "Just as everyone knows that the earth goes around the sun, so everyone knows that gay people are promiscuous, that American Indians are alcoholics, and that women are good with children" (Young, 2010, p. 42). In as much as straight white men can avoid demarcation as members of minoritized groups, they're the only ones who can remain individuals in a culturally imperialistic society.

Many groups in the United States suffer oppression by systemic and barbaric *violence*. In the United States, women, African Americans, Latinx people, Asians, Native Americans, people with diverse gender or sexual identities, and Muslims live under constant threat of such violence that has no other motive than to harm, degrade, or destroy. You have all seen or heard about this type of violence, or have been personally subjected to it: raping or assaulting women, severely beating gay men, killing African-American men and women at the hands of law enforcement officers, assaults and killings of Muslim Americans, assaulting or killing transgender men and women, mass shootings by white supremacists targeting people of color, or the use of police force against Native Americans peacefully protesting the construction of an oil pipeline are perpetual parts of our American culture. Individual violence itself is not oppression (although it's just as unacceptable), but the systemic and historic nature of targeting the same groups of people over generations has made violence against oppressed citizens an American social practice (Young, 2010). I may even go as far as saying that this abhorrent violence against our fellow citizens has become an American pastime, one that is encouraged by politicians and condoned by state and federal governments, and one that is watched as a spectator sport by millions of Americans indifferent to the human carnage. No other civilized country on this earth has done so little to avoid the violent deaths of its citizens over generations.

Toxic masculinity certainly fits into the system of oppression because it not only norms masculine behavior to be aggressive, competitive, and dominant, but it also perpetuates whiteness and maleness in who has access to resources, goods, or opportunities. The glaring overrepresentation of white men in politics, law, education, and corporations is a symptom of systemic oppression against women and people of color. By a wide margin, men are also the main perpetrators of rape, assault, and violence against other humans, a further indication of the pervasiveness of the oppression by men.

Perceived Drawbacks of Being a Straight White Man on Campus

Turning now to the findings from my study, this chapter reports data emerging from the answers to the following focus group questions: "What's it like to be a straight white man on this campus? Talk about some of the drawbacks and benefits you perceive." The answers the men provided let us glimpse into their perceptions of white men as potential victims of societal or campus-based diversity efforts, as well as into the beginning exploration of their own privileges. If you're a straight white male college student, ask yourself the question about benefits and drawbacks to being who you are on your own campus. How would you answer? The question also works for all other readers. How do you conceive of yourself and your salient identities in your family, your workplace, and your community?

White College Men as Victims

Larry Roper (2004), former Vice Provost for Student Affairs at Oregon State University, administered a survey to undergraduate students to assess whether they supported campus diversity programs. About three-quarters of all respondents strongly supported diversity efforts at the institution; however, participants also displayed confusion and skepticism about the institution's commitment to, management of, and instruction in matters of diversity and equity. I have frequently used the following quote from a straight white male student in Roper's study in my teaching and scholarship on white college men:

> I'm a straight, white male. As such, I am the least celebrated ethnic group. When people talk about diversity, they mean everything except what I am. Before I came to OSU, I had no idea that I was the sole cause for all the problems in other people's lives, but that is what I have been made to feel like in the past four years.... In classes I have been made to feel like my opinion is not as highly valued because I'm a straight, white male ... I had no idea people hated me because of what I am, but I've had to learn to deal with it ... I have had discussions with people about all the reverse discrimination going on that I am supposed to ignore, while celebrating "diversity" (everything except me). It isn't fair, but, unlike so many minorities, I'm willing to simply accept the fact that life simply isn't.
>
> (cited in Roper, 2004, p. 50)

This particular student adamantly perceived campus diversity efforts in direct opposition to his own identity as a straight white college man. He was just one of Oregon State's thousands of students during the semester of the survey's administration and, in his senior year, we might hope or expect to see a more discerned notion about his standing on campus and in society. Fact is, there are lots of straight white male students on our nation's campuses who feel slighted, neglected, or even discriminated against by their institutions or by society (Vaccaro, 2010). What should we as educators do about this? Stamp them as whiners and, as they would put it, continue to ignore them? Engage them and their opinions, risking the potential of outward or violent resistance? If we engage them, should we do so openly in classrooms or in one-on-one or small-group meetings? And who should do the engaging? Faculty, advisors, mentors, coaches, peers, or all of the above? We will get to the answers to these questions by the end of this book. First, let's take a look at whether the participants of my study also perceived themselves as victims of diversity efforts on their college campus.

Affirmative Action

In only four of the focus groups, participants discussed affirmative action as a potential detriment to straight white men in college. The only student who seemed to speak from personal experience about the perception of being directly affected by an admission process he thought favored a high-school classmate whose family immigrated from Iran was Stuart, a senior at St. Margaret University:

> I applied to [a highly selective university on the West Coast] because that is the engineering school for [our state] and I didn't get in.... So, it's just interesting how I'm just another white guy applying to be an engineer and then there is this [Iranian] guy.... Because he's more ethnic, they needed to have a certain diversity quota.

In Stuart's perception, the only difference between him and his Iranian classmate was the (slightly more exotic) ethnicity. Stuart didn't know any more detail on the institution's decision, but he made up his mind about why the decision was made. Stuart didn't share whether he continued to hold a grudge against the other institution four years after the fact that he didn't gain admission. He also didn't share whether his Iranian classmate actually attended the other institution. And, for all intents and purposes, Stuart seemed to thrive at St. Margaret's. But his perception of losing a spot to a student of a different ethnic background was significant enough of an experience to mention during the focus group.

Talking more generally about affirmative action during college admissions, Brian, a senior at Lucas College, shared his perceptions about a potential drawback of being a straight white male college student:

> I'd say potentially [in] admission. When you start selecting for cultural diversity. When it comes down to it at the end of the day, if, from what understand, if Lucas doesn't feel like they have enough diverse population then equally qualified heterosexual white male may not take the place of an international student. Just things like that.

Brian may not have understood the purpose of affirmative action as a traditionally American policy under which institutions or organizations seek to create or improve educational or career opportunities for traditionally excluded populations, such as women and people of color. Most white college men likely don't realize that white women are also covered under affirmative action auspices, including their admission to colleges and universities. Affirmative action goes back to an executive order signed by President Kennedy in 1961, and was initially created to improve opportunities for African Americans on the heels of Jim Crow laws and the *separate but equal* doctrine.

But has affirmative action really leveled the playing field for racially minoritized individuals? Based on data from the National Center on Education Statistics (Musu-Gillette, de Brey, McFarland, Hussar, Sonnenberg, & Wilkinson Flicker, 2017), the immediate college-going rates of white, Latinx, and African-American high school seniors have only become closer in the last decade. As early as 2000, the immediate college enrollment rate for white high school graduates was 65%, compared with 56% of African American, and 49% for Latinx graduates. In 2015, these rates totaled 70% for white, 67% for Latinx, and 63% for African-American students (Musu-Gillette et al., 2017). These percentages are not meaningfully different or statistically significant, but it's clear to see that programs like affirmative action don't propel black or Latinx students beyond the chances of college enrollment for whites. Especially at predominantly white institutions, where application and enrollment rates of college-bound students of color remain low, the probability of many whites getting supplanted by even more students of color is highly unlikely. During a focus group at Lucas College, Tony, a senior, may have been thinking about this probability when he pointed out:

> I think as far as white heterosexual males go, I think 99 times out of 100 we're not oppressed. Discrimination, I think, against white people still happens. I think any time you're sorting by race you're discriminating … [But] I think if I were not able to get into college because I was white, I wouldn't consider myself oppressed.

Jacob, a senior and resident assistant (RA) at St. Margaret University, shared this experience about the potential drawback of affirmative action from the perspective of college employment:

> So, there are seven RAs on my staff and there's two white people … there's a Spanish girl, an Iranian girl, there's an Armenian girl, there's a black girl. [Some of them were] pulled off the wait list and some of them are not right for the job.… When housing hires people, they hire a diverse group and I have five really good [white male] friends who would be incredible RAs that didn't get the job. So … where they have a quota to fill, so I think that can kind of harm the straight white males.

Jacob's perceptions show that despite not knowing all the intricacies about why three women were hired, he has crafted a negative opinion of the hiring authority, the institution, and also of the women who were hired. He may also mistake the hiring of the women as a form of quota-keeping or affirmative action when, in fact, the reasons for hiring women in this case may have been related to make-up of the dorm or floor to be staffed, or fit of the specific candidate over another. I don't have an account of the women to share here, but it's possible they may have faced a chilly climate on their staff working alongside men like Jacob who had his mind made up about why they were there in the first place.

Apparent Ubiquity of Race Scholarships

Aside from the possible drawback of affirmative action policies, participants also discussed the potential of lack of scholarships as a drawback white college men faced in institutions of higher education. Evan at Southern State University shared an encounter when he applied for scholarships: "You go online looking for scholarships and there is maybe a list of 50 scholarships and I was able to apply for, like, 15 of them because within the first three words I'm already tossed out." Dean, a Danbury College student, expressed a similar notion: "There's a lot of scholarships out there for Asian people or Latino people or black people. And you'd be kind of hard pressed to find straight, white, male middle-class scholarships." Nate, also at Danbury, shared this in a different focus group: "There are scholarships out there that are awarded based on performance and then there are scholarships out there that, my interpretation is, that they are trying to diversify [the institution]."

At Riverside State University, Jason indicated,

> more scholarships [are] available to minorities. I got a black friend that because he had a certain GPA [grade point average] and he was African American, he got a free laptop to college and they don't have that for white men.

Without knowing the specifics of the scholarship program and whether only African-American students got laptops, Jason assumed no institution offered similar programs for white students. These assumptions feed into the perception that college students of color may reap more benefits than white students. And if we as educators don't challenge white college men on their misinformation, we will continue to perpetuate the notions of unfavorable treatment toward white men during the financial aid process.

The majority of white complaints for not receiving enough financial aid are actually unfounded. Based on data from the last administration of the National Postsecondary Student Aid Study (NPSAS), white students, who represent about two-thirds of all college students, receive more than 75% of all institutional merit- and need-based financial aid in the form of scholarships or grants (Kantrowitz, 2011). The numbers look similarly in the awards of private scholarship and funding. According to Kantrowitz (2011), and based on 2007–08 information that's a bit dated, white students receive more than 69% of private aid, despite representing only 61% of all college-going students. In contrast, students of color receive 30% of private funding while representing 38% of all college students. These data suggest that we as educators must do better at dispelling the myths of ubiquitous race-based financial aid and advocate for equity in financial aid awards.

Why do some white college men perceive they're being slighted in the college admission process or the process to gain financial assistance to fund their education? Kimmel (2013) suggests that "angry white men" in our society view affirmative action or other policies that attempt to establish some level of parity or equity for past wrongs as reverse discrimination. White men do this because they feel entitled to their fair share, to get admitted to the college of their desires, and to receive the financial aid they think they're due. This "exposes something important about these legions of angry white men: although they still have most of the power and control in the world, they feel like victims" (Kimmel, 2013, p. 17). Simply because they're middle class, white, male, and hard working, white men today may feel they get to take their God-given place in our economic system. These are the meritocratic myths and ideals they have been fed, consciously by parents, the media, perhaps even by educators, and unconsciously by a structured social system created and perpetuated by generations of their cultural white male forebears. I'm sure you've heard statements like, "people have equal opportunities in this society", "pull yourself up by your bootstraps to be successful", or "hard work delivers results."

The myth of meritocracy also asserts that if you are a member of minoritized communities (race, gender, sexual orientation, ability), your standing will have no bearing on your life's accomplishments (Sue, 2010) and that all people have equal chances in life to be successful. The myth suggests that intelligence, effort, motivation, or family values are the only keys that contribute to success (Sue, 2010). Those who don't succeed are seen as possessing deficiencies that made it impossible for them to thrive in a given context. Whites often struggle or fail to understand that poverty, unemployment, or low educational achievement are connected to larger systemic forces like institutional or societal racism, and some whites regard people of color as lazy, not smart, or lacking discipline (Bonilla-Silva, 2014; Feagin, 2013; Sue, 2010).

It is outside of our purview as secondary or post-secondary educators to inspire the middle-aged white men Kimmel (2013) describes in his book to have a change of heart and develop critical consciousness, empathy, solidarity, and advocacy behaviors. But it is most certainly well within our abilities to commit to challenging and encouraging straight white male college students who are just beginning to participate in this economic, social, and political system. They still have time to critically disrupt and help transform American society to reach equity and true democracy.

Perceived Benefits of Being a Straight White Man on Campus

Aside from some participants' potential feelings as victims of affirmative action or reverse discrimination during the college search and enrollment processes, we also asked the straight white men in the sample to discuss the perceived benefits of being who they are on their specific campus.

Sense of Comfort as Majority

The sense of comfort, fit, or ease participants felt as white men on a predominantly white campus was palpable during the focus groups. Consider this comment by Chris, a student at Mason College:

> We don't have to think about our identities in every situation.… But just walking around, [or] in most classes … there are so many people who look like us and our way of being is sort of a cultural norm. We just don't have to be thinking about it and interrogating how our identity is affecting the way we are moving through social spaces.

Chris addresses what you will find throughout this theme: white students represent a cultural norm on predominantly white campuses, and straight white men don't have to be cognizant about their identities or probe further how these identities may affect their experiences in college.

I would like you to pay attention to how important this sense of comfort as the majority was for the students, including the emotional importance they assigned this feeling. Consider this interaction at Southern State University:

> KIPP: I can walk down the street here and see mostly people who I think are generally like me.
> JÖRG: And what does that do?
> BILL: It makes me feel comfortable, first off.
> JÖRG: And is that important?
> BILL: Absolutely [*emphatic*].

Max, at Riverside State University, used the word "easy" to describe his experiences of being a straight white man on his campus: "if you want to blend in, it's easy to do. Cause you look just like everybody else. More or less, you act just like everybody else and have the same interests, more or less."

Blending in was the topic of this exchange at Southern State University:

> OWEN: It's kind of a corny metaphor but I feel like my skin is kind of like camouflage because I blend in with 85% of the people on this campus; I don't stand out whatsoever.

JÖRG: And what's that like?

EVAN: I don't feel out of place.

MARTIN: You don't feel like you have to hide anything, you can just be yourself.

Beyond feeling a sense of comfort or ease, and not being judged or looked down upon, the ability of being able to hide or blend in was important to the participants. This point emphasizes, not only empirically but also figuratively, that whiteness is often seen as invisible by whites, and being white affords us the luxury of not being noticed, bothered, or discriminated against. Several participants realized this. Jamie, a senior at Lakeside State, indicated that being who he was meant he had "a larger group to go with" and didn't "have to find a group," stressing that making or finding friends is an important benefit of being a white guy on campus. To potentially avoid loneliness, fitting in was important to Alex, a senior at Riverside State University:

> I guess [a] benefit, would just be fitting in because, obviously it's not a diverse campus, we all pretty much look the same ... I guess the benefit is just, there's a ton of your own, you don't feel lonely I guess.

Feeling comfort; feeling a sense of fit; blending in or even hiding; not feeling lonely; a sense of ease. All of these descriptors of being the norm or feeling comfortable as the norm were important to the participants. These expressions of emotion or feelings speak to two things that may be going on with straight white men on college campuses. First is their sense of vulnerability about their own human needs and sense of belonging, despite their socialization as men to have specific masculine traits that traditionally have not included comfort or vulnerability. Emotional needs of belonging are typically not socialized male behaviors. Second is the notion that white men need to feel they belong to their homogenous in-group of other white men because some haven't yet learned how to interact with and befriend peers in their outgroup, including students of color, or gay, lesbian, or transgender students. Their needs as whites who want to connect are tied to a group of other whites, many of whom are also male and straight.

Minoritized Peers don't have Comfort

Some participants were able to differentiate between their own sense of comfort as part of the majority and the potential lack of comfort students of color, women, or peers with diverse genders or sexual orientation feel at the same institution. Cliff at Mountain State addressed how a peer student with an underrepresented identity may feel in classrooms at predominantly white institutions:

> As a white male it's kind of like a light switch. So, being in a classroom full of white people you feel like your ideas are going to be expressed, so,

therefore, you may not feel like you need to [add anything]. Versus having a marginalized identity, such as African American or Latino in a classroom. People look to them to understand their perspective, but that is a lot of pressure, and because of that pressure to speak out we marginalize them even more, not making it a comfortable environment.

The pressure on racially minoritized students grows when we hold them responsible to educate us on what it's like to be a person of color, or when we ask them, as individuals, to represent their entire social group. I'm going to make the assertion that such microaggressions happen every single day on American college campuses, and students like Cliff may be able to disrupt these misplaced and insensitive pedagogical strategies. Anthony, a junior at Riverside State University, shared this experience about a diversity course: "I had to take Ethnic [and] Racial Studies and Understanding Human Differences. I felt awkward for the people who were of a difference race, like, how they're feeling while the professor is talking about [issues that pertain to them]." This sense of empathy Anthony expressed here is an important foundation on which to build further exploration of privilege and oppression by straight white male college students.

Related to their own comfort as white men who are comfortable on a predominantly white campus is Ron's statement about how his peers of color may feel in college classrooms: "A black kid going into a class of 50 white kids might not feel as comfortable as the 49 white kids there.... You definitely have to overcome that if you're a black student at [Southern State]." The notion of the *lonely only student* of color in a sea of white faces on a historically white campus is well established in the literature (Harper & Hurtado, 2007; Strayhorn, 2012). The fact that white students also realize this conundrum of their peers from different racial or ethnic groups appears in the literature far less frequently.

In the same focus group at Southern State, Micah and Thomas shared the following perceptions:

> JÖRG: So, you fit, you walk on campus and you see 80% of people look like me.
>
> MICAH: It's comfortable.
>
> JÖRG: Comfortable. All right. Is that something you think about when you walk outside? You go, "Oh, it's comfortable because I'm not in the minority."
>
> THOMAS: I think so because it feels the exact opposite if you're the minority. It would feel strange. It would almost feel not normal.

Fewer than half of the participants were able to match Thomas's recognition of the difference of campus climate for underrepresented students. His understanding and empathy also have key implications for developing solidarity among privileged and oppressed college students. We as white educators can build on, work with, and easily engage students who have begun to interrogate their own privileges and who may be ready to help other white men do the same.

Racial privilege is not the only issue the participants addressed in the study. In a focus group at Riverside State, Peter discussed his sense of comfort about his identity as a straight man:

> We never have to be afraid to be who we are. If you were a gay man, maybe you wouldn't want to hold your partner's hand because you could be made fun of. If I'm holding a girl's hand, no one thinks twice about it.

Peter has begun to understand that a heterosexual couple has a plethora of privileges compared to a same-sex couple.

Two of the participants discussed their perceptions of safety for women on college campuses as a way of contemplating how minoritized students may experience the campus environment differently. Trent at Callahan College shared:

> I know one [female] friend, she said that, especially if it's one of her first times going somewhere, she wants to be walked there by someone.... Having a guy in the group, in general, helps because [women] automatically feel safer.... They're worried about a guy coming up and raping them. You don't have that worry as a guy of rape.

Dennis, at Lucas College, provided this quote about safety on his campus:

> Several times at night I'll be walking across campus and it will be like 1:30 a.m. and I realize that I feel totally safe in this environment, or walking home from downtown really late at night.... But yet, talking to enough of my female friends, I know that there is just this constant worry if they're out that late. When I'm walking back late at night, I go, "Geez, I can enjoy this but other people can't."

It may be indicative of the way straight white male college students conceptualize diversity if they, here and there, talk about issues unrelated to race or ethnicity. Issues facing women-identified students, or students with diverse genders or sexual orientations, didn't typically surface for the participants in this study. I am optimistic about the fact that the (few) preceding perceptions focus on sexual orientation and gender; however, how rarely white college men bring up gender and sexual orientation implies that we as college educators have critical work to do to engage men more widely in questions of diversity, privilege, and oppression. Race is the category in our last excerpt on issues minoritized people would perceive differently on campus or in society. Leonard at Southern State offered this insightful comment on the benefits of being a white man on campus:

White privilege is a saying, but it is specifically white male [*more emphatic*] privilege ... I had a buddy [who was black] all throughout high school and we would go apply for the same jobs. And we would be the same exact kid ... I would get the job and he wouldn't. And it's not my fault, but I still feel that burden.

Here, Leonard interrogates his professional (getting a job) privileges as a white man compared to his black male friend. This account stands in stark contrast to some of our participants, who reported that they're becoming victims of reverse affirmative action because people of color or women are actually preferred as employees or students. Based on this statement, I would consider Leonard someone who is in solidarity with people from minoritized backgrounds. I would also think he would be able to challenge other white guys who may struggle to understand privilege and oppression. Leonard's statement also makes a transition to the last theme of perceived white male benefits in this section.

"We Don't Have to Worry About Discrimination"

Think for a second about the terms whites have used to hurt people of color; that men have used to hurt female-identifying individuals; and that heterosexual people have used to hurt folx with diverse genders or sexual orientations. Can you think of some of these slurs? Now think of equally hurtful terms people of color, women, or gay, lesbian, and transgender people have used for whites, men, or heterosexual individuals. How many can you think of? Even if we could identify some, the difference in effect on the person facing the slur is infinitely worse for individuals with minoritized identities. Offending heterosexual white men may be possible, but no words will ever truly oppress us. We have created pejorative terms for all people of color, for women, and for gay people, but no similarly oppressive words exist in the English language to put down straight white men.

Emerging from my study was a similar theme dealing with participant perceptions of the impossibility of white men being discriminated against or oppressed in college and in the community. Jay at Southern State University referenced a well-known American comedian when making his point: "Daniel Tosh was talking about how you cannot crack down on white men, there's not a joke to be said about our background, and his response was, 'Oh, darn, I hate being entitled and making money.'" George at Lakeside State shared a similar point about his understanding of white male advantages on his campus: "I guess an advantage would be that the biggest thing we have to worry about is our social status, as far as wealth and if you're, like, in middle class, lower class." Abe and Milton, two Callahan College students, had a similar conversation about how truly limiting offensive jokes about whites could be compared to generations of oppression:

ABE: I think the benefits of being white here, being white and a male here, are similar to anywhere. The large demographic [group] generally doesn't face oppression in society or faced oppression in history.... There is no sort of stereotype bias for white males ... that keep them down and keep them from performing at their best.

MILTON: I think there are a good number of stereotypes that go with being a white, heterosexual male, but the question is, how much does it get in the way? And I think you're right, not very much.

Dean, a student at Danbury College, stated: "Sometimes I feel like a lot of the black students [on campus] kind of get judged. [They] kind of have a lot of negative stereotypes about them. So, as a white male you don't really get that."

Discussing a recent blackface video incident on his campus, Brad, at Lakeside State University, shared:

[As a white male], you don't have to worry about stuff like that happening. Um, and so one day, like, this video gets posted up, and there, like, the painted faces on it and, and we just don't have to really worry about that situation.

I appreciate Brad's acknowledgment of the fact that straight white men are typically not forced to engage or to care about issues of oppression like a blackface video. However, language or awareness that the oppressive system (or oppressive peers) can be challenged, confronted, or even stopped by other white men on our nation's campuses is still missing from his statement. What would it take for Brad and other straight white guys at Lakeside (or any other campus for that matter) to openly express concern and to express solidarity with the students who are silenced by the video? That, in essence, is what this book is about: raising one's awareness about issues of oppression (Brad seems to have done that), disrupting the normative white culture that condones this behavior by challenging it, expressing empathy and solidarity for and with the victims of such treatment, and continuing to educate self and others after the incident. These steps from awareness to potential action, however, can and must be communicated and taught.

Naming Oppression

Very few of the participants had experienced overt prejudice, stereotyping, or discrimination before or during college. However, a few personal encounters may have helped the participants to become more aware of issues of power, privilege, and oppression. Justin, a senior at Lucas College, shared a story about his stepfather, an African-American man: "[My] stepdad is black ... and you notice more things. You'd like to think that it's not there, but ... walking somewhere with my stepdad, or going to the gas station, you notice eyes on you." Ken, at Midwest University, shared his experiences growing up as a Muslim:

> I was very close to getting oppressed in middle school and bullied but I managed to deflect it. I was a typical kind of chubby nerdy foreign kid and it didn't help that my family is Islamic. And the jocks were starting to take notice and poke fun at me. It could have escalated but luckily enough the movie *Borat* came out so I started imitating him and that's how I got into the jock clique in high school. So, I luckily managed to not get oppressed.

This is a powerful account about how a straight white male student had to play false in high school not to get bullied by peer students. By making light of his own heritage (a son of immigrants from Bosnia), he was able to deflect the ridicule he faced. I have no illusion that this book will stop young men from bullying others. But I hope the students' accounts appeal to the bullies' humanity to redirect their behavior and focus on living in community and harmony among one another.

During a focus group at Southern State, Clay shared this experience about noticing homophobia on his campus:

> I think there's a lot of homophobia on this campus, for sure. You see it every day. "Oh, look at how he dresses, he must be gay" or "Oh, look at those tight skinny jeans, he's got to be gay." My roommate just moved in. He was still with his family in Miami [but had moved some stuff in], and he had like a zebra crock pot, and [my friends] were like, "Oh, your roommate must be gay." ... I don't understand what makes someone afraid, or look down upon people like that.

Clay's encounter with homophobia on his campus speaks to me as I reflect on my research with white undergraduate college men. Many of them may perceive issues of injustice in their environment; in fact, they may be negatively affected by it. But do they confront these issues, or do they simply listen and passively witness the prejudice of others, their friends? We don't know if Clay confronted his friends about the homophobic comments targeting his new roommate, but we hope that sooner, rather than later, he would find the courage to speak his mind to his friends, as he was able to do in the focus group.

Also at Southern State, Paul shared an encounter with what he perceived as racism. He and a black friend of his visited a fraternity party together when the following ensued:

> PAUL: My [black] friend came up to me and said [the frat guys] told him, "Hey, not enough room, you've got to head on out." So, then he kind of looked at me and he's like, "What do you want to do?" I was like, "All right, let's just go." So, we just walked out, we didn't

argue with them or anything. It was their house, it was their entire fraternity there, so even if we did put up an argument it would be 90 of them against us two.

JÖRG: What did they tell him was the reason, or what did they tell you was the reason he had to go?

PAUL: They wouldn't. They would find a way around, they'd be like, "Oh, well, too many people here." And you'd look around and there'd be plenty of space everywhere.

Paul showed solidarity to his friend by leaving the fraternity party with him, but did not confront the members directly because he was afraid of the potential consequences. Many straight white men, I included, would likely choose the alternative that Paul picked in the situation. This is why it's important that institutions of higher education have mechanisms through which such an incident can be reported and followed up on, in this case by members of the Greek Life office or the Dean of Students staff. Showing solidarity to a friend who is minoritized due to his racial background is important, and making sure student organizations don't continue to perpetuate racism or other forms of oppression is just as vital.

Few students in the sample divulged that they displayed oppressive behaviors toward others. Justin, at Lucas College, was different:

I think in my experience, I definitely think if you've ever been bullied or have bullied someone then you've experienced oppression. But, in my life, I've been more oppressive than oppressed, like even something as small as using derogatory language in the confidence of friends can still be oppressive.... In general, it's a bummer because it's a position that I've inherited through my race.

Here, Justin reflects on his actions and behaviors toward others in his environment over quite a long period of time for a senior in college. This type of self-awareness, albeit downplayed by words like "small" or "bummer," is of critical importance in the education, development, and growth of today's straight white male college students. As the focus groups have shown, it isn't very difficult to get men talking about these issues, showing vulnerability, and raising their consciousness on matters of power, privilege, and oppression. But we as educators need to be willing to have these conversations, and allow white college men to share their anxieties or fears around not expressing themselves with the kind of faultless language many diversity educators seem to expect these days.

Invisibility of Whiteness and Colorblindness

The participants' conceptualizations of whiteness as norm confirm decades of research on the seeming invisibility of whiteness or the difficulty for whites to critically interrogate and engage their white racial identity (Bergo & Nicholls, 2015; Cabrera, 2011, 2012; Feagin, 2013; Feagin & O'Brien, 2003; Hughey, 2012; McKinney, 2005). "I have never really thought about it," is a common response whites utter when asked to describe what it feels like to be white (Hughey, 2012), and white men have often not thought about how maleness or whiteness show up in their lives (Feagin & O'Brien, 2003; Vianden, 2009). In her book *Being White: Stories of Race and Racism*, Karyn McKinney (2005) identifies whiteness as a *prompted* identity. That is, whites don't typically think about their race unless they are asked, or prompted, to do so. Most people of color in the United States do not have this luxury. They are most always painfully aware of their racial background.

Whites' lack of engagement with their own racial or gender identity stems in part from the racial isolation we discussed in a previous chapter. Not having deep or long-lasting interactions across racial differences, or spending time mostly with other white people, means that we aren't aware of the everyday effects of racism and other forms of oppression in the United States and, in turn, white becomes mundane, the majority, unimportant, normal. However, being white men is anything but trivial in the context of current American and European political and social predicaments. White college men who are not challenged to interrogate their race or gender privilege will continue to live their lives in an unquestioned and seemingly normal state. The danger, Feagin and O'Brien suggest, is that this will perpetuate white and male hegemony over time: "Whiteness as a racial identity maintains its privileged position in part by remaining mostly unexamined, yet at the same time being the standard by which racial 'others' get measured" (Feagin & O'Brien, 2003, p. 66).

Another danger that may develop from an assumed automatic white identity and the denial of any issues attributed to race is colorblindness, the most recent form of racism in the American society (Bergo & Nicholls, 2015; Bonilla-Silva, 2014; Hughey, 2012). Not critically exploring whiteness may go along with whites not wanting to focus on race or racism, while declaring that we've arrived at a racially egalitarian state (Hughey, 2012). That race (or any minoritized identity) no longer affects the opportunities Americans have is a dangerous myth politicians and the media are keen to assert. The participants of this and other studies (Feagin & O'Brien, 2003) have shown this is the case. Many of the white men in my study are not oblivious to the differential treatment faced by their peers of color, women, or students with diverse genders or sexual orientations. White educators must critically explore and challenge whiteness and help our students do the same. Not because we want them to become like us, but because we want to create an anti-racist, anti-sexist, and anti-homophobic nation, and their prompted white identity should become a readily discussed one.

I side with other researchers who have asserted that we need to stop taking whiteness for granted and stop overemphasizing white racial unconsciousness (Hughey, 2012; McKinney, 2005). After all, my book's subtitle infers that we need to hold straight white men appropriately accountable for reflecting on their role in present-day oppression, support and challenge them to help realize a more socially just society. To this point, Bonilla-Silva (2014, p. 308) offers this call to action:

> [T]hose committed to racial equality must develop a personal practice to challenge [whiteness]. If you are a college student in a historically white college, you must raise hell ... you must organize to change the racial climate and demography of your college.

Summary

I started this chapter with a discussion on power, privilege, and oppression in contemporary America. I provided empirical evidence on race privilege, as the term or description *white privilege* has become a thorn in the side of politicians and citizens who feel attacked by discussions that straight white men hold more social privileges than most others. I leaned on other scholars to delineate who, by definition, can oppress whom in this country. Using the equation of *prejudice + power = oppression*, people in power who are prejudiced against others can oppress. It follows that blacks can't oppress whites on race (or in barely any other thinkable way), that women or transgender folx can't oppress men on gender, and that people with diverse sexual orientations can't oppress straight people on being straight. Despite the widespread myths in this society that all people can basically oppress all others, other scholars will agree with me that power is the variable that gives oppression its insidiousness.

In this chapter, we've also got to know our participants from the Straight White College Men Project more. Asking about perceived drawbacks and benefits to being straight white men on their college campus, we learned that a few of them fear they're getting the short end of the stick in the college admissions or financial aid race because of affirmative action or race-based scholarships. Debunking those myths is an important task for high school and college educators who work with straight white men ready to embark on their higher education journey.

The participants articulated they benefited from having a sense of comfort as the majority social group on a predominantly white campus, including fitting in or not sticking out as one or a few among many. This, some of them attested, must be how their peer students with minoritized identities feel. Not fearing any possible discrimination was another benefit of being straight, white, and male. Some participants also identified their understanding of how oppression works on their campus, and what oppressive attitudes and behaviors they had witnessed or been part of. I must say, in this part of the study, I was impressed with wide swaths of my participants. Their empathy for their peers who face oppression shone through, a foundation on which solidarity and advocacy for social change can be built. In the next chapter, we will learn more about the willingness of our participants to challenge this oppression at their institution or in their communities.

As I close this chapter, I want to leave you with a question in case some of you continue to waiver whether privilege really makes a difference in people's lives or whether all of this is just academic or liberal gobbledygook. Here goes. Knowing what you know about social, cultural, economic, and political issues in the United States, can you pledge you would be willing to assume the identities and life of someone from an oppressed social group, tomorrow? For example, if you're a middle-class straight white man, would you, without a qualm, slip into the life of a black lesbian or a Latino transgender man. Be truthful to yourself. My guess is nearly no whites would switch because we know we'd be treated differently, we'd be discriminated against or oppressed, and we'd be forced to lead entirely different lives. If you, in fact, would not assume the identities of someone who is minoritized in this country, don't you think lots of work remains to make this nation more inclusive, equitable, and socially just? If that's what you think, then let's commit to doing that work together with family, friends, colleagues, and others who face daily oppression in this country.

5   It's Hard to Speak Up

Challenging Racism, Sexism, and Homophobia

> DONALD TRUMP: I better use some Tic Tacs just in case I start kissing her. You know, I'm automatically attracted to beautiful [women] — I just start kissing them. It's like a magnet. Just kiss. I don't even wait. And when you're a star, they let you do it. You can do anything.
> BILLY BUSH: Whatever you want.
> DONALD TRUMP: Grab 'em by the pussy. You can do anything.
>
> (*New York Times*, 2016)

One of the most publicized acts of sexist, misogynistic, and male predatory behavior was this infamous exchange between Donald Trump and radio host Billy Bush on their way to a publicity event in 2005. We could spend a whole book discussing the vitriol Trump spews frequently, not only about women but about nearly all people with minoritized identities. Giving this much attention to Trump and chronicling his dishonorable misuse of language and abuse of individual American citizens, however, is not the aim of this book.

Yet it is critically important to examine and challenge the go-to, perennial, and often flippant response of white men after they've been criticized for inappropriate language or actions: "It was just a joke" or "Where is your sense of humor?" or "Don't take it so seriously" (Feagin, 2013; McCann, Plummer, & Minichiello, 2010; Picca & Feagin, 2007). *It was just a joke* is what we white guys get away with too often. Some men apologize, more or less genuinely; others take their hats after cases of criminal or civil litigation. In Trump's case, the behavior was stamped as "locker room talk." Once some men hear "it was just a joke," the case is closed and we move on – perhaps because we're tired of hearing about it, or because we've said similar things in the past, or because we think we can't change anything about "those guys" anyway. But should we move on so quickly?

No doubt, not all men use this kind of language to denigrate women, people of color, or individuals with diverse genders and sexual orientations. But they are a vociferous and powerful minority, especially when they also have political, social, or economic power. Can we show some forgiveness to college students who use inappropriate language? Probably. Should we hold the same yard stick to presidents, senators, governors, judges, CEOs, or other elites? Surely not. We need to express our outrage and hold them accountable for their language and behaviors. Moreover, we need to speak with one another, in our classrooms, locker rooms, fraternity houses, and off-campus apartments, about what kind of culture we as men want to create on college campuses and in our communities. I doubt that most white college men want to continue to live in the oppressive climate men have created for diverse individuals.

We should expect college students to have a certain predisposition to learning, critical thinking, interpersonal development, and certain life skills. However, the ordinary white men in my study are also inculcated, socialized, and trained to behave, act, feel, and respond a certain way based on the patriarchal culture into which they were born and of which they are part. The racist, sexist, and homophobic behaviors we see in public settings in the United States we also witness on our nation's college campuses.

White Male Misbehavior in College

"No means no, yes means anal." That was the chant heard on the campus of the prestigious Yale University in October of 2010, uttered by pledges of Delta Kappa Epsilon fraternity as they marched through Yale's Old Campus where most first-year women lived. The fraternity got banned from any campus activities for five years. In March of 2015, a group of pledges of Sigma Alpha Epsilon fraternity at the University of Oklahoma were filmed performing a racist chant about African Americans and lynching on a bus. The university closed the fraternity's chapter. In the fall of 2015, members of Sigma Nu Fraternity at Old Dominion University displayed banners calling for "freshmen daughter drop off" from the balcony of an off-campus building. The university suspended the fraternity.

Hateful, racist, or misogynistic behaviors are not exclusive actions of college students alone, nor of fraternities alone. They are, however, nearly exclusively male behaviors (Feagin, 2013; Harper & Harris, 2010). The racial and sexual frames under which men operate are deeply ingrained in our culture and in our masculinity. An overabundance of reprehensible bias- or hate-motivated incidents, including shootings, assaults, hate mail, blackface parties, racist and homophobic posters, or vandalism, happen on U.S. college campuses with alarming frequency. Racist, sexist, or homophobic slurs and graffiti are a near-daily occurrence in college dorms, in bathrooms, on campus grounds or chalked onto sidewalks. If you are a college student, reflect on the frequency with which you witness this kind of behavior on your campus. Who are the typical originators of this behavior? Who intervenes, if anyone? What are the typical outcomes? The victims of this behavior, many of them students, faculty, and staff, sharply condemn these acts as detrimental to their success, to the institution, as well as to alumni and the local community. The defenders of such actions refer to this behavior as covered under the free speech provision of the First Amendment. Wherever you fall on the continuum of hate speech and free speech, perhaps think about the demeaning, traumatizing, and silencing effects of the above incidents on the victims. Just because you've got the right to free speech doesn't mean you need to use it. I also highly doubt that most overt acts of racist, sexist, and homophobic slurs or verbal attacks are done to exercise one's free speech; these acts mean to hurt people, and the intention is hardly ever just to voice an opinion.

College men have long been the primary instigators of campus unrest, and the primary and disproportionate offenders in college conduct processes (Harper, Harris, & Mmeje, 2010; Ludeman, 2004). Compared to women, college men overwhelmingly perpetrate sexual assault and rape, they are more drawn to dangerous or violent behavior, and they are more prone to using and abusing alcohol and drugs (Capraro, 2010; Harper & Harris, 2010; Ludeman, 2004).

According to reports by the National Sexual Violence Resource Center (2016), 1 in 5 women will be raped at one point in their lives; during college, the rate rises to 1 in 4. Most of us probably assume that the numbers of men who sexually assault women are negligible or very low; after all, most men likely see themselves as incapable of assaulting, harming, or raping women. However, studies on sexual assault since the 1980s suggest that between one-quarter and more than half of men report perpetration of some form of non-consensual sexual contact, and between 8% and 14% of men typically report behavior that meets legal definitions of rape (Mouilso, Calhoun, & Rosenbloom, 2015). Moreover, more than one-third of college men have reported they would consider raping women if they could get away with it (Newsom et al., 2015).

Men tend to perpetrate nearly 95% of all sexual assaults in the United States, and more than a third of all offenses are perpetrated by men between 18 and 29 years of age. Between 1994 and 2010, the average number of white perpetrators of rape was 62%, making whites the dominant racial group among rape and sexual assault offenders (Planty, Langton, Krebs, Berzofsky, & Smiley-McDonald, 2013). And at predominantly white colleges and universities, the unit of analysis of this book, more rapes and sexual assaults will be committed by white men than by men of any other ethnic or racial background. This also holds true for all other acts of violence or discrimination perpetuated by college men.

Even when found guilty of committing a crime, white men often receive sentences that seem too lenient given the heinous act they committed. This was most evident in 2016 when Brock Turner, a former Stanford University swimmer and Olympic hopeful, raped an unconscious woman in an alley on campus. The judge levied a six-month sentence and Turner was released after serving half that time. But Turner isn't the only white male perpetrator of sexual assault or rape who gets off easily in courts of law. For a chilling but fascinating study of the intersections of college rape, masculinity, and college sports, consider Jon Krakauer's (2015) book *Missoula: Rape and the Justice*

System in a College Town. This bestseller chronicles the stories of several women, the nights they were raped or assaulted, the gruesome shunning they faced after coming forward, and the abhorrent negligence of the courts in some of their cases to enforce justice.

Although we have a clear preponderance of white male violence on college campuses, we also need to acknowledge two irrevocable facts my friend and colleague Ryan McKelley, psychologist and masculinity scholar, points out about men. First, yes, men perpetuate extreme acts of violence; second, no, not all men do (TED Talk, 2013). However, all men in the United States are raised and socialized in a culture in which violent and criminal acts happen on an all-too-frequent basis. Even men's inactions around issues of hate and violence may do their part to inadvertently condone the injustices. In this context, most socially unjust behaviors by one group onto another take place; that is, the behaviors occur through the often-unpublicized actions or inactions of ordinary people in mundane settings, including personal, educational, or professional arenas. It's also in these settings, like college campuses, where the capacity for solidarity, empathy, real social change, and advocacy for social justice is possible.

Straight White Men as Campus Climate Creators

If you're a college student who identifies with one or more privileged identities, think about how your campus "feels" to you. Is it safe to walk about the grounds, even at night? Are faculty and staff inviting and welcoming? Are your peers creating an environment in which friendships are established easily and in which learning can take place? If you have answered affirmatively, good. Your campus likely has a positive campus climate in your estimation. Now, put yourself in the shoes of your peers with minoritized identities, like students of color, students with different genders or sexual orientations, students with non-Christian religious views, students with physical or cognitive disabilities, or students from foreign countries. How would they answer the question about how the campus feels?

Campus climate can be defined as the attitudes, behaviors, standards, and practices of members of the campus community, including faculty, staff, administrators, and students (Rankin & Reason, 2008). Renowned campus climate researchers have suggested that campus climate is a complex concept, and one which includes the dimensions of institutional history, structural diversity, as well as psychological and behavioral climate (Hurtado, Clayton-Pedersen, Allen, & Milem, 1998). Most campus climate research focuses on the racial or ethnic climate on college campuses (Harper & Hurtado, 2007; Hurtado et al., 1998; Rankin & Reason, 2008 Solórzano et al., 2000; Van Dyke & Tester, 2014; Woodard & Sims, 2000), on the climate perceived by women (Allan & Madden, 2006; Whitt, Edison, Pascarella, Nora, & Terenzini, 1999), and the climate perceived by campus community members with diverse genders and sexual orientations (d'Augelli, 1992; Brown, Clarke,

Gortmaker, & Robinson-Keilig, 2004; Evans & Herriott, 2004; Rankin, 2004, 2005; Stotzer, 2010; Tomlinson & Fassinger, 2003).

Students, staff, and faculty from underserved groups tend to report similar impressions of the climate at their institution: on all predominantly white campuses, forms of racism, sexism, and homophobia exist inside and outside of the classroom. Racist, sexist, or homophobic campus climates affect minoritized students in a variety of negative ways. Primary among them are stress, isolation, alienation, stereotyping, blunted cognitive or developmental outcomes, reduced engagement in educationally purposeful activities, or dropping out of college. Faculty and staff with underrepresented identities also suffer from chilly campus climates, including negative career or job attitudes, decreased health and well-being, or attrition.

I have often called straight white college men the main creators of campus climates at predominantly white colleges and universities. These climate creators include white men in classrooms or residence halls, athletes on sports teams, student organization or student government leaders, and men in some traditional white fraternities. Campus hate incidents of an ethnic or racial nature tend to be more prevalent on predominantly white campuses and on those that have a large Greek population (Van Dyke & Tester, 2014). Campus climates are also influenced by white male faculty, coaches, advisors, and staff who teach, advise, supervise, guide, and mentor college students. Finally, campus climate creators include the administration, the disproportionately white and male leadership of institutions, including presidents or chancellors, their right-hand vice-presidents or vice-chancellors, provosts, deans, and directors. The latter group, along with the boards of trustees or regents, represent the most power at the institution; they direct the goings-on at a college or university, and they are responsible for what happens on the campus.

Before you condemn me for painting with too broad of a brush castigating *all* white men on campus as awful community members, let me explain. We as white men don't only create chilly or oppressive climates for individuals from underrepresented social groups. We also have the ability, and many of us do this already, to create welcoming environments for students, staff, and faculty from a variety of traditionally minoritized backgrounds. However, we as white men also have to realize that not only our actions create chilly or welcoming climates. Our inactions do as well. These inactions typically include condoning oppressive behavior or not supporting the welcoming behavior we witness. Considering their power and privilege on campus and their abilities to influence its climate, white male college students, staff, faculty, and administrators need to commit to learning more about how to condemn acts of violence, how to create environments in which individuals from minoritized groups are no longer minoritized, and how to help disrupt the system of oppression inherent in predominantly white institutions of higher education.

Beyond assessing campus climate and its effects on campus community members, researchers have also examined how students, staff, and faculty from traditionally privileged backgrounds, specifically whites, perceive the campus environment (Harper & Hurtado, 2007). White participants in campus climate assessments have tended to overestimate how welcoming and supportive their specific institution is toward racial, gender, or sexual diversity (Cabrera, 2014; Harper & Hurtado, 2007; Vianden, 2009). Whites on our nation's campuses also differ on their perceptions of the level of oppression facing students, staff, or faculty from minoritized backgrounds in their campus community (Harper & Hurtado, 2007; Hurtado, 1992; Rankin & Reason, 2008). Many whites struggle to conceive the myriad ways in which oppression manifest on campus or in the community for their peers or colleagues who are members of oppressed groups.

Reasons why straight white male students, staff, and faculty may be overestimating the welcoming nature of a given campus climate include their beliefs that oppression is no longer a problem in American society (Hurtado, 1992). Consider data from the Straight White Men Project on this point. Adam, a student at Riverside State University, discussed his impressions of campus climate at two points during his focus group. First, he surmised, "um, as far as women, there's, there's [sic] no, uh, I guess like biased attitudes towards women, that I see." Later, when talking about one of his friends who was gay, Adam stated, "I mean everyone's friendly to him, I've never seen anyone be mean to him, or anything like that." Alden, a sophomore at Danbury College, sensed a similar welcoming climate on his campus:

> There's not really many issues … that I've experienced or seen personally, nor have I really heard any stories of anyone being racist, sexist, or homophobic…. There are individuals on campus that have issues with it but they never vocalize those issues or publicized them in any way.

For a moment I want to ask white readers of this book to reflect on their own experiences. If you're also of the impression that racism, sexism, or heterosexism are no longer a problem, we should ask ourselves, *How do we know?* Straight white men are typically not the targets of the oppression I'm discussing here, yet some of us think we can speak confidently about its apparent non-existence or even eradication. Reflect on this next time you're having a conversation about race, sex, or sexual orientation with someone who may actually be directly and personally affected by oppression. To what level of systemic oppression are we as white men really privy to be able to judge how welcoming the campus climate is?

Some straight white college men may willingly or at least unconsciously create hostile climates because of a sense of competition they feel with students of color, women, or students with diverse genders or sexual orientations (Van Dyke & Tester, 2014). Most institutions of higher education herald their missions to increase diversity, to be or become inclusive campus environments, or to serve all students, staff, and faculty equitably (Roper, 2004). Since the late 1970s women have outnumbered men on college campuses. In fact, in every age, racial, and income group in the United States, women earn more baccalaureate degrees than men, and by 2015 women were projected to earn 78% of all four-year college degrees (Kellom, 2004). And at many institutions, white male students may also witness a steep rise in the enrollment of students of color signaling the perception of competition for funds (Van Dyke & Tester, 2014). Is it possible that some white college students, and white college men in particular, have come to view their campuses as white-only spaces? And is their conduct, including threats, intimidation, discrimination, and microaggressions, symptomatic of this perceived threat?

Many white men who actively resist campus diversity efforts may do so because they're convinced of American meritocratic ideals: hard work always garners success. This means using "fair" hiring procedures including always finding the best person for the job, irrespective of diverse identities (Vaccaro, 2010; Vianden & Gregg, 2017) and admitting students to universities based on academic qualifications only (Vaccaro, 2010). In this kind of resentment of diversity efforts and positive campus climates, some white college men clearly show their privilege, but also indicate the underlying notion that whites are always more qualified than people or color.

Racist, Sexist, and Homophobic Joking

Think, for a second, of your favorite carnival or funfair games (an interesting prompt, I know). Can you picture a game where you throw a ball into a pyramid of cups or cans trying to get all of them to fall? What's the best strategy to achieve this goal? If you throw the ball at the very top of the structure, you may knock down a few cans, but won't get the base to fall. Throwing the ball at the middle likely will have more success, but some of the base will remain. Finally, if you aim the ball directly at the base you have the best chance of toppling the entire pyramid. We can use this image of the can structure (system of oppression) and the ball (intervention) to explain how specific methods of violence prevention or eradication could work on a college campus.

Targeting the most extreme behaviors at the top of the pyramid, where homicide, assault, and rape reside, does not end systemic oppression, because these manifestations of violence are rare compared to more frequent acts of verbal interpersonal violence in institutions in which structural oppression thrives. Verbal violence, such as harassment or joking, are found at the center of the pyramid. These behaviors rest on the foundation of cultural microaggressions, the normalized, subtle, and sometimes intentional messages individuals with social privilege send to individuals with minoritized identities. To be sure, for any type of interpersonal violence to end, men must be held accountable to not violate others. However, if we want the men who don't offend, discriminate against, or hurt others to help end violence against traditionally marginalized individuals, we must engage the broad foundation of the structure, the place where human attitudes and beliefs (e.g., racism, sexism, and homophobia) live. Only that way we can topple the systemic oppression the pyramid represents, and with it the more and most extreme forms of interpersonal violence.

To engage this wide base of the structure of the violence pyramid, I will share data describing our participants' experience with telling or hearing inappropriate language and joking, most often in their friend group. I'm talking about inappropriate language and behavior because that kind of behavior is ubiquitous, specifically among white college men (Cabrera, 2014). Critics may counter that joking is clearly not harmful behavior, certainly not as harmful as overt harassment, assault, or discrimination. Maybe, but research has long shown that men who laugh at or participate in telling jokes, specifically sexist ones, have a higher proclivity for sexual or relationship violence toward women (Romero-Sánchez, Durán, Carretero-Dios, Megías, & Moya, 2010; Ryan & Kanjorski, 1998). Unchallenged joking, objectification, and dehumanization may be harbingers for more serious forms of male violence (Banyard, Plante, & Moynihan, 2005). Racist joking, or the apparent jovial expression of racial thoughts, covers up the menacing truth that racial jokes are the vehicle to communicate deep-seated bias for racial others (Feagin, 2013; Picca & Feagin, 2007). A joke thus becomes a representation of the systemic, 400-year-old American white supremacy. And left unchallenged, jokes are an insidious reminder of how the system of oppression continues to perpetuate itself.

White Backstage and Frontstage Performances

In their 2007 book *Two-faced Racism: Whites in the Backstage and Frontstage*, American sociologists Leslie Picca and Joe Feagin conceptualized the way whites perform racial performances, like telling racist jokes. According to the authors, racial performances involve the "activity of a white person at a particular place and time and attempts to communicate racial views and images to others" (Picca & Feagin, 2007, p. 4). The reason whites perform racial joking in front of their key reference group (friends or family) is to relate to others, to gain social capital, as well as to influence the attitudes and behaviors of other group members (Picca & Feagin, 2007). Our racial performances are based on centuries of white racial framing of others, including stereotyping, overt hostility, and discrimination. The main American target of racist joking are African Americans, featuring in more than three-quarters of the white college student journals Picca and Feagin collected in their study (Feagin, 2013).

Picca and Feagin (2007) conceptualized those racial performances taking place in two different spatial settings. In the *frontstage* (public spaces that are often multicultural), many whites seem to know that joking, microaggressions, or overt racism are inappropriate. Or at least their racial performances are subdued or characterized by politically correct language. In the *backstage* (private, behind closed doors, and mostly white spaces), whites often ruthlessly joke about race and ethnicity with much condoning and without much dissent. Cabrera (2014) finds that whites tell these jokes in the back-stage because they think individuals with different racial backgrounds are too sensitive about race and don't get the humor. Cabrera (2014) adds that whites may feel free to tell jokes if they move in white-only spaces that are generally free from criticism of people of color. As we have seen in data from the Straight White Men Project I have been sharing in this book, many of our participants have spent most of their lives in these white-only environments, in which displaying stereotypical or prejudicial racial views becomes normal.

The excuse of "I was just joking" or "Don't be so sensitive" is one that whites will make often when confronted on their language and performances (Cabrera, 2014). Yet whites tend to be the only racial group that tells racial jokes. African-American or Latinx racial joking about whites is virtually non-existent (Picca & Feagin, 2007). And racial joking clearly goes beyond poking fun about the stereotypes of one racial group or another. The snippet at the outset of this chapter about the fraternity at the University of Oklahoma featured the chant, "There will never be a [n-word] at SAE, you can hang him from a tree, but he will never sign with me." Such vicious racist representations are a keystone in the ways whites have thought about, talked about, or treated racial others, including century-old white images, stories, and performances of black men as oversexed, animalistic, or dangerous human beings (Feagin, 2013).

Although *racial* joking likely predominates the performances of straight white college men, we need to also look at their performances about individuals with different genders and sexual orientations. I would like to suggest that white racial framing parallels the gendered framing we as men have done with women-identified individuals, and we as straight beings have done to sexually frame members of diverse sexual orientation groups. The common denominator in all the framing: white, straight men who assert their role as the oppressor, and other white, heterosexual men who witness, often passively. To end this widespread form of oppression, all whites must learn to become more vociferous dissenters to joking. Too often, though, when oppressive joking is challenged, the dissenter tends to be admonished by the perpetrator or the group: "Instead of the joke teller being held accountable, the challenger often must defend [their] intervention" (Picca & Feagin, 2007, p. 250).

Bystanders Influenced by Normative Peer Culture

If we as straight white college men create campus climates and enact or witness racist, sexist, or homophobic performances, it's essential to explore and understand how to become more active in holding ourselves accountable. Part of this exploration includes illuminating under what circumstances or in which contexts white college men act as active or passive *bystanders* during incidents related to systemic oppression.

Have you ever watched ABC's *What Would You Do?* with John Quiñones, a prime-time show where actors perform inappropriate or illegal public behaviors to observe if and how bystanders intervene? There are nearly 250 video clips of episodes on YouTube if you would like to take a look. Now think of racist, sexist, or homophobic behaviors (the show features these a lot) and how you may react when you witness these behaviors performed by family, close friends, peers, or even strangers. What would you do or what have you done during these types of events?

Most of the available literature on men's bystander behaviors and interventions focuses on sexual harassment, assault, violence, or rape. In the context of sexual violence, bystanders can be defined as individuals who interrupt situations that may lead to sexual assault, who confront peer or social norms that support rape, and who have acquired skills to be effective supporters to survivors (Banyard, Moynihan, & Plante, 2007). Many colleges and universities have instituted bystander intervention programming and training (sometimes mandatory) for students to address issues of potential injuries, violence, and sexual assault, specifically in the context of off-campus parties (McMahon, Banyard, & McMahon, 2015; Silver & Jakeman, 2016). For the purposes of this book, I will extend the definition of bystanders and their behaviors to include college men who witness actions or incidents that connote racism, sexism, or homophobia within their family, in their friend group, on their campus, or in their community.

Early research on bystander behaviors suggested that highly masculine men may not intervene in an emergency in fear of embarrassment or because they prefer to remain stoic in the face of a crisis (Tice & Baumeister, 1985). Other studies asserted that masculinity plays an important role in bystander behavior, specifically in sexual assault situations (Carlson, 2008). Men often understand the need to protect women, but also weigh appearing too weak or sensitive to their peer group in their decision to intervene. Carlson (2008) pointed out that the setting in which men intervene is an important factor in bystander behaviors. If the intervention takes place in a public setting where women- and men-identifying individuals are present, men may consider challenging sexual violence appropriate and necessary. However, "for some of the participants intervening in a private setting where only other men are present is considered too weak and therefore unmasculine" (Carlson, 2008, p. 14). College students, and college men specifically, may also be more likely to support the victim after a specific incident than to challenge the perpetrator (Hoxmeier, Flay, & Acock, 2016).

The peer group or culture is perhaps the most important factor in predicting positive bystander behaviors by men or interventions against oppression. Brown, Banyard, and Moynihan (2014) find that students who believed their peers supported bystander intervention were more likely to intervene against sexual violence. Other researchers suggest that, as new college students focus on establishing a peer group, they may not be willing to confront or challenge their peers in fear of lacking or losing their social support system (McMahon et al., 2015).

Why does it seem to be difficult for men to confront other men on inappropriate language or behavior? What are the reasons for the lack of action on behalf of men? Answers may lie in examining the power and influence of the male peer group, or same-sex friend group. The age group of traditional-aged college students (roughly 18 to 30) is key in men's development as they experience and deal with the shift from adolescence to adulthood. Men are often thought of as unemotional and inexpressive, and typical American characteristics of masculinity include independence, self-reliance, and emotional stoicism (Smiler & Heasley, 2016). Many college-aged men desire friendships with other men that are based in trust, emotional intimacy, and shared interest, but the masculine-norms-enforcing peer group often sways men to hide these desires. Early research on men and masculinities suggested that friendships between men may be based in the lack of self-disclosure, mutual understanding, and affection (Mazur, 1989; Williams, 1985); not a strong foundation for sensing the ability to confront peers on possible inappropriate behavior. In addition, friendships devoid of trust and confidence in one another may not emphasize personal responsibility for any attitude, behavior, or action (Williams, 1985).

As they vie for acceptance and social capital among their friends, college men resort to performing masculinity in specific contexts. This performance adheres to the cultural conventions of the *boy code* (Pollack, 1998) and *guyland* (Kimmel, 2008) and avoids the expression of emotion, takes fewer risks in showing vulnerability, and practices the covenants of desperately avoiding to appear gay or feminine (Smiler & Heasley, 2016). Men may participate in heteronormative or white normative behaviors like joke-telling or name-calling to be accepted by their friends, and given our knowledge of pre-college male environments, college men are raised in contexts in which such behavior is prevalent (Pascoe, 2007; Pollack, 1998).

Once in college, men find themselves in a peer-enforced atmosphere in which they at least perceive that other men are policing their behaviors. In this setting, men engage in a cost–benefit analysis of sorts to weigh certain actions against what they perceive their chosen peer group would find acceptable (Kehler, 2007). In college, this may mean that men weigh the potential consequences of confronting their peers on racist, sexist, or homophobic joking. This atmosphere is potentially so norming that men perform bystander behaviors to gain (or at least not lose) social capital. However, this often comes "at the loss, for many [men], of social consciousness and … emotional intimacy" (Smiler & Heasley, 2016, p. 576). In the specific context of confronting or challenging racist, sexist, or homophobic humor, little empirical research exists that could instruct educators on college men's experiences. Still, McCann and colleagues (2010) suggest that challenging homophobic joking can be detrimental for men who don't already conform to toxic male norms: "if [men] were isolated because [they] were already considered to be non-hegemonic, the risks of standing any further out could be damaging" (McCann et al., 2010, p. 514). Men who want to belong to a peer group but feel pressure to conform are likely to choose "laughing with the crowd" (McCann et al., 2010, p. 514) over open dissent and feared shunning.

These findings hold key implications for school and college educators. Not only do we need men to explore their desire for more emotional friendships, we also must encourage them to take the risk of confronting the members of the peer group for attitudes and behaviors detrimental to their own humanity as well as the humanity of their peers with minoritized identities.

Standing by or Standing up: Straight White Men's Perceptions of Intervening Oppression

As I turn to my participants, let me say that the data in this chapter stem from questions about how participants had responded or would respond to issues of racism, sexism, or homophobia on campus or in their communities. To get the conversations started in the focus groups, we often began by asking a question about how participants respond to joking on issues of race, ethnicity, sex, or sexual orientation inspired by the frontstage–backstage concept (Picca & Feagin, 2007). Tony, at Lucas College, provided a fitting example for this concept and the ways in which white college men may conceptualize what is considered appropriate public behavior. This encounter deals with a situation he noticed working in the college cafeteria:

> We have an African-American cook, who had just come back from a vacation.… A white female chef, said, "Hey, look who's back. Look at the nice tan he got." She got written up for that.… If I would have gotten written up for things that we've said in our friend group, I probably would have been expelled by now. We do make these jokes with our friends, but we do it to only our friends.… Just to make light of the fact that our friend is [racially] diverse.… He laughs, it's not like we're picking on him.

Tony and his peer group seemed to have figured out at what point racial joking is acceptable as the comment fittingly explains the frontstage–backstage concept. However, we may wonder whether his friend of color really has the ability to buck the influence of the peer group. In this focus group, at least, we did not follow up on that important question.

Finding the Line between Oppression and Humor

I start this discussion with the participants' perceptions of how to navigate the line between oppression and humor in joking among men. Considering whether he would challenge his friends on offensive language, Alex at Riverside State pointed out:

> I don't know if they would take me seriously, because, you know, when you're that good of friends, almost everything we do is joking around

with each other, so I don't know if they would take it seriously at all.... You know, on the weekends when you're drinking, they would just end up making fun of you for it basically. [They] definitely wouldn't take it seriously.

Important in Alex's statement is the confirmation of empirical research findings about male same-sex friendships: much in male friendships is about fun, joking, teasing, and humor (Greif, 2009; Vianden, 2009). If joking plays a central part in male friendships, how will men be able to differentiate between what is supposed to be an acceptable form of joking and what is not? In his statement during a focus group at Lakeside State, Nathan explored the line between offensive and funny:

> We all have fun, like, with our little jokes at each other, but that's the thing; like, we know each other so well that we can, like, you know, kind of throw in those, you know, stereotypical jokes, and, like, sometimes it may cross the line, but I think, like, when it's your friends and it's a joking setting, the line is where that person is actually starting to get hurt.

When white men joke with one another about individuals with different racial or ethnic backgrounds in the backstage, it may be difficult for some in the group to acknowledge a line has been crossed.

Greg, at Lucas College, shared his thoughts about the crossing of the proverbial line in this comment:

> There's obviously a line where we may make a joke that someone doesn't feel comfortable with and we've established a boundary that we don't cross. I feel like in public where people are not comfortable with that boundary starts off at zero and that can move. So if somebody is insensitive or really doesn't like jokes about their race for whatever reason, then that needs to be respected. But as you build a comfort level with somebody, you can find out what that level is.

Greg seems to say that joking about identity is acceptable once a peer group has established the line that is not to be crossed. Interesting here is Greg's pondering the idea that some peers from a different racial background may, in fact, approve of some form of racial joking. In the same focus group Tony picked up this discussion and provided another example:

> For example, we have our gay black friend. So, he's in our group, kind of a double minority, and if we make a joke towards him, whether it's a gay slur or racial comment, we're not trying to hurt him.... In our group of friends we have a good understanding of how comfortable we are with each other and what we can say. He has said before, "Can you not say

this sort of thing?" We apologized and we don't. Within our group of friends, we'll say these jokes, but we know not to say them outside of our friend group.

Not only does Tony (and presumably his friends) know what the line of joking versus oppression seems to be, he also knows that the joking is likely inappropriate to begin with. Further, he knows not to make these kinds of cracks in public. Important, though, for our understanding of college men and masculinities is that white men seem to "try out" or "practice" what they can and cannot say in front of their friends with multiple minoritized identities. What we didn't gather from Tony is whether he thought his gay black friend may have been offended many times before first asking the group not to "say that sort of thing." In the following comment by Nick at Lucas College, the apparent diversity of his friend group is remarkable given the general lack of deep interactions whites have with individuals from minoritized identities I discussed earlier. Yet joking with and about one another is still prevalent.

> I think it just depends on the group of people. I watch football games; it might be me, a couple black guys, white guys, I've got an Indian friend and a couple gay people. We'll all be watching the game, we'll throw jokes at each other and laugh; whether it's about, "Well, that's a white thing to say," or, "That was pretty gay," or so forth and so on. So I guess it depends on the group you're with, but we'll crack jokes all the time.

Once white men have negotiated what peer behavior may be appropriate, challenge-worthy, humorous, or offensive, they may decide to dissent or let it go. Here are a few thoughts of the participants that explain how, when, and if they would make the decision about challenging a joke. In my conversation with students at Danbury University, their lack of experience with confrontable situations of inappropriate peer behavior or joking was evident:

> DUSTIN: Just kind of like tell them … like dull [the joking] down a little bit. It's pushing it.
> JÖRG: Has that happened before?
> DUSTIN: Not really.
> DALE: Hasn't really happened [for me] but I think sometimes you can tell when it's just a joke and when it's meant in a more serious way. And when it's meant in a more serious way it's not okay.

Key here is Dustin's attempt to explain how he may intervene. His intervention doesn't seem forceful or direct but buddy-like and respectful of the potential offender and their feelings. This type of intervening behavior may be typical in men who are fearful of consequences they face from peers, or worse, getting fired or ostracized from the man group they're part of

(Kimmel, 2013). Joey, at Lakeside State, didn't sound more forceful when he described his way of confronting a peer on an inappropriate joke: "It depends on like the line they cross. If it's not that bad, I'm not going to be like, 'You guys should probably stop.'" Joey may condone inappropriate joking until it has reached a line at which point he may politely ask his friends to consider ceasing the joking. Educators ought to discuss these issues with men in and outside of classrooms to gain a deeper understanding of what men experience when they're weighing whether to challenge behavior and to help build their skills in practicing dissent (Cabrera, 2014).

What potentially happens when men challenge peer joking is evident in Leo's response during his focus group at Riverside State University:

> Yeah, I've heard a friend like say something, like a gay joke, and he just took it too far. I'm like, "Whoa, like come on," and he's just like, "Oh, why do you care? What's your deal? Like why don't you think that's funny?" "Well, I think you just took it too far." And [he said], "Well, you make fun of me all the time," like you know friends give each other a hard time, like, "What's your deal?" ... I don't know, you try to set a level and people think that, uh, you're being a hypocrite.

First of all, good for Leo to begin challenging his peers on homophobic joking. His comment confirms the literature cited earlier in the chapter. Male dissenters who challenge their friends on racist, sexist, or homophobic joking may become the person having to defend their actions, not the perpetrator. I understand why challengers think twice about confronting a next time if they're called humorless or hypocritical. Yet this dissension is crucial in reducing and possibly even ending white male behaviors that perpetuate an oppressive system for people of color, women, and people with diverse genders and sexual orientations.

It's Hard to Speak Up: Challenging Family

In the following sections, I share data which emerged from follow-up questions during the focus groups when we asked participants to describe if and how they would confront family, friends, and strangers on inappropriate language or behavior.

Given my bond with my own family, loved ones, and friends, it doesn't surprise me that the participants may have struggled confronting potentially inappropriate language and behavior. I've struggled with this and continue to do so, even in my late 40s. The people we challenge when we say, "Please stop" are those with whom we tend to have the most special relationships, a stronger connection than with anyone else. Why, then, would we dare to infringe on this relationship to perhaps face long-lasting consequences? Yet it's important to find ways to exert influence in one's personal sphere as straight white men develop solidarity with others and find ways to advocate for social justice. Because of our strong relationships in the personal sphere, challenging here may actually be most effective. As you read the following statements from our participants, reflect on whether you can identify with their perceptions, given your own experiences with family.

One of the participants at Riverside State expressed difficulty confronting parents when he said, "It's hard to tell your parents not to say something [people laughing]. They've been telling you what to do your entire life." In his focus group at St. Margaret University, Derek shared this fascinating experience with his brothers at home in the Midwest:

> Going back home, it's different. Because you watch what you say out here and watch what you say around minorities and around other groups but going back home, I test my brothers to not say words like faggot and stuff like that. I'm like, "Ouch, dude, that really hurts people." And they're just like, "Oh shut up, you pussy." So, it's different trying to fit into two opposite groups of people.

Startling in Derek's account, although not totally surprising, is the misogynistic language his brothers use to counter his challenge. Once again, the challenger has to defend himself while the perpetrators go unchecked. What's more, college men of any identity, but especially of non-academic families, express difficulties they experience when they return home after having spent time at college (Vianden, 2009; Vianden, Kuykendall, Mock, & Korb, 2012). Many of them feel out of sorts in the home environment, find the anti-intellectual comments they face from loved ones hurtful, but are unable to challenge family. Alex, at Riverside State, expressed that his family members' judgment makes it difficult for him to confront potentially inappropriate language:

> I don't think I would [confront]. I just feel like, say, if I would say something, they would just immediately judge me. Like you know, "He goes to college and now he's just, you know, does he feel smarter than the rest of us?" type of attitude.

Max, also at Riverside State, expressed a bit of resignation in describing the decision-making process he considers when possibly challenging joking, language, or behavior of family:

> If you're the only one that's going to stand up, like at home, I know for a fact I'll be the only one to ever say anything, 'cause my whole town is racist and doesn't care what anyone else thinks.

If Max's town is the way he describes, it might be a perfect place to begin sowing seeds of challenging racist behavior or language. Yet I also understand why he may be reticent to do so on his own. One key would be for him to identify other white male family, neighbors, or friends who think similarly about their community. Those folks exist, I know, but the task of identifying them may seem too arduous for Max.

Challenging Friends or Strangers

An equally large set of data emerged from the focus groups on participant perceptions of potentially challenging friends or strangers on racist, sexist, or homophobic language or behavior. Specifically, the men discussed whether it would be easier to confront friends or strangers and, as you will see in this section, there was no consensus among the participants. Some thought confronting friends would be easier than strangers; for others the opposite seemed to be true.

To begin, consider Peter's comment on the power of confronting friends; in his case, on his residence hall floor at Riverside State University:

> [When] you can get [friends] to recognize that [they should consider their language], it changes what people say so quickly. And I don't know if it carries on when I leave my wing ... I like to think at least, that it makes a difference.... Every once in a while, you can get a couple guys to buy into it and it makes a huge difference. If you can just get those two guys, if they're in the room, and they can call somebody out on something ... everything changes.

On the one hand it's reassuring that Peter considers the importance of confronting friends on language and behavior; on the other it's disappointing that he seems unsure of the lasting positive effects of standing up to friends. Educators have the opportunity, and likely the obligation, to find ways to make the effects of peer confrontation stick much longer than a year and into adulthood. Equally important in Peter's comments is the apparent influence of one or two men on the entire peer group or, in Peter's case, his residence hall floor. Strategically placed interventions with specific male students can thus have an essential effect on the entire group or community.

At Mountain State University, Aaron shared his perceptions about the difficulty of confronting friends:

> What I've learned at high school is if you embarrass someone in front of their friends by calling them out, you have less of a chance of changing their heart than if you take them aside and explain to them. It's something more loving. Overcome evil with good. Challenging someone openly in front of others, people tend to get offensive and harden anything to change.

Aaron's explanation of how we should confront others on their use of language shows a lot of grace. Compare that to the chilling lack of grace we as straight white men in the U.S. have shown to people of color, women, or people with diverse genders and sexual orientations over the last few hundred years. Aaron may be correct in his conceptualizations of the effectiveness of standing up to oppressive language and behavior, but the way he describes it almost implies fault in the confronter, not the originator of the behavior.

Some of the participants shared that it may be easier for them to confront friends on language and behavior because of the established relationship. Consider the following exchange during a focus group at Lakeside State University:

JÖRG: So, is it easier [to challenge] good friends or easier with strangers?

NATHAN: Easier with good friends.

KELLEN: Good friends.

ELI: Yeah, I agree.

JAMIE: Yeah, definitely easier since you know them.

JAMIE: Yeah, you have a one-on-one relationship with them, and then you can approach them about it. You know, as opposed to someone I don't know.

Approaching friends about inappropriate language and behavior was also the topic of discussion of the following focus group at Riverside State University:

STUDENT A: Yeah, I feel like I'd be way more comfortable if my friends were bullying a kid to be like, "You know what? That's not cool. You got to stop that," because I think that he would respect my opinion and then that would actually be more effective.

STUDENT B: Well, and you have something to hold over their head too. I mean you have a friendship versus someone bullying [someone].

STUDENT A: Yeah.

Notice the men discuss confronting their peers in a cordial and supportive way, one that hopefully sticks but one that doesn't admonish or criticize the perpetrators for the language or behavior. Owen at Southern State seemed a bit more forceful in this specific experience:

My best friend I grew up with in [home state], we both joined the Marine Corps at the same time. He was an infantryman and then I was in Com.... We [got put] on the same base. He saw a Lieutenant Colonel, didn't care about the rank, and she corrected him about something on his vehicle and he just blew her off. He got in some shit about that, in his unit. He told me about it and was laughing about it … I told him, "You're ignorant, you're not going to succeed in life because no matter where you go there's going to be diversity. Female, male, black, white, it doesn't matter."

College does not afford all students the opportunity to be surrounded by their best friends. In fact, for many college students, college is a place where new friendships are forged but these friendships are also often formed for life. Owen's intervention hopefully had a lasting effect on his best friend, and as educators we must help guide college men to have similar effects on one another no matter how fresh the relationship is with someone else. The positive outcome of such a challenge is too important not to try.

The following are data from participants who discussed confronting strangers on inappropriate language or behaviors. Abe, a student at Callahan College, shared that, "It's easier to [confront] a stranger ... than to say it to someone you have more of a connection with [because the] relationship you have with [them] is now on the line because you're criticizing what they said." Next, notice Peter's (Riverside State) sense of resignation that intervening with a stranger might not bear any fruit at all, and potentially cause more harm:

> People are always like, "Well why wouldn't you call this guy out in public?" 'Cause it's really not going to make a difference. I mean if anything it's going to retaliate to make it a worse situation for the people in there.

The following exchange from a focus group at Southern State University exemplifies a similar idea:

> JÖRG: Yeah, so it's easier to [confront] strangers? If somebody crosses the line, somebody is going to say, "All right, that's too far."
> GROUP: Yes.
> JÖRG: But it's harder to do that out in the open right in public, right?
> GROUP: Yeah.
> JÖRG: Why is it harder to do that in public?
> OWEN: You don't know what that person has gone through, their experiences. If you say something that might be like their last straw that they have for that day and just snap on you.

Anxiety around confronting strangers was also a topic in this focus group at Riverside State:

> STUDENT A: If I saw a guy graffiti-ing something hate crime-wise, I'd look at him and be like [*sigh*] and keep going. You can't be doing that but I'm not [going to] confront the man about what he is writing on the wall or whatever.
> STUDENT B: It's not worth the risk of someone pulling a knife out or a gun or something.

The fear of confronting strangers who pull knives or guns is all too real and unfortunate for many bystanders in this country. Some of the participants were clearly weary about that, as am I and likely you. Perhaps that is why it is most important to begin the advocacy, dissent, and challenge with folks who are in our inner circles: our families, loved ones, and friends.

But the men in the study were not only alarmed or unnerved by someone potentially attacking them after a confrontation about racism, sexism, or homophobia. They offered more mundane reasons for not choosing to confront anyone – family, friend, or stranger.

Choosing not to get Involved

For several participants, accepting the behavior they're witnessing or simply choosing not to get involved were reasons to not challenge inappropriate language or behavior. Consider Leo's statement from a conversation at Riverside State University: "Most people just accept [the behavior] and they don't try and change it, don't say anything, they just accept it that it's the way it is, it's not going to change." Do you hear resignation in his comment about the futility of trying to change others' minds? During a focus group at Lakeside State University, the participants discussed a recent sporting event during which Lakeside students heckled the other team with inappropriate language referring to Native-American history and culture:

> And like Jamie said, you can stand up for yourself, like honestly, you can attempt to talk to your friends, depending what state of mind they're in. I know [my friends] sit at the games, so normally, I like yelling. But when I hear something, I'm just like, I think about it first, and I'm just like, "Um, is that pushing the line a little bit?" But it's just like Jamie said, you can be that role model, you can maybe try and take your friends away from that, but other than that you're not going to stop all those students.

This specific issue was so important to the institution that high-ranking administrators became involved in studying crowd behaviors at Lakeside State sporting events. The institution then discussed with students the inappropriateness of certain chants and professed the values of diversity and inclusion of Lakeside State. Notice Nathan's uncertainty of whether confronting his friends would change anything. It's clear to him, however, that confronting the entire student body on their chants would not be fruitful. Men like Nathan – and I bet he is one of many at his institution – are perfectly capable of noticing inappropriate peer behaviors. Yet he and his friends don't intervene because they waver on whether dissenting would have any effect. They're even unsure if they should challenge their own friends when chanting inappropriate language, as Jamie's response shows:

> I know that for me personally, if it's, like, you know, a chant that I really disagree with, I might not chant it, but I'm probably not going to be like, "Hey guys, it's really not cool that you're saying that."

Chanting at the opposing team may be part of sports; chanting oppressive, identity-based, and racist language is utterly inappropriate and should be stopped. Our participants, by and large, knew that. The next step is help convince them that they are not alone in their opinions and that their challenge can, in fact, change others and bring about more equitable campus and community climates. This kind of step would assist in building solidarity with students from minoritized backgrounds, would help disrupt the white supremacist and patriarchal norm, and would pave the way for straight white men to develop social justice advocacy behaviors.

During a focus group at Callahan College, Trent described his thoughts about potentially confronting someone else's language or behavior:

> In general, I think the way that I react, it tends to be kind of slow. If I hear something that I think might be wrong, I have the tendency not to do anything right away because I'm trying to not make more trouble than there needs to be.

Instructive here is the phrase "more trouble than there needs to be." To me, Trent's comment implies that he considers the benefits and drawbacks of his potential dissension, and then may decide that dissenting comes with unwanted results.

Martin, a student at Southern State, offered this comment about his choice to confront others:

> I would probably just not involve myself. For someone of the majority to involve themselves, it could be misconstrued as possibly adding insult to injury. Generally, that's my personality anyway, to just kind of stay out of things like that.

Martin is clearly thinking about how it might look if he challenged other's racist, sexist, or homophobic performances. I'm not sure whether he thought the trouble with his possible challenge would be that it could be construed as centering his whiteness and maleness, but that is an important consideration.

Remember Paul's experience about how he and an African-American friend were kicked out of a fraternity party for dubious reasons? This exchange chronicles the aftermath of being shown the door by the white fraternity members:

> JÖRG: You and your friend, you're walking away from [the party] and … ?
> PAUL: I just said don't even worry about it, it's not even worth the time thinking about it.
> JÖRG: What did he say?
> PAUL: Obviously, growing up in [large Southern city], if you're not white then you're going to have some discrimination against you.… It's a shame though because some of my friends are in the fraternity and even

they couldn't do anything because it was the majority of the fraternity against three people I knew in it. It was just one of those things, you shake it off. You don't give it the time of the day to think about it.

Paul left the fraternity party with his African-American friend. I take that as an expression of solidarity and a confirmation of their friendship. In terms of social justice advocacy, leaving the party together is a good step for a white college man to take. However, I wonder if Paul's friend would have felt better about the situation had Paul expressed his disapproval at the party, or had he, perhaps quietly, confronted the chapter members who asked his friend to leave. Rather than shaking off the incident, straight white men like Paul ought to be encouraged to not only reflect on this experience, but to also learn how to find their voice in disrupting deeply rooted systems of oppression. Even on the spot.

Not getting involved was also a topic of conversation during this focus group at Midwest University:

STUDENT A: I played sports in high school [and] … made a lot of friends through that. So I didn't really reach out of my group too much. [When] there were people who were acting out or acting weird, I kind of would leave the situation.

STUDENT B: I mean, when you see something like that happen it's just, like, and you're part of the group that's doing it, I mean, it's kind of wrong so you kind of step back but you don't want to do anything to stop it. It just feels weird.

Repeatedly, our participants can recall experiences in which they identified their own or others' discomfort around inappropriate language or behavior. What they had not begun to articulate, however, were ways to dissent and challenge others' actions. Greg, a student at Lucas College, made a comment in this regard. Notice the difference between acknowledging behavior and doing something about it:

I would like to say that I would confront that individual even if there wasn't someone of that race … in the room … I'm a pretty shy person so I don't know if I would have the guts, if you will, to stand up and say, "That is wrong." If it was continued or if it was directed at somebody, I think I would, but if it was a passing joke, I feel like I wouldn't be able to bring myself to stand up and say, "Hey, that's not [cool]."

I appreciate the vulnerability of men to fully disclose, often with strangers in the room (for sure I as the researcher, but also other men they have not met before), about their inability or reticence to challenge inappropriate behavior though they may want to. This has non-trivial implications for learning and development of college students, as well as for college teaching, advising, and coaching. Men, who are socialized to be rough and tough on one hand, are also forthright about their inability about leading the charge to disrupt racist, sexist, and homophobic language and behaviors. It should make us optimistic that straight white college men may continue to be capable of building solidarity with others and fit to advocate against oppression. Yet it will require more specific reaching and teaching by teachers, faculty, advisors, and coaches.

Moreover, their individual inability to dissent implies what I raised earlier in the book. As men, we need to begin to sense, articulate, and show that we're part of a gender that has been perennially dominant. At the same time, we need to embrace that we have the power, influence, and ability, as a group, to challenge oppression and its perpetrators. But we also need to be open with other men about our perceptions of racial, gender, or sexual injustices. If all of our participants had sensed that other men in their friend group felt similarly about the inappropriate behavior they witnessed, they would have likely found dissent easier to do as part of a group.

Next, I turn to showing why it may be so difficult for men to intervene or confront family, friends, and strangers who are perpetuating systemic oppression. As a transition, consider Leo's comments from his focus group at Riverside State University:

> It's hard to speak up. Especially if you don't like conflict. If you don't want to be labeled as, like, [for] lack of a better term, the dick. Like you don't want everybody to think, "Well, that guy doesn't have a sense of humor. He just doesn't like to play along with anything." And then you get labeled yourself, and then, then nobody really wants to deal with you.

"You Don't Want to be That Guy": Fearing Social Consequences

Leo's trepidations about showing solidarity to oppressed people and confronting inappropriate language and behavior are common in men. Human beings who are part of a peer group from which they seek support, affirmation, and validation will likely not risk that friendship by actions that may not be supported by the group (Kehler, 2007; McMahon et al., 2015). In addition, many of our actions are driven by how we perceive our reference group will react to what we do, rather than by how the group actually reacts. Men specifically are scared that their outward dissension will not be accepted by their friends and will get them ousted from their reference group (Kimmel, 2013). So they remain silent, even when witnessing what they know is inappropriate peer behavior (Kimmel, 2008). Just how important the peer group is to college men is evident in this statement by Jamie at Lakeside State:

> If [strangers] are saying something that is inappropriate, then for me personally, it's easier to confront a stranger than a friend, just because I don't really care about their opinion. They mean nothing to me. Yeah, they

mean nothing to me, whereas my friends [and] their opinion of me, just mean about everything.

Considering what most of us know about male socialization in a Western context, we often fail to understand why assumed independent, assertive, competitive, or self-sufficient men seem to have trouble challenging others' inappropriate behaviors. What we're often unable to explore are the complex and intricate processes at work in the male peer group. We also tend to underestimate the emotional connection many men have with one another because too many of us believe men are bereft of emotion (Smiler & Heasley, 2016). Jamie's quote above shows how important his friends are to him, and that connection is one of emotion, even though he may not overtly acknowledge the emotional component. These complex male relationships hold key implications for educators working with men.

The following data explain why straight white men may, in fact, be reticent to openly dissent to racist, sexist, or homophobic performances in their peer group (Carlson, 2008). Discussing why white men may hesitate to confront inappropriate language by friends, James shared this comment during a focus group at Lucas College:

> And then there's actual repercussions. Like, if you're in your friend group and you're the only guy who [throws] the first wet blanket on the joke that everybody else gets. There could be serious repercussions [if you're] the guy who ruins jokes every time. You don't want to be that guy.

As you will continue to read, many college men think about their actions around their male friends and potential consequences of those actions (Kehler, 2007). During his focus group at Lakeside State, Jamie made this comment about condoning or accepting inappropriate joking: "If [I] felt [the joke] was offensive, well, I mean, it's just kind of that thing where you want to make everybody happy, you want to make your friends happy, so you go along with [it], yeah." Brad, in another conversation at Lakeside State, said: "We should be able to [confront], but we won't. We want to go along with it, we want them to like us in a sense, and by laughing they think that [we like them]." Here Brad describes a behavior McCann and colleagues (2010) called "laughing with the crowd" to avoid scrutiny by the friend group. For Abe at Callahan College, confronting strangers was easier than friends because challenging friends would mean to jeopardize the relationship: "It's easier to [confront] a stranger than to say it to someone you have more of a connection with. [The] relationship with [your friend] is now on the line because you're criticizing what they said." For Zane at Lakeside State, confronting friends on language could potentially end the friendship:

> I think it's a hard thing to do, like, to confront friends [when] they make a comment that crosses the line. Because you don't want to say

something and then they get really angry at you, and you're just like, "I just wanted to let you know." You don't want to make things weird or awkward, or potentially ruin a friendship because some people are just that sensitive.

The fear that "the violence just might be turned against them if they voice their opposition too vehemently" (Kimmel, 2008, p. 61) is one reason why men may not challenge their peers as much as we might expect. Educators have a lot of work to do with college men who assume someone would end a friendship because they have been confronted on inappropriate language. Those who do were likely not good friends to begin with; yet many of our participants would have rather not tested the relationship over a confrontation on racist, sexist, or homophobic language or joking. Above all, the "You don't want to be that guy" trepidation outweighed the wish or desire to confront, no matter whom, where, or what.

Summary

This chapter started with a discussion of white male misbehavior in college, including perpetrated racism, sexism, and homophobia by a preponderance of white men. I pointed out that not all straight white men on campus are culprits of these behaviors, but all are part of a social group that collectively does commit these acts. Compared to women and people of color, white men on campuses, overwhelmingly, are the originators of sexual assault and rape.

Straight white college men are creators of campus climates in three specific means. First, they can behave in ways that are welcoming and supportive of peers who tend to be oppressed at predominantly white institutions. Second, they can be the oppressors themselves, thus contributing to an environment that affects their minoritized peers in a variety of negative ways. Third, straight white men can remain inactive or passive when they witness acts of oppression, thereby condoning and perpetuating the campus as an oppressive social system.

I addressed racist, sexist, and homophobic joking as a behavior at the mid-level of the violence pyramid based on a foundation of microaggressions stemming from a white male hegemonic culture. Our participants admitted they struggled finding the line between oppression and humor, as well as confronting family, friends, and strangers on jokes or inappropriate language. That's to be expected because friends and family represent the people with whom our participants had the most intimate relationships. Yet it is in the close personal sphere, among friends and family, where I argue most change can happen if straight white men were to try to exert influence there.

Let's close this chapter with an insightful exchange I had with Brad at Lakeside State University about his thoughts on the reasons why college men may struggle to challenge oppressive language and behaviors:

> BRAD: I think there are very, very few white straight males who actually
> would challenge a racist or sexist joke or comment.
> JÖRG: What does that come from? What's the difficulty with that?
> BRAD: I think a lot of [is about] just wanting to please people, wanting
> to be a part of the group. [Otherwise it] might seem like you're no
> fun or something like that. I think that has a lot to do with it. And
> also ... it's obviously not funny. But we haven't had that experience
> where a joke like that [relates to us].

We have learned that many straight white men may recognize oppressive language and behaviors, but few articulated they would challenge or intervene. We also heard from them about why they wouldn't, and from some participants the reasons provided were actually poignant and signaled their vulnerability. Men struggle with confronting jokes because they don't want to be shunned by their friends for not conforming to what the group finds acceptable. The desire to belong is important in college men and they will weigh sticking out, showing solidarity, or advocating for social justice against expected behavior by the peer group.

Combine this with their – as Brad stated – lack of relatable experience in diversity or social justice matters about race, sex, or sexual orientation, and we have a conundrum where straight white men may continue to provide little challenge to their family and friends, as well as to strangers who perpetuate systemic oppression by their language or actions. The final chapter will feature strategies readers can use to increase the sense of responsibility to speak up and out about issues of oppression, and to make oppression more relatable or proximate to straight white college men.

6 What's my Responsibility? Strategies to Engage Straight White College Men in Social Justice

After hundreds of years of anti-racist struggle, more than ever before, non-white people are currently calling attention to the primary role white people must play in anti-racist struggle. The same is true of the struggle to eradicate sexism – men have a primary role to play. This does not mean that they are better equipped to lead feminist movement; it does mean that they should share equally in resistance struggle. In particular, men have a tremendous contribution to make to feminist struggle in the area of exposing, confronting, opposing, and transforming the sexism of their male peers.

(bell hooks, *Feminist Theory: From Margin to Center*, 1984)

The preceding chapters have led us to the point where we will now contemplate how straight white college men will build solidarity with peers from minoritized backgrounds and learn how to advocate for social justice. Even though our 92 participants are not a representative sample of the entire U.S. college population of straight white college men, we have enough data to draw some plausible conclusions about their attitudes, behaviors, and experiences around racism, sexism, and homophobia on their campus or in their communities. In this chapter, I will also advance strategies that teachers, coaches, professors, counselors, or individual straight white men can use to increase their propensity to get engaged in social change.

Straight White Men's Critical Consciousness

More than 30 years ago, bell hooks, famous American social activist and author, made the call to white men you see displayed at the start of this chapter. To help eliminate the social problems our cultural ancestors created, we as white men must heed hooks's call, now more than ever. It's clearly time.

Before we can build solidarity with others and begin to advocate for social justice, we need to raise our consciousness about social issues like privilege and oppression, as well as race, gender, and sexual orientation. First, straight white men have to understand that we're active members of a system that perpetuates oppression. These social inequities hurt our partners, kids, friends, and colleagues, as well as us. What we as whites have long failed to understand is how much we have benefited from social inequities throughout the history of the United States (e.g., slavery, Jim Crow laws). Throughout 82% of the life of the United States as a nation, slavery and Jim Crow were in existence (Feagin, 2014), staggering statistics white Americans have to be conscious of as they live their lives in this nation.

Feagin (personal communication, May 1, 2019) uses the term *social reproduction* to refer to the enrichment whites inherit from their cultural ancestors. Had African Americans had equal opportunities to gain prosperity as their white counterparts did over time, there would be nearly no wealth gap today between black and white families. Whites, and specifically straight white men, need to understand and critically interrogate the foundation of this country as a system of inequities in which whites continue to reap benefits.

Some research exists on the consciousness raising of counselors, teachers, or faculty (Brown & Perry, 2011; Hinchey, 2004; Landreman, Rasmussen, King, & Jiang, 2007; Lazar, 2014; Stachowiak, 2015) but we have little empirical knowledge about how to raise the critical consciousness of straight white college men. Freire (1970) coined the Portuguese term *conscientização*, or *critical consciousness*, to explain that critically conscious individuals develop awareness and personal concern around topics of social justice, which could result in action to disturb and end systems of oppression (Landreman et al., 2007). Critical consciousness includes personal awareness of historical, political, and social implications of a given situation or context; awareness of one's own location in or predisposition to the context; awareness of one's own multiple and intersecting identities (e.g., race, ethnicity, gender, sexual orientation, class); as well as awareness of the tensions between the envisioned justice for people and societal reality (Landreman et al., 2007). For many scholars, developing "critical consciousness is the first step in contesting and changing the status quo." (Lazar, 2014, p. 735). Hinchey (2004) suggested that developing critical consciousness means we accept that our own ideas come from our own life experiences and not from universal laws. This also means that we need to accept that others' experiences are equally as valid, even if they're different from our own. For example, straight white guys in college need to accept (and be outraged about) the fact that 1 in 4 of their female-identified peers will be sexually assaulted during college, rather than engage in victim blaming that she was assaulted because of what she wore or what she drank. And we need to accept the fears of students of color who feel oppressed on a predominantly white campus because of racist graffiti they read on dry-erase boards or in bathroom stalls, rather than saying, "Get over it, it was just a joke."

A key component of raising the critical consciousness of individuals is to understand and address how issues of race, ethnicity, gender, sexual orientation, class, ability, age, religion, or national origin influence our own personal and professional goals and identities (Brown & Perry, 2011). As you have seen in this book, this could, at first, be difficult to do for straight white college men because they may not consider themselves as connected to such issues of diversity; or they may consider themselves virtuous, good, and anti-racist (Applebaum, 2010; Feagin, 2013). What's more, depending on the specific male peer or friend group, "consciousness raising is not perceived as valuable and is indeed threatening to those in power" (Segal, 2011, p. 272).

Raising white men's critical consciousness is largely a cognitive or intrapersonal feat. It's difficult, no doubt, but if we're successful we must not rest there. The next step, a more physical or interpersonal task, is to activate white men's social empathy. Both are necessary if we want straight white guys engaged in understanding their own awareness and position vis-à-vis social justice, equity, diversity, and inclusion, as well as moving toward action.

Straight White Men's Social Empathy

Most of us would likely agree that empathy is a good thing. And those who seem to be devoid of empathy, many of us would castigate as socially or psychologically pathological. Yet lately we've heard a lot in the news and social media about how individual and collective human empathy may be dead or dying in the United States and in other Western countries. If it weren't dead, why do nations sit idly by as refugees drown in the Mediterranean Sea? If it weren't dead, how come Puerto Rico needed to wait to have their electricity restored nearly 12 months after Hurricane Maria? If it weren't dead, why has the Flint, Michigan, potable water crisis continued for nearly half a decade? And if it weren't dead, how can we jail toddlers in metal cages at our southern borders, not allowing anyone to comfort them when they cry?

The common denominator in all of these (and most other) social crises is the "other," specifically members of communities of color. The other as Syrian or African refugees risking life and limb in search for a better life; the other as Puerto Ricans, brown-skinned so-called U.S. citizens with hardly any political rights; the other as penniless Flint residents, nearly 40% of whom live below the poverty line; and the other as Central American asylum seekers who attempt to cross the border in search for a life free from danger. Ask yourself if Flint's water fiasco would have lasted this long if its citizens were largely upper-class whites, or if we would dare to separate infants and toddlers from parents of white European refugees.

In *The Empathy Gap: Building Bridges to the Good Life and the Good Society*, American philosopher and professor J. D. Trout defined empathy as the "capacity to accurately understand the position of others – to feel that 'this could happen to me'" (Trout, 2009, p. 21). The aim of empathy is to place ourselves in the situation of others or to take their perspective. Compared to more self-focused emotions such as anxiety, anger, or distress, empathy is directed toward others (Trout, 2009).

For decades, empirical research has confirmed that empathy has physiological components. Human beings react by physiological arousal when they witness others in pain or being hurt, and the arousal increases when the subject who's suffering is more similar to us (Trout, 2009). As white Americans, we are more likely to display empathy toward a white child in pain than a child of color, or we are more likely to act empathically toward a homeless man on the streets of Chicago than toward one on the streets of Bangkok. However, more recent research findings give reason to be hopeful about empathy. Humans may, in fact, be hard-wired for virtuous, prosocial behaviors and emotions like empathy (Segal, 2011). Neuroimaging of human brain patterns suggests that the same non-conscious system that monitors human biological processes also drives the motivation for virtuous behaviors like empathy or social responsibility (Segal, 2011). In *Social: Why Our Brains are Wired to Connect*, Matthew Lieberman (2013) suggested that empathy is the peak of human social brains: empathy, he said, calls on us to understand personal emotions of others and then behave in ways to help them and the relationships we have with them. Our neural mechanisms need to function in a coordinated state to not simply know, but feel, the other's experience.

This means that empathy may manifest as innate human biological traits. However, simply being born with empathy or having a biological propensity to develop or show empathy doesn't mean we all act empathically all the time. Main barriers to active empathy are perceived social values and perceived acceptable peer-normed behaviors (Segal, 2011). Especially in college men, the latter point is key. Just because white college men may think about acting empathically toward a ridiculed gay or black friend doesn't mean they will stand up to their peer group if the empathic response is perceived to be unacceptable. Challenging straight white men to reflect on living more empathically and to actually behave in more empathic ways should be a key goal for all educators.

Segal (2011, pp. 266–7) defined *social empathy* as the "ability to understand people by perceiving or experiencing their life situations and as a result gain insight into structural inequalities and disparities." Social empathy rests on social responsibility, the sense of connection to people outside one's close circle of family and friends that includes an obligation to help those in need or oppressed in the local community, society, and the nation. To promote social empathy in straight white college men we must find ways to increase proximity and to improve their familiarity between members of diverse communities (Segal, 2011). The college campus, along with its curricular and co-curricular engagement of students, is the perfect setting to promote these key prosocial behaviors.

To begin to explore where straight white college men stand in terms of articulating a sense of responsibility to engage in solidarity building and social change action, let's turn to our data.

What's My Responsibility?

On every campus, we asked the participants to reflect on racism, sexism, and homophobia at their institution or in their community and what, if any, responsibility straight we as white men have in eliminating these issues. The findings can be grouped into three sections that best describe the overall responses. A few participants sensed little responsibility (*"What I say won't Matter"*) in curbing oppression, primarily because they felt they were in a powerless position in society based on age and social standing. The majority of the participants sensed some responsibility (*Respectful Role Models*), specifically being a role model for others, being open minded and respectful, as well as educating themselves. This second category also included statements from men about their lack of certainty about what exactly to do to engender social change. A final category included a small group of participants who sensed they had much responsibility (*"It's Up to Us"*) to eliminate social issues by educating and confronting others and hopefully to change thinking.

"What I say won't Matter"

Contemplating their sense of responsibility to end oppression, this participant at Riverside State shared his perception about having a positive effect on others: "Obviously bullying is a huge problem. Yes, one person might be able to change it, but if some guy really has that kind of animosity towards a gay student, what I say probably won't change his mind." In a different Riverside State focus group, Jack pointed out:

> Well, you can obviously see that there is maybe a way that we should act to inhibit discrimination, but there's more toleration of it than anything. I mean, we understand that we shouldn't let someone pick on someone else, but it's much easier to just let it happen or not say anything about it and just kind of look the other way.

Both students seem helpless in their statements that what they might do to confront others' oppression won't bear any fruit.

Jamie at Lakeside State made this comment about his own influence as a white man to change others' viewpoints:

> I try to not to be racist as hard as I can. Like everyone to a degree, like every single person has racial stereotypes. [White people] can't make a stink about it because people are going to be like, "So what?" you know? No one cares, you know, you're not the minority, so if you make a stink about it, people don't do anything about it.

Jamie's perception holds important implications for college teaching and learning. If whites are under the impression that one has to be a person of color to be more believable in disrupting racism, they will likely continue to leave the advocacy up to already-minoritized individuals. As I've shown in this book, and as you will read on the following pages, whites indeed can do the challenging, specifically of other whites.

During the following fascinating discussion at Southern State University, the participants shared that their powerlessness in helping advocate for social change stems from a lack of stature in society:

JÖRG: What do you mean? Like [social change] will come with time?

CLAY: It's a process.

RON: Yeah, it's a process. There's still enough [oppression] lingering from generations before us that advocate hate, that advocate inequality, that advocate, "Let's keep the money where it is. Let's keep the power where it is." It's like he was saying earlier, I don't know if you can just break into something if you're not a powerful person yourself. You can lay down your job, but then what? Now I don't have a job and he doesn't have a job. So what did I really accomplish?

AUSTIN: Nothing.

RON: Whereas, over time, if we begin to work and establish ourselves and our names and our credibility, then it's our burden. And then we can actually do something about it. Because I do feel like there is a burden, but I don't know what I can do about it. I … like…. You know what I mean? It's hard for me.

As I discussed in Chapter 2, an increase in more racially diverse Americans alone probably won't eliminate racism. I can understand young men, just out of college perhaps and in their first professional position or job, who might not want to rock the boat. However, if we appeal to their collective identities as men, and maybe to men who work for the same company, sewing seeds of change among co-workers or even supervisors is possible. And dissenting among friends or colleagues on the same rung of the ladder is always helpful. Done appropriately, this disruption will succeed, and fairly immediately. I get men who want to climb the professional ladder first to be able to usher in positive social change, but we don't have that kind of time.

The concept of time was also a topic of discussion among these two Lakeside State students:

ZANE: I think it is worthy [to advocate for social change], but it's just a very difficult thing to do because you can't change people's minds, or in any quick way, it takes time…. There's no quick fix, it just takes time and people need to become more, I guess educated on, you know, I can't think of the word, like not diversity, but you know, on other people's outlooks.

KELLEN: Interpretations and beliefs?

ZANE: Yeah, you have to be more open to other people's beliefs and everything.

Philip, a student at Riverside State, made this comment about his sense of helplessness about what to do next: "I agree, we shouldn't be doing these things [oppression, bullying] but I don't know where to go from here." Educators reading these lines need to hear the call for action in Philip's words. Men who want to contribute to social change or advocate against oppression but don't know where to start need to be engaged on the steps they can take. The strategies offered later in the chapter may help educators with that endeavor.

Respectful Role Models

The majority of the participants understood that straight white college men had some responsibility in bringing about positive social change on their campuses and in their communities. Kellen at Lakeside State put it this way: "We do have a responsibility, we have to try our best to not make the problem grow, but make it just shrink a little bit." Micah, a student at Southern State, knew that the struggle for social change was going to be difficult but necessary: "You can't force someone to think something, it's their decision. You can shove it in their mouth as much as you want to but if they don't accept it, that's their decision. So we have to be convincing." In his focus group at St. Margaret's, Jacob shared his thoughts on the necessity of respect:

> [Everyone] equally has a responsibility as human beings to be respectful to other people. And I think as white males … seeing as we are the majority on this campus, I think we have the most power, possibly, to make a difference because such a large number of the students are straight white males. So I think that's the responsibility could come into play. If everyone felt the same responsibility, we are the majority, so we have the power to make a change.

During his focus group at Lucas College, Greg discussed his perceptions of the need for respect, especially for women in professional settings, like computer science:

> If I have a career in this, is realizing that that is an issue that has to be solved and [women] aren't in this profession because they're not smart enough or they don't like it. It's just that either society says they can't or that's not something they should do, or they didn't have the chance to when they should have gotten involved in this stuff. So, I think, [men should] know if there is a female, make sure that they … are not being discriminated against.

It's clear that many of the participants knew that openness and respect for others were important human as well as professional values in this society. Making sure that other straight white guys in college also could have similar notions emerged from a few discussions around the responsibility of role modeling appropriate behaviors to peers.

Knowing white men can influence other white men in college, Abe, at Callahan College, made this impassioned plea to his white male peers:

> The biggest group to impact you are your peers in college, it's not your parents or even your professors, it's the people you identify with and the people you spend the most time with. So I think an important way for this to happen is for men who really care about this to share it with their other white, heterosexual male friends about why this stuff matters and what it means to you. 'Cause I think often there's sort of a lack of conversation and interest in caring about minority issues and subjugated populations and stuff, and this understanding among ourselves that "We're not a part of this, we're above this, we don't need to talk about this, this isn't of any pertinence to us. In fact, this is kind of annoying when you bring this up to us, so don't." When I talk to people at home, they just do not want to hear it. They're the kind of guys who are much less politically correct and are always throwing around gay and racial slurs. So I think the peer – it's hard because you don't want to be a nuisance to your friends – but the peer approach is really effective.

Delivering another key quote of the entire book, Abe underscores the importance of working on generating social change collaboratively, and letting peers be partially responsible for the education and continued development of straight white college men. Abe was correct in his assessment of the peer effect. Since the early 1990s, scholars have attested to the powerful and positive effects of peers on college students and in most student outcomes (Astin, 1993; Pascarella & Terenzini, 2005). We as educators must make sure that college men get to engage in this work with their straight white male peers.

"It's Up to Us"

The third and final data category relative to the participants' sense of responsibility for social change included comments that emphasized the men knew they had a clear responsibility as straight white men to help bring about social change on their campus and in their community. Note here that this group of men was smaller than the previous two. This means that fewer of our participants accepted their responsibility as white college men to do something about social change than those who didn't know whether what they said would matter or those who thought they needed to be respectful role models.

Brad at Lakeside State didn't hesitate to answer the question on straight white male responsibility for social change and did so emphatically:

> Absolutely, there's a responsibility. It begins with even just recognizing that these things are happening every day. It also begins with making

personal changes, if you are having troubles, um, not seeing racism or sexism or anything, just realizing that it exists, and then connecting with, with other groups to kind of understand what their challenges are. It also is, you know, calling it out when you see it. Just if someone is saying something racist, like just let them know that, "Hey, that is hurtful."

Ryan, a student at Riverside State University, made this comment about how white college men can help bring about equity:

> For me, I do [think I have responsibility]. That's just my social ideology, I guess. I like a fair playing field. Being a straight, white male, I already have an edge up on a lot of other demographics and that's not fair. I feel like I really have a role to be a voice and stand out and actually stand up for someone, whether it's a minority or whatever it be, to elevate their status in a way. Not to suppress mine at all but bring them up as well.

In the beginning of the book I talked about the zero-sum game some politicians want to make us believe actually exists in a society striving for social justice (Norton & Sommers, 2011). According to the rulers, members of oppressed communities only get more when others get less. Ryan shows here that he doesn't believe that myth, which is a good starting point to engage him and his peers who feel similarly about being in solidarity with others and in social justice advocacy.

During his focus group at Danbury College, Dale pointed out that it should be up to straight white college men to disrupt racism:

> Well, I feel like it's up to us to maybe break the mold of how things used to be. I think it's already progressing towards people being more open minded and more diverse. I think it's up to us to continue the trend.

Dale seems to understand the role straight white college guys must play to end oppression and to advocate for positive social change. However, we can also notice that he is not entirely certain on how to begin going about becoming more active in living this advocacy. Kyle, in discussing the issue of responsibility with his focus group colleagues at Riverside State, shared this thought about confronting oppression:

> I'm sure you've seen a lot of it where, you know, you read a news article and it's like, "High school teen commits suicide after being made fun of three years for being gay." I think that's a huge problem because that's many years of people not confronting it. Obviously, people heard the jokes in class, heard them in the hallways and no one ever said anything, and now someone's dead.... Just because no one would ever stand up for him.... So it really does take someone from the norm group, I feel, to intervene.

Jacob, at St. Margaret's, seemed more certain about and active in his role of advocating to end oppression and to stand up against discrimination:

> I had guys [on my floor who] had racist tendencies, they would make racist jokes and things like that, but I would just stop them in their tracks and it kind of felt uncomfortable at times.... We do have a responsibility and I think that as you get higher up in positions, I think it gets even more responsibility.

Perhaps Jacob's role as a resident assistant on campus allowed or, in a way, obligated him to challenge his students' language or behavior. But not every straight male college student lives on campus, and not all of them have positions like resident assistant, orientation assistant, peer mentor, or peer advisor. In fact, the vast majority of college students don't hold these positions. College classrooms are one of the only spaces where we have a captive audience of students on our campuses. That is, academic courses and major programs of study are not voluntary spaces. Students are going to class because they're required to attend. In the classroom is where most of this education on issues of diversity and social justice must happen. And the learning must certainly be supplemented outside of the classroom in dorms, in student organizations, on sports teams, or in fraternities.

In Chapter 3 I introduced the ways in which the participants conceived of their potential engagement or participation in campus diversity efforts. Attending events is something all straight white men can do, specifically with others who may also be reticent to attend diversity initiatives alone. As we move into the final sections of the book, I appeal to straight white guys in college reading this: get some friends, attend events on campus, and afterwards talk about what attending meant to you and what you took away. Not all events or activities may be equally meaningful, but I guarantee you will learn something about yourself or think about something in different ways than you did before.

In sum, the data show that several of our participants could articulate their responsibility as men in helping to engender positive social change. Some even seemed to be fairly active already. However, there is a caveat to the study. We only explored participants' attitudes, perceptions, impressions, or thoughts. We did not measure or explore their actual engagement in social justice advocacy. So before we move to the strategies to engage more white college men in this advocacy, we ought to consider that, while most white men on our nation's campuses may be able to *talk* about responsibility, fewer may in fact be active in *living* that responsibility.

Strategies to Engage Straight White College Men in Developing Solidarity and Advocacy for Social Justice

I want to finish this book with specific strategies educators can use to help straight white men build solidarity with those oppressed, and to challenge them to advocate for social justice. I hope these strategies will be helpful for white male students and those who work with them.

Focus on Productive Masculinities

This is a book *about* men. They're straight, white, and in college. But this is also a book *for* men. For those who read it and challenge themselves to not only become more reflective and prosocial men, but to also become better citizens of their campuses and their communities. Perhaps you have watched the recent Gillette commercial advocating for more positive masculinities. It shows men intervening on other boys' and men's behavior (a group of boys bullying another boy; a man trying to make a move on an attractive woman; a father keeping two boys from fighting). The public outcry against the commercial was amazing; it was as if Gillette had declared a war on men. What could ever be wrong with boys or men who bully, show predatory behaviors toward women, or settle disagreements by fist fighting? What Gillette aimed to do was, sure, sell more product, but also focus on ways men can become more productive in their everyday lives as men and exude more positive masculinities. I don't use Gillette products for other reasons, but I consider the commercial a good example of a jumping-off point for more discussions on contemporary masculinities.

As you have read throughout this book, straight white male college students, in general and as a social group, are responsible for many inappropriate behaviors. We need to instill in them that they demand accountability from themselves and their peers who identify with similar privileged social identities. Stopping men who commit acts of sexism, racism, and heterosexism is the responsibility of other men and we don't have to ask women, gay, lesbian, and transgender individuals, or people of color, for permission to let us intervene with men who behave in these ways. I'm certain many would appreciate if straight white men intervened more often with other men to get them to cease their oppressive behaviors. We as straight white men are capable of these positive prosocial behaviors toward our fellow citizens, peers, friends, family, and loved ones.

When we show these positive behaviors, we will help usher in new kinds of American masculinities scholars have discussed for a while. This new masculinity, sometimes called *positive* or *productive masculinities* (Harris & Harper, 2014; Kiselica, Benton-Wright, & Englar-Carlson, 2016) provides a lens to view men's attitudes and behaviors that aren't focused on the deficit-model-minded rough-and-tough toxic masculinity we've become so used to in this American context. Men who show characteristics of productive masculinities tend to express their needs; tend to be confident and self-reliant yet unafraid of being ousted or having to prove their worth to other men; tend to have high self-awareness; tend to interact with other men on an emotional level; tend to recognize the experience, worth, and power of others, including individuals with minoritized social identities; and tend to be supportive partners, friends, and fathers (Kiselica et al., 2016). As I mentioned earlier, opponents of feminism or critics of men exploring new ways of masculinity are afraid of guys who show the behaviors I just mentioned. Faultfinders who lament that somehow men aren't allowed to continue to behave in rough-and-tough ways, and that the development of the sensitive guy ushered in some kind of male gender Armageddon, are simply afraid. They're afraid of losing their patriarchal supremacy, political and economic power, and social capital to men, citizens, and families who want to be done hating, discriminating, and oppressing and who want to live in peace with others. Productive masculinities characterize men who seek to build solidarity with others and who are active in their advocacy for a more socially just society. This focus on positive masculinities should not distract us from the many issues we as men must grapple with and for which we bear responsibility. Productive masculinities provide a way to address all men, their ambitions, goals, and dreams, without focusing on the detrimental behavior of a few men, and how their actions should not be the yardstick to measure all of us.

Productive masculinities should be trained or developed in men, and male-only groups (e.g., athletic teams, fraternities, dorm floors, male staff groups, male counseling groups) are perfect venues for these discussions. Harris and Harper (2014) advocated for critical reflection as a strategy for supporting positive masculinities in men. Educators should provide spaces and opportunities to critically explore and discuss men's perceptions of their identities. Using films, books, commercials, music videos, or other audio-visual materials in which gender looms large are good tools to bring about critical discussion. Service learning or volunteering projects can also be fruitful venues to explore social, economic, and class differences, as long as the activities are critically examined, discussed, and debriefed in the group. As we've seen in other studies on confronting oppression or bystander behaviors of men, peer challenge and support are vital. Men will be more likely to rise up against systemic injustice when they see their peers doing the same (Harris & Harper, 2014).

In Chapter 5 I addressed bystander behaviors of straight white college men and noted that our participants perceived confronting others, whether friends, family, or strangers, was not easy to do. To engage white college men who are witnesses to systemic oppression on their campus or in the community, we must break the culture of silence around masculinity (Kimmel, 2008). Men show inappropriate behaviors in part because they perceive they can get away with them and that other guys won't challenge them. To effectively train active dissenters, we must drive a wedge between the originators of the problematic language or behavior and those men who observe the performances (Kimmel, 2008). Kimmel suggests that men should be empowered to find one or more friends or accomplices who might feel similarly about the racist, sexist, or homophobic performances of others and together confront the perpetrator. The strength-in-numbers aspect of confronting oppression may be important for educators to emphasize when working with college men. McMahon et al. (2015) indicate that not all men have been passive witnesses to inappropriate peer behaviors. In fact, many white men may already have experience with challenging others. We need to identify these men and ask them to share their experiences with others who are just beginning to develop active bystander behaviors.

Create Proximity to Achieve Empathy

A little while ago, my partner and I watched *The Post* (Spielberg, Krieger, Pascal, & Spielberg, 2017), a historical drama set in 1971 featuring Meryl Streep and Tom Hanks in the main roles. Streep plays Katharine (Kay) Graham, owner of the *Washington Post*, and Hanks plays Ben Bradlee, editor-in-chief. Summarizing the plot briefly, Graham and Bradlee make the much-criticized decision to publish classified materials unearthing years of collusion of the American government in the Vietnam conflict. Nixon's White House seeks an injunction against the *Post*, the Supreme Court fast-tracks the case, and decides 6 to 3 for the paper in a landmark decision.

As I was watching the movie, I reflected on the topic of this book and the outrage of the American people in the 1960s and '70s against the American government, mostly fueled by non-transparent, collusive, and dubious policies in the Vietnam War, which took nearly 60,000 American lives (National Archives, 2018) in a near-20-year conflict. Today's White House under President Trump is not engulfed in a warlike conflict like Vietnam, yet the administration is fraught with human rights violations, and a host of racist, ethnocentric, sexist, and homophobic executive orders, policies, and roll-backs of previous laws. During the Vietnam era, thousands of Americans protested the policies and decisions of the various presidential administrations, especially in the late 1960s and early 1970s. These demonstrations also happened on college campuses, including the infamous Kent State University shootings on May 4, 1970, by Ohio National Guard forces, killing four and injuring 13 students. These demonstrations included people of color, women, and they certainly included white men. Today's protest marches for social movements, including Black Lives Matter, #MeToo, or Women's March, certainly include white men, but the vast majority of the marchers are likely individuals with one or more minoritized identities.

Why were white men more apt to protest, march, or speak out against the American government in the 1960s and '70s? I argue that they were engaged in the fight against injustice and senseless American deaths because their brothers, cousins, nephews, or friends were either in Vietnam fighting or they had been shipped home in body bags or coffins. They had *proximity* to the injustice. They could feel what is was like to lose loved ones, family members, and close friends. This was motivation enough for them to protest, challenge, dissent, and disrupt. Today's white male college students don't have the same sense of proximity to issues of systemic oppression. By and large, they're not close enough to the struggles of black Americans whose community members die at the hands of police officers. They're not connected to asylum seekers from Central America whose toddlers are ripped from their clutches and moved to different holding pens, or moved across states and away from parents. Today's straight white college men don't have proximity to the LGBTQ rights movement, or to stop sexual assault. They don't have proximity because they're not the ones targeted in social (or governmental) injustices. The others are the targets. We as white men are often only the idle bystanders. One of our participants at Riverside State put it this way: "If someone was making a joke about my Mom, I would definitely stand up, but if someone is making a joke about a female I don't know, I might not."

How do we increase the proximity of straight white college men, not only to social movements, but to daily injustices and inequities faced by many of their peers from disadvantaged communities? How do we as white men get closer to issues of social, political, or economic injustices? Bryan Stevenson, American lawyer, social justice activist, and professor, calls this *getting proximate*; that is, we must get closer to "suffering and understand the nuanced experiences of those who suffer from and experience inequality" (as cited in Fernandez, 2016, para. 4).

In a Western context, men are typically socialized to not focus on developing emotional self-awareness, expression, or sensitivity to others (Goodman, 2011). This means that men tend to have underdeveloped empathic connections with others and overdeveloped emotional armor to safeguard against discomfort and vulnerability. Against this backdrop, I'm calling on educators, coaches, advisors, counselors, and peers of men to not only increase empathy and critical consciousness, but to activate a sense of responsibility for social change. Research suggests that when male peers approach men in positive ways to build alliances with one another (e.g., in sexual assault prevention), their empathy increases (Piccigallo, Lilley, & Miller, 2012). As mentioned above, proximity to or knowing someone who has been affected by systemic oppression will help cultivate empathy and engagement in anti-oppression work. Yet, as Piccigallo and colleagues (2012, p. 511) pointed out, "it is neither possible nor preferable to rely on this personal link in order to engage men and foster empathy on their part." Oppression against one's loved ones is still oppression that targets all people with minoritized identities, whether they're close to us or not. Straight white men must understand that and find ways to develop proximity to all oppressed people.

Having men read or watch testimonies or experiences of victims of oppression may also increase empathy. These stories can be from victims of racism, ethnocentrism, sexism, homophobia, ableism, sexual assault, or any other systemic inequity or criminal behavior, including from male victims of such forms of discrimination or violence. Showing men as potential victims has shown to increase empathy in other men (Foubert & La Voy, 2000; Piccigallo et al., 2012). One respondent in a recent study explained the connection between empathy and male behavior this way:

[It can] help … men understand what it might feel like to be raped, help them realize that it can happen to anyone, including those they love, and you can really start affecting the way they go about their own personal prevention efforts.

(Piccigallo et al., 2012, p. 513)

Empathy-based, rather than blame-based programs with college men have shown success in increasing their willingness to engage in advocacy against sexual assault (Foubert & Perry, 2007). This type of approach could also be used in advocacy against oppression. Foubert and Perry (2007) described a program on a college campus that helped male participants understand the weight of the word *rape*. After the program, participants refrained from telling jokes about rape and several participants challenged rape jokes told by others. Showing men as potential victims of sexual violence enabled the male participants to put themselves in the shoes of women who had been the victims of rape and developed greater empathy.

Broockman and Kalla (2016) recently published a groundbreaking study that confirmed what Allport's (1954) contact hypothesis has claimed for more than 60 years: reducing prejudice in people, even if for a short time, can actually work. Perspective taking is the thought process that has been found to decrease prejudice in the research Broockman and Kalla (2016) reviewed. The intervention the authors described focused on reducing prejudice against transgender individuals, or transphobia. The research procedure involved canvassers going door-to-door in Miami after the city had passed a non-discrimination ordinance for transgender people in 2014.

Fearing backlash among residents, canvassers engaged in strategies that included defining transgender identities, asking residents to explain their side on the issue of transgender protection by the city, and involving the residents in perspective taking by asking about a time when others judged them for being different. The intervention lasted only 10 minutes on average. Respondents were then involved in an experiment in which they filled out surveys that assessed their levels of prejudice toward transgender people. Findings revealed that the canvassing intervention was broadly successful with large effect sizes, irrespective of whether a transgender canvasser spoke to the residents, whether the residents identified as Republican or Democrat voters, or whether the residents were subject to attack ads against transgender individuals. Surprising about the results was the lasting nature of the reduction of prejudice up to three months after the canvassing event. If strangers canvassing door-to-door can have this kind of enduring effect, educators in schools and colleges ought to feel good about working with students on reducing prejudice in classrooms and lecture halls. Part of any discussions on reducing prejudice, building solidarity, and developing advocacy for social justice may include some grace on the part of the educator for the level of development and knowledge of the student.

Too often we as educators use the sledgehammer with men whom we believe must finally understand their roles as oppressors of every other subordinated human being on this earth. As the saying goes, every toolbox needs a hammer, but the hammer is not the best tool for every job. I am not advocating against teaching and challenging men about their roles in the oppression of others. However, hitting them over the head with a hammer will lead most of them to resist, hide, or disengage from the educational initiative to begin with. Their social privileges allow them to do that. I have seen too many college classrooms in which men, once challenged hard on issues of race, gender, or sexual orientation, retreat from the discussion and hide in the corner with the proverbial blanket over their head. They will likely be reticent to engage in similar discussions again and they will leave the class no more educated on issues of systemic oppression than when they entered. Using blame, aka the sledgehammer, only reifies straight white men's privilege to remove themselves from discussions in which we need them to participate. I'm especially calling on straight white male educators to leave the hammer in the toolbox and find other ways to challenge their straight white male students.

In addition to using a nonblaming way to engage men in important conversations on diversity and social justice, we must also appeal to their diverse humanities if we want to activate their sense of responsibility for social change. Feagin (2013) presented several strategies through which we as educators may attempt to engage men. First, we should appeal to men's moral obligation toward other human beings. In many individuals, especially in the United States, this morality stems from tacit religious beliefs that have been fostered by families for generations. *Love thy neighbor as thyself* or other commandments in the Christian tradition, as well as moral ideas from other faiths, are cornerstones of prosocial human attitudes and behaviors. Calling on religious men to evoke these principles when reflecting on systemic oppression may be a way to engage them more directly.

Another strategy to create proximity and empathy is to appeal to the liberty-and-justice frame Americans tend to use to make sense of the world around them (Feagin, 2013). We are interested in fairness, equal treatment, and justice, specifically when our own self or our loved ones are concerned. We must involve straight white college men in this framed thinking and remind them of their better values when they seem to have forgotten that the sense of fairness afforded to them should also be afforded to every other human being, regardless of their diversity.

Another form of invoking empathy in straight white college men is to foster the identification *we* versus *they*. For centuries, the Christian white male ruling class has propagandized people of color, immigrants, and people with different religious backgrounds as the "other" who is to be avoided and feared. Recent political elections in the U.S. and beyond have continued this sinister propaganda for personal and political gains, and we as citizens have fallen prey to the politicians' cunning plans. Rather than listening to politicians who want to divide us, we should begin to build solidarity with people who are closer to us economically. For college students, "we" are likely college peers on similar rungs of the socioeconomic ladder rather than others who are perched comfortably above. "We" includes college students who are people of color, people with different genders and sexual orientations, and students with different abilities, ages, national origins, and religious beliefs. "We" doesn't include elite politicians, CEOs, or fat-cat financiers who aren't interested in the day-to-day struggles of college students anyway. If we can get white college men to identify with and show solidarity to their college peers from minoritized backgrounds, we will have taken a big step toward achieving a more socially just society. As a result of this identification with and commitment to their peers, when our so-called leaders attack the "other" they're in fact attacking all of us, and college students will express their commitment with votes for those who stop hate and discrimination, once and for all.

Join, Don't Disassociate

One of the biggest problems in social justice advocacy work are white men who deem themselves too evolved or too arrived to engage with those of us who are not as far along, or who display racist, sexist, or homophobic attitudes and behaviors. These white *madvocates* often engage in distancing behaviors to show solidarity with individuals with traditionally minoritized identities (which is a good thing); yet they likely also distance in hopes they can demonstrate their own innocence in the social injustices of this society. Distancing yourself does not exonerate you from being part of a society in which all of us are responsible for ending oppression or enable you to give back your privileges based on your race, gender, or sexual orientation.

But whites who distance themselves have had (bad) role models who have shown similar behaviors for decades. A recent example came from former New York Senator and Secretary of State, Hillary Clinton, while on the 2016 presidential campaign trail. At a fundraiser in New York City she distanced herself from Trump supporters in the following statement:

> You know, to just be grossly generalistic [*sic*], you could put half of Trump's supporters into what I call the basket of deplorables [*laughter and cheering from the crowd*]. Right? The racist, sexist, homophobic, xenophobic, Islamophobic – you name it. And unfortunately, there are people like that. And he has lifted them up.
>
> (Reilly, 2016, para. 2)

I have two major issues with this kind of disassociating comment, but the second one has more bearing on this book. One, it's not smart as a politician to be so aloof to desecrate a large number of American voters, for whom one would serve as president. Two, disassociating oneself from Trump supporters for their apparent hatred doesn't make us any better. Neither does it abdicate us from our obligations to help eradicate social, political, and economic injustices. Judging by the statistics of voter groups for Trump, I wonder if Clinton would take her comments back if she could have a do over. White male voters of all ages, in large parts, were responsible for putting Trump in the White House (Tyson & Maniam, 2016) – not that hard to understand when reading the transcript or watching the video of Clinton's speech.

By the way, this white disassociation from perceived cruder or simpler whites was not only a dominant force in winning Donald Trump the presidency of the United States. It also helped decide the outcome of the Brexit referendum in the United Kingdom in 2016, facilitated the election of the highest percentage of right-wingers to German parliament since 1933, and nearly won populists the political supremacy in France. We as whites, and specifically those of us who identify as straight white guys, cannot afford, ever, to disassociate ourselves from other straight white men. Chris, one of our participants at Mason College, made this fitting comment:

> [One thing that] perpetuates this stereotype that white straight males don't care is that, um, when addressing culturally misappropriating jokes and Halloween costumes is that sometimes, when dealing with these situations, we feel like the easiest solution is just to distance ourselves from the people making these inappropriate jokes. And I think, what that leads us to is a tendency to ignore the [fact that] we aren't actively trying to educate ourselves more or actively becoming engaged in these issues.

Consider this personal story to reflect more on the joining versus distancing behaviors of white men. The year was 1994. I was 22 and in my first semester at my undergraduate alma mater in Iowa, having transferred from the university in my hometown in Germany. I remember hanging out one night in my friend Andrea's room. Several of her friends were also present. Andrea was from the Midwest, white, and I assumed she was straight. We were friends and I enjoyed her company because of her jovial nature. She and the friends in her room were members of some of the choirs for which our college is well known. When Andrea asked me whether I liked to sing, I responded, "Not really, because I sing so high that it makes me sound gay." That was not the first time I had ever ridiculed members of different sexual orientations, but it was the first time my joking garnered the kind of response Andrea provided.

Her face grew visibly upset, and she yelled, "Don't ever say something like that again." At this point we were standing just a few feet apart, and even though Andrea was more than a foot shorter than me, she was a force to be reckoned with.

"Oh yeah," I said laughingly, "what are *you* going to do about it?" (I know how this sounds, and I am sure Andrea received it similarly, like uttered by a complete jerk).

"I'm going to punch you in the face," she snarled back. At this point I didn't know whether she was serious or joking, but I decided she could only mean the latter because we had often laughed and had fun together. "OK," I said, "hit me right here," pointing at my right cheek and bending forward a little. Before I could react or avoid Andrea's fist hitting my jaw, I felt my head snap from her left hook. It clearly wasn't a friendly tap, but an enraged blow that made my ears ring. Silence fell over the room and Andrea and the rest of the people in the room looked at me worriedly, wondering what I would do next.

Smiling nervously, I stammered, "Uh, I better go now," turned around and left the room. That was the last time I spoke to Andrea until we found each other on Facebook nearly 10 years later. After she punched me, I couldn't figure out why it hurt her so much that I made a joke about someone sounding gay when they sing. Did she identify as a lesbian? Did some of her friends or family? Or did she simply not want me to tell offensive jokes in her presence?

As a straight white male educator who has committed to teaching college students, I have to remember my own shortcomings from 25 years ago and those I continue to make on a frequent basis. I cannot afford to distance myself from today's straight white men who act the way I did when I was at that age. That would not only be hypocritical but detrimental to the education of young people, because in my interactions with them they might learn something that allows them to avoid making the same mistakes I made. So I'm calling on other educators, but most definitely on other straight white men who are in my line of work: do not disassociate from straight white male students, their attitudes and behaviors, even if you want to. Stick with them and do the best you can in helping them develop and learn. It will be difficult work, but the fruits are too important to not engage in the labor.

Facilitate Disorienting Dilemmas

With Andrea, I experienced what Jack Mezirow (1991), late renowned American sociologist and professor at Columbia University, called a *disorienting dilemma*. A disorienting dilemma can be seen as a single event or a series that make individuals aware they are viewing the world through a limited or distorted perspective. Disorienting dilemmas trigger transformative learning in the sense that we examine the limited view critically, accept the possibility of alternative ways of thinking, and then change the way, or part of the way, we see the world (Taylor & Cranton, 2012; Mezirow, 1981, 2000). This kind of transformation Mezirow (1991, p. 167) describes as a "more inclusive, discriminating, and integrative perspective" that includes, "finally, making choices or otherwise acting upon these new understandings."

Although likely too violent (but not undeserved) than what college educators have in mind when we're thinking of disorienting dilemmas, Andrea's fist to my cheek was a transformational learning experience for me. My worldview seemed to indicate that it was acceptable to joke about someone else's sexual orientation among friends. Her opposition to my language and apparent indifferent attitude about individuals with marginalized identities was the first confrontation of this worldview I can recall. Reacting so vehemently must have meant that I hurt her, and if I had the potential to hurt Andrea, I likely had hurt or would continue to hurt others with similar comments. As a result of the punch, I began to refrain from joking about sexual orientation and thought long and hard about in what other ways I needed to adjust my thinking about and behavior around human difference.

Much like I needed it in college, today's straight white college men need disorienting dilemmas. In my nearly 20 years as a professional college educator and as a researcher of men and masculinities, I have encountered countless college men who were influenced by peers, family, friends, co-workers, faculty, and staff to think in a specific way without fully exploring their own viewpoints on events or phenomena. Social norms theory (Berkowitz, 2004), specifically tested on college men, implies that men act or don't act based on how they think others will act. So I may not be comfortable as a white college man with hearing sexist, racist, or homophobic jokes, but I won't confront the joke teller because other men in the group seem to be okay with what they hear. This is what we heard from many of our participants in Chapter 5.

Today, many men are uncomfortable with traditional male gender role socialization and masculinity (e.g., independence, aggression, competition, being in control, acting tough) but falsely think that other men are actually comfortable with these attributes (Berkowitz, 2004). Education is the key to help men unearth these mistaken perceptions and explore their peers' true feelings around power, privilege, and oppression. College classrooms, residence halls, sports or intramural teams, fraternities, and other student activities are perfect settings to seek out disorienting dilemmas, transformative learning, and authentic peer-group interactions.

Education that brings about disorienting dilemmas or transformative learning experiences may sound to some readers like brainwashing. Often today, college educators are criticized as liberals who push their students to think or act in specific ways, and often the critics lament that we want students to think more liberally, or even become liberals. Certainly, in order for white college men to be more engaged in making this nation and society more socially just, some may have to change their thinking. However, the choice to engage in this thinking, learning, and to potentially experience a perspective transformation is up to each individual student. In other words, for college students this perspective change is negotiable. What should not be negotiable is that college educators continue to present issues of diversity, social justice, power, privilege, and oppression from a variety of perspectives and in a way that spurs critical thinking (perhaps a more widely known term for perspective transformation) so that learners may make up their own mind about whether they should change their perspectives.

Sherry Watt (2015), professor of higher education and author, established the Privileged Identity Exploration (PIE) model as a way to increase disorienting dilemma for people with socially dominant identities. The PIE model helps folks interrogate how they become aware of the effects of oppression and how they may move that awareness into advocacy for social change. Engaging in learning spaces with learners who present different privileged and oppressed identities creates a kind of push and pull, or a deconstruction and reconstruction, of our values, ways of knowing, and ways of behaving. Watt said that "this sense of disequilibrium comes from having to reconceive the self in relation to others in ways that are counter to one's understanding of one's social and political position in society" (Watt, 2015, p. 42). The PIE model includes four assumptions, including the interrogation of privilege as an ongoing and never-ending process; the need to involve learners in "self-awakening difficult dialogues" about oppression (Watt, 2015, p. 43); the fact that learners put up defense mechanisms as a normal reaction; and that an intersection of oppression and privilege resides in each learner. Educators working with straight white men need to be aware of these tenets and help learners navigate the difficult dialogs, defense stimuli, and the intersections of their identities. Perfect spaces for these in-depth conversations are college curricula and classrooms, specifically in the major program of study.

Require Diversity in Major Programs of Study

Given that our participants' experiences may be somewhat representative of white male collegians in general, we must contend with a serious question and major predicament. In this book, I have argued that many of today's straight white men may leave college no more prepared to interact successfully across difference than when they entered. This may be especially true in interactions with peers from communities of color or with individuals from diverse genders or sexual orientations. If this is true, it spells one of the biggest shortcomings of higher education, particularly considering the vast demographic changes the United States is experiencing.

Think of the current set up of a college education as a buffet line in an all-you-can-eat restaurant. The curriculum at your institution includes a smorgasbord of opportunities, including some items you have to take (you'll have to eat something, otherwise why go?), others you should (vegetables and fruit), and yet others you won't (the stuff you don't like to eat). For instance, students are required to take specific courses in their major program of studies, and most, if not all institutions typically require a certain amount of general education requirements. Considering options that cover diversity, inclusion, equity, or social justice, most institutions offer different courses, if they even have diversity requirements. At the same time, many major programs of study may not have designated courses on diversity-related content or require such courses of their students. What happens, then, as students meander down that buffet line of options? Generally, straight white men, as this study has shown and as 15 years of data of the National Survey of Student Engagement confirm, don't choose buffet items that include diversity, social identities, race, gender, sexual orientation, equity, or social justice beyond what they're required to take (Vianden, 2018). And as they're walking down the buffet line, no one stands behind it offering additional options "on the house" or "from the kitchen." Options are good, but colleges and universities in today's economic and political landscape must step up and put more diverse curricular opportunities in front of students, specifically exploring current social topics of privilege, power, and oppression. And there's no better place for this than in the major program of study.

It's likely that most programs of studies in the social sciences, education, humanities, and arts include some aspects of human difference, inclusion, equity, or social justice. However, I'm not certain that natural sciences, engineering, computer science, or business do. A diversity course in sociology, psychology, or communication studies? Of course. But in accounting, management, or computer science? Absolutely!

Students, once they have declared a major, will likely spend between 10 and 15 courses in that program, frequently interacting with the program faculty and smaller groups of peer students. In this setting, diversity coursework should be incorporated or required, thus supplementing the required courses in the general education arena. However, this in-depth treatment of diversity topics may not be occurring in the major program of study at some of the research sites.

In his focus group at Callahan College, Mitch stated, "I think your challenge as a faculty member is to integrate diversity and not have the special 'Diversity Day.' You have to integrate it into the curriculum." Because diversity coursework may not directly appeal to all straight white male college students, incorporating topics of human difference in major programs of study may be the best way to get them to engage in the topic in more depth and throughout their college careers, specifically if the outcome of the course is tied to career-related ends.

During the Straight White College Men Project, we asked participants to provide recommendations about how to get more white guys involved in campus diversity initiatives. An important theme in their answers emerged when many men said, "Require diversity in major programs of study."

> JÖRG: If [your] program said, "Each year there is going to be a required diversity component," you wouldn't worry about it?
> BILL: I wouldn't pay for it.
> JÖRG: It's required for your major.
> BILL: I'm going to a different school if I have to pay for that.
> RON: [to Bill] No, it's part of your 120-hour plan basically.
> JÖRG: If it's part of your curriculum just like the courses....
> RON: Instead of financial accounting you have to take a diversity class. It wouldn't be a big deal at all.
> KYLE: Yes, everyone would just take it.
> JÖRG: It's part of your major.

RON: If … it's part of my major, it's a fact of life. [If] it's going to get you a job, you're going to take it.

Like Bill, not all straight white men may be excited to take diversity courses in the major, but very few would consider leaving their program of study to avoid or resist engaging in diversity content in the classroom. We need to capitalize on the captive audience of students our major programs of study provide and offer diversity content where students must engage in it.

This kind of prescribed approach to diversity education may be a suitable way to engage more straight white men in diversity content than they are used to; however, it also points to a problem. If diversity education in the major continues to be viewed only as a means to an end, college men may not necessarily engage in it more deeply than before the requirement. To realize the altruistic nature of learning about power, privilege, and oppression, college administrators and faculty have to carefully communicate the human and ethical obligations of engaging in diversity in the major and beyond the associated career-related promises.

My colleague Robert Reason (2013) discussed ways to infuse social responsibility into the curriculum and co-curriculum of American colleges and universities. He argued that social responsibility includes the dimensions of empathy, or perspective taking, and making contributions to a larger community. Many institutions and individuals are already engaged in this initiative in the form of service learning, community service, and volunteering. Perspective taking includes understanding and become active in forming one's own judgment, as well as getting involved in studying diverse perspectives in learning, at work, and in life (Reason, 2013). Extant research shows that college students typically endorse the importance of contributing to their community at high rates. They also get that they should engage differing perspectives when creating their own. However, far fewer college students actually participate in service learning or community service, build skills and awareness of community engagement, or deepen their commitment to social change. Colleges and universities should include tenets of perspective taking and community engagement in their coursework, or perhaps requiring service-based learning, such as the University of Wisconsin-Eau Claire. Most important, however, is that educators actually engage students in critical and reflective conversations before, during, and after their engagement in service or experiential learning. Simply requiring such activities and then leaving the students to their own devices in figuring out what they learned is poor practice. Moreover, engagement without reflection may actually perpetuate systemic oppression or the privilege of white students who enter and leave oppressed communities during their learning. See Reason's (2013) article for good institutional examples for infusing social responsibility and perspective taking into their curriculum.

Utilize Pedagogical Models for Privileged Learners

All strategies suggested here take into account that straight white college men are privileged in their salient social identities and, as such, may have different learning needs than individuals with one or more oppressed identities (Curry-Stevens, 2007). If we want to reach straight white college men and engage them in discussions, behaviors, and actions that have been heretofore foreign to many of them, educators must employ teaching mechanisms that fore-ground privileged identities and propose that men with such identities can change in fundamental ways. Several of these models have been advanced by scholars (Allen & Rossatto, 2009; Goodman, 2011; Keddie, 2006; Kimmel, 2002; Nurenberg, 2011; van Gorder, 2007). It's important that educators help privileged learners move away from positions of paternalistic allies to ones characterized by collaboration, interrelation, and solidarity (van Gorder, 2007). Educators must realize that "oppressor student[s] [are] different from an oppressed student. And any pedagogy that fails to account for this differ-ence is unlikely to contribute to meaningful social change" (Allen & Ros-satto, 2009, p. 179).

Pedagogy for the privileged (Curry-Stevens, 2007) makes intentional the engagement of privileged learners to assist their transformation as accom-plices of individuals who struggle for social justice. The pedagogy is predi-cated on the fact that privileged learners bring their social power to bear in the learning environment and to use this social power to help advocate for change. Curry-Stevens (2007) developed a step model to be used by teach-ers, coaches, advisors, or supervisors to transform the learning of primarily privileged individuals. This pedagogy targets cognitive development and encourages learners to become aware of their privilege. First, this includes acknowledging structural systemic oppression by asking questions such as, "In what ways are we oppressed as students at this university?" and "In what ways do we act as oppressors as students at this university?" This first step recognizes the self as oppressed and aims to build solidarity among learners by focusing on universal ways in which all or many college students are dis-advantaged or oppressed (e.g., incurring debt while in college; working on campus and providing cheap labor to the institution; being exploited as student athletes). Once learners have recognized oppression, locating one's own universal privilege (e.g., being in college, age, religion, ability), its benefits, and how privilege implicates the self in the oppression of others are the next steps of the model (Curry-Stevens, 2007). Here, it's important to ask questions such as, "In what ways are we as students of this university privileged?" and "How do we benefit from our privileges?" The third step, co-conspiring for change, involves motivating learners to identify with one another to affect positive change. Questions to ask at this juncture include, "In what ways can we connect and together create change?" For educators going through this exercise, a question may include, "How can we come together and empower our students to engage in social change?" The final step of Curry-Stevens's (2007) model calls for mutual commitment of the learners in a given space. This ensures that learners are reminded of their mutuality and solidarity with other learners and of the commitment they made to one another to carry forth the advocacy for change. Important questions here include, "To what will I commit as I leave this space (classroom, locker room, chapter house)?" and "What specific support would I like from others (who share this space with me)?"

Foster Identity-Based Caucusing

About 15 years ago I attended a conference for professional college educators in Atlanta, Georgia. Leafing through the conference publication for workshops to attend that day, I noticed the title "White Men's Roundtable Discussion." Given my interest in whiteness studies and masculinity, I was excited to attend the session and converse with other white male administrators in higher education. I still remember the room. It was small and the chairs were set up in a circle. One by one the attendees filed into the room, appearing to be somewhat apprehensive about the session. Participants greeted one another, but not much conversation took place until the workshop facilitator, my colleague Z Niccolazzo, higher education professor and scholar of transgender issues, welcomed the attendees. We weren't a large group, perhaps eight or 10, all of whom I perceived to be white and male. As we began introducing ourselves, the door opened and an African-American woman entered the room. I still remember the looks on some of the faces. I wonder if the participants thought that the woman's attendance changed their impression of what they might be able to share. She introduced herself as a higher education administrator and mentioned that she didn't want to crash the group or influence what attendees might say. I caught myself hesitating several times to contribute to the conversation in fear I might say something offensive. I know this was not the intention of the woman educator at all, but I wondered about whether it would have been better to keep the group exclusively white and male (I also know that this is impossible at conferences). Not to scheme in fanatical ways to perpetuate oppression, but to be open and honest about what we wanted to say. The focus of this identity caucusing should be to begin open and honest conversations that aim for learning, development, solidarity building, consciousness raising, empathy, and advocacy. Don't get me wrong: I don't want to avoid conversations with members from minoritized communities in the room. But there are times and places when well-facilitated identity-based caucusing can be helpful and should be used. And once the conversations among straight white men have taken place, often over months or semesters, sharing space in conversation with individuals with minoritized backgrounds is also needed.

Empirical research has long suggested, and our focus groups with the participants have confirmed, that today's straight white college guys are not inexpressive. They want to share their thoughts, even on topics like diversity and social justice, to which they don't organically seem connected. And they seem perfectly comfortable sharing their perceptions with perfect strangers: the researchers, as well as other male students in their focus groups, who were students on the same campus, but they had not necessarily met or knew one another well. I also argue, and research affirms, that the men were freer to share their opinions on potentially difficult topics like diversity and social justice with other men whom they assumed identified along similar characteristics, such as race, gender, and sexual orientation (Gulati-Partee & Potapchuk, 2014; Hudson & Mountz, 2016). I contend they would not have disclosed so honestly had women, students of color, or students with diverse genders and sexual orientations sat around the same focus group tables.

This context holds important implications for working with college men in conversational settings with male-only groups. Specifically, male-only cisgender athletic teams, male-only cisgender dorm floors, and cisgender fraternity chapters provide the near-perfect spaces to engage straight white men in challenging but important discussions with their peers. Identified in education literature and practice as *identity caucusing*, men in these conversation groups benefit from the fact that they're engaged with other students who identify similarly across characteristics, at least across the intersecting identities of race, gender, and sexual orientation. Careful and trained moderators should pose challenging questions and provide environments in which honest dialogue can exist. The questions we asked in focus groups during the Straight White Men Project could be an appropriate jumping off point for these caucused conversations.

I don't only advocate engaging straight white college men in exclusive male-, white-, and straight-only groups. Identity caucusing can be spaces for the "self work" straight white men have to do in order to avoid taxing folx with minoritized identities with the labor of educating us on issues of diversity and social justice. Once groups have been divided by identity characteristics, students in each caucus should be encouraged to talk about and unpack feelings, openly share personal experiences, discuss current events relative to systemic oppression, and ensure accountability among the members of the caucus to commit to advocating for social change (Gulati-Partee & Potapchuk, 2014). If you're an educator wanting to use identity-based caucusing, you could break students into groups by salient identities, have them discuss in these groups for a given amount of time, and then bring the groups back together to debrief. This creation of *intergroup dialogue*, or the connection, conversation, and communication of members of several diverse groups after the single-identity caucusing, is necessary to explore and understand differences and similarities in group perspectives on a specific topic. Bringing the groups back together may also enable students with generally oppressed identities to speak, as a group, about what they expect from students with privileged identities relative to diversity, inclusion, equity, and social justice.

Some scholars have questioned whether men are capable, by themselves, to stem the tide of sexism specifically (Jordan & Luzader, 2016). Men-only groups, in their opinion, may be problematic in fostering an anti-sexist agenda and successfully disrupting gender oppression. It's important to combine men-only or caucused-group approaches with those that debrief the experiences or learning in the whole group where all social identities reconvene.

Create Intergroup Dialogue

As I addressed early on in the book, Allport's (1954) tried-and-true contact hypothesis is still important today. He purported that meaningful same-level contact (e.g., economic standing, college students) across human difference has the power to deconstruct and diminish stereotypes and prejudice. The more we engage with our peers who identify across racial, ethnicity gender, sexual orientation, ability, age, national origin, or veteran status backgrounds, the more we increase the potential to understand others and decrease our own stereotypical thinking and behavior. We know that many of the participants of the Straight White College Men Project didn't interact meaningfully across such differences while growing up. Specifically, their racial isolation from people of color was startlingly apparent. Now in college, these men have the chance to interact with and learn about and with individuals with a variety of intersecting identities, and we as educators have to create and foster the environments where this learning can occur.

Intergroup dialogue can take place in formal and informal spaces. Formal spaces may include special programs that several colleges and universities create outside of the classroom to enroll individual students with different identities and have regular discussions over a specific period of time. At one of my former places of work, we had a six-week Conversations on Race program which enrolled a group of diverse students who assembled weekly for two hours to discuss all kinds of social issues in the group, to learn about and cherish the perspectives and life experiences of others. This program was voluntary, meaning only those who wanted to participate did. Students also received no additional academic credit. Based on the findings from the present study, many of our participants would likely not have engaged in such a program. For them and other students who would likely not stretch their comfort zone in this way, informal spaces work well. Informal spaces are typical classrooms, athletic team meetings, student organization or fraternity chapter meetings, where the group leaders (e.g., professor, teacher, coach, fraternity or student organization president or advisor, peer leader, resident assistant) have a captive audience. In other words, the participants are voluntary in the sense that they could have opted not to enroll in the class, not to play on the athletic team, or not join that specific fraternity chapter. However, the audience is also captive because the men are required to attend class (at most institutions at least), or to be present during team or chapter meetings.

Engaged listening is key in intergroup dialogue situations (Zúñiga, Lopez, & Ford, 2012). Especially intergroup dialogue group members of privileged social groups realize immense learning takeaways during these sessions. Zúñiga and colleagues (2012) pointed out several possible activities for intergroup dialogue events. Members of privileged social groups recalled that they learned to actively listen during the sharing of testimonials, an activity where participants write about their thoughts, feelings, and experiences of two or more social identity groups and then share with one another. The "fishbowl" activity also engendered engaged listening on the part of the group members. Here, learners are split into evenly sized groups by identity and assemble in two concentric circles, one inside of the other. Those on the outside of the circle listen silently while those on the inside share feelings about privilege and oppression (or any other topic the facilitator or participants want to address).

Critics of intergroup dialogue indicate that the outcomes are too focused on making members of privileged groups feel better about themselves by finding commonalities with minoritized peers. Other critics assert that group members with dominant identities rely on their peers from marginalized groups to educate them on issues of privilege and oppression. It's true, intergroup dialogue members with privileged identities have gained and learned from members of minoritized communities (Zúñiga et al., 2012). This is why intergroup dialogue groups ought to be facilitated using the pedagogy for the privileged (Curry-Stevens, 2007) or other forms of critical pedagogies to help and challenge privileged learners (Allen & Rossatto, 2009; Kimmel, 2002). Once group members have identified in which ways all may be privileged and all may be oppressed, the search for commonalities of experience to bond and align and together advocate for social change may begin.

I want to leave you with a powerful intergroup dialogue type of exercise that was featured and went viral on several social media outlets. A few years ago, TV2, a Danish television station, invited and assembled groups of people who were different by profession or identity in an effort to combat stereotyping and prejudice: nurses, students, senior citizens, immigrants, sports fans, athletes, trades workers, among others. As they entered the television studio, the producers had drawn boxes on the floor in which the participants were to assemble by identity (the concept of caucusing). After the participants had some time to look at one another (likely with some trepidations, stereotypes, and prejudice), the facilitator began to ask questions to the entirety of the group. Those participants who would affirm the question would move from their caucused box to a larger box at the front of the room (intergroup space). Little by little, members of the different groups began to interact with their fellow participants on questions that were first fairly benign, but later more personal. In the end, all participants understood that they had first acknowledged their differences and then shared their commonalities; the biggest of them all, that they loved Denmark and being Danish. Now, Denmark is not the United States, and Danish social issues (in a country that didn't have slavery or severe racial hatred) are different than those in the U.S. But caucusing the groups, having them acknowledge who they are and how they identify, and then, little by little, bringing them together to identify common characteristics can work in any college classroom in this country.

Listen and Follow

A recent essay by a student at Dickinson College in Carlisle, Pennsylvania, set off a national debate on the topic of white men's ability to listen in college classrooms, rather than spout their dominant ideologies in attempts to receive validation. In her essay, *Should White Boys Still be Allowed to Talk?*, Leda Fisher (2019) aptly calls out her white male peers who seem to have an opinion on everything, including on issues that don't seem to be part of their own experiences, such as issues faced by women or people of color:

> I cannot describe to you how frustrating it is to be forced to listen to a white boy explain his take on the Black experience in the Obama-era. Hey Brian, I'm an actual Black woman alive right now with a brain. In what world would your understanding of my life carry more weight than my understanding?
>
> (Fisher, 2019, para. 3)

If you're a college student at a predominantly white institution, think about your classroom environments. During discussions, who is the first one to speak to a professor's question? Who speaks early and often even on topics including race, gender, or sexual orientation? In my experiences of teaching in a college environment for more than 20 years, white men tend to be the most confident, vociferous, and frequent speakers. This is also the case, by the way, with white male faculty and administrators, even when women and people of color share the space. I would argue that straight white men in college as in all other areas of society get plenty of airtime. In classrooms as well as boardrooms and lunchrooms, white men talk more, decide more, and lead more than members of communities of color or women. The key for white students is to listen to conversations, not to dominate them, yet to remain engaged (Allen & Rossatto, 2009). Developing consciousness and empathy won't happen unless whites learn how to listen and follow rather than to speak and lead.

A growing literature on the politics of listening suggests that white listening in and of itself is not the solution to ending systemic oppression (Dreher, 2009; Swan, 2017). Dreher (2009) suggested that listening requires whites to allow other experiences and realities to surface and circulate, and to not expect members of minoritized communities to teach. In practice, straight white male listening should include doing important self-work to learn about privilege and oppression, how they operate in the institutions in which we work, letting go of control and dominance, and engaging in reading and learning about non-white discourses (Swan, 2017).

To have straight white men build solidarity with others includes showing humility. Goodman (2011) argues individuals need to relinquish their potential feelings of superiority, listen to others, and trust their wisdom and experiences. The results may include straight white men who admit they aren't the experts on everything, who let others lead, who work *with* people rather than trying to be their savior, and who are non-defensive when receiving critical feedback.

Villalobos (2015) coined the term *white followership* to focus on whites assisting or following people of color who work to bring about racial understanding. Using concepts including white accountability and white humility, Villalobos (2015) argues white followership is a path to white leadership. The model asks whites to "actively center the experiences, sensibilities, interests, methods, critiques, and vision offered by peoples and communities of color who are invested in making racial justice" (Villalobos, 2015, p. 167). Straight white men should focus on the experiences and voices of people of color, women, or people with diverse genders and sexual orientations specifically regarding their experiences with systemic oppression. Those who experience racism, sexism, and homophobia should speak, and those who don't should listen, support, and follow. Villalobos's (2015) model features specific tenets whites ought to take to heart to build followership practice, including interrogating white supremacy and its effects on people of color; being authentic, engaging in critical humility, and being vulnerable; and, focusing on the needs of people of color without requiring recognition. By adapting the core tenets of white followership, straight white college men can lead while centering the voices and experiences of minoritized individuals.

Incite Revolution

Paulo Freire (1970) argued that education alone will not be the panacea needed to set oppressed people around the world free. More education will certainly lead to more beneficial outcomes, but the vice of oppression may be too strong to be turned loose by people who simply learn more about themselves and others. What's needed, in Freire's (1970) estimation is a revolution. In a U.S. context, this will not be a quick process brought about only by demographic changes that take effect when young people of color outnumber older whites. We need to get ready for a steady process that unlearns our white racist and cisheteronormative frames of thinking which have, for generations, determined how we regard our fellow human beings with diverse racial, gender, and sexual identities.

Our real enemies in achieving a more socially just and equitable society in the United States are not people of color, women, immigrants, Muslims, or people with different genders or sexual orientations. The real enemy are the 1% elites that have the most social, economic, and financial power. They make and enact the laws that oppress all others. They create systems that don't allow those who are not rich white men to ascend to the same status in life, or at least not at proportional rates. They erect barriers and bars so people of color or individuals from low-income backgrounds don't have access to the same education they had the privilege of receiving. They need to know, once and for all, that the rest of us will no longer stand by idly and watch.

This revolution should be led by people who are oppressed by a system, such as people in the United States who have been minoritized, put down, and silenced for many generations. Freire (1970, pp. 126–7) said that "revolution is achieved with neither verbalism not activism, but rather with praxis, that is, with *reflection* and *action* directed at the structures to be transformed." Straight white college men must be accomplices in this revolution and show solidarity to people with minoritized identities. After we have raised our consciousness and developed empathy, we must band together with individuals with whom we have more in common than with the white male socio-economic elite, including the special interest lobbies, disgraceful politicians, and oligarch CEOs.

Don't get me wrong, I'm not calling for violence (although the elite's path to power and riches certainly contains lots of violence against oppressed people), but for other means necessary to topple and unseat those unscrupulous big money men and to take their power away. We must do this in the voting booth for sure, but we must also do it in every institutional space we're part of, including meeting rooms, board rooms, classrooms, locker rooms, fraternity chapters, lunch rooms, dining rooms, and living rooms. Actively disrupting systems of oppression, questioning authority, and speaking out against racism, sexism, and homophobia are ways to begin this revolution. People of color, women, and members of diverse gender and sexual orientation communities have long been engaged in this fight. It's time we as straight white men join them.

Conclusion – A Call to Action

The purpose of the Straight White College Men Project was to explore and understand the levels of engagement of straight white college men in issues of diversity, inclusion, equity, and social justice on their campus or in their community. Considering the findings, I draw the following conclusions about the participants' experiences. In the beginning I noted in which isolated and segregated ways they grew up, away from people of color and with few meaningful relationships across racial or ethnic difference. Some participants had not spoken to an individual with a different skin color until college. Even when they grew up in larger metropolitan areas or communities with more racial or ethnic diversity, their interactions with members of communities of color were mostly superficial. Some of our participants grew up in racist households and communities that socialized them to think less of those from different racial backgrounds. The findings from the current study confirmed much recent research suggesting that since the high point of desegregation of American communities and schools in the 1980s, an insidious re-segregation has taken place, leaving today's schools separated by race and ethnicity at alarming rates.

Beginning in high school, and for sure in college, straight white men began thinking about, discussing, and learning about diversity. Most of our participants defined human diversity along physical and invisible characteristics. The most common characteristic of human diversity was race and ethnicity, followed by gender. One of the most consistent answers we received when asking the participants how they fit their own definitions of diversity included that diversity didn't seem to be about them as straight white men or that they had nothing to contribute to the conversation. This finding confirms decades of research on whiteness as invisible. A few participants fell in line with typical colorblind notions of defining diversity; they deemed the focus on diversity as unnecessary and rather wanted society and education to focus on the commonalities as humans we all share, without first studying the differences.

Once in college, some participants shared that they could learn and benefit a great deal from diversity, specifically relative to personal and professional growth. Despite their indications of potential learning, the men's interactions across racial or ethnic differences didn't dramatically increase during college compared to their high school days. This finding is especially surprising given their campuses and college communities are places with more multicultural diversity than most of the participants had ever been used to growing up. Their lack of interactions across racial or ethnic difference didn't just hold true for their early college experiences. Given that nearly three-quarters of our participants were college juniors or seniors, we must conclude that most of them remained racially or ethnically isolated during college, just like they had in their homes and schools. Several participants seemed reticent or resistant to get engaged in diversity initiatives or to enroll in additional coursework. They decried a lack of depth in diversity coursework and some seemed to criticize their instructors for a lack of skills or for publicly shaming white men in the classroom.

Examining the findings further, we conclude that some participants perceived straight white male college students face disadvantages because institutional foci seem to rest more on bringing about diversity than supporting members of dominant social groups. As a result, some of the men perceived themselves as victims of campus diversity efforts. The apparent ubiquity of race-based scholarships and policies such as affirmative action contributed to this understanding of the, in their mind, subordinated role white men place on campuses. When discussing potential benefits of being white, straight, and male on campus, many participants indicated that their race, gender, and sexual orientation privileges allowed them not to worry about discrimination or oppression. This provided a sense of comfort and fit for them. Some participants were able to articulate that their peers from minoritized backgrounds don't have the same privileges and a few others could identify specific experiences of witnessing oppression on their own campus or in their community.

Chapter 5 dealt with the participants' difficulties or reticence to challenge their family's or peers' racist, sexist, or homophobic joking or other inappropriate language or behaviors. They struggled identifying the line between humor and oppression, and standing up to family, friends, and strangers seemed difficult. Findings were inconclusive about whether the men thought friends or strangers would be easier to confront on joking or other inappropriate behaviors. Reasons for not confronting anyone included choosing not to get involved or fearing social consequences from their peer groups.

Against this backdrop I attempt to issue a call for action for straight white college men and the educators who work with them. At the start of this chapter I included a quote from an influential African-American author, professor, feminist, and activist, bell hooks, from the mid-1980s. Why did I include such a dated appeal in this current book on seemingly contemporary white male experiences in college? Because, regardless of when women authors or authors of color began making pleas to men (and especially to white men) to get off their behinds and to start becoming active in the fight against social systems of oppression, we still haven't done it, or at least not often or enough of us. Why should straight white college men become more active and stand up to issues of discrimination and oppression in America, compared to simply standing by? Because we hold positions of power, because our humanity requires it, and because the outcome is a more socially just society, one from which all citizens benefit, not simply a chosen few. As Feagin and Ducey (2017) implore, white men in the United States must begin to critically problematize the insidious racist, sexist, and homophobic framing elite white men have used so successfully over decades and centuries to establish systems of oppression. We as white men have to call out elite white men who have:

> long exploited and subordinated ordinary working people, people of color, and women … For centuries they have created empires for capitalistic and racist exploitation, … built undemocratic political systems, … and rationalized … the oppression of massive numbers of people.
>
> (Feagin & Ducey, 2017, p. 249)

Ordinary people, including straight white college men, should no longer passively witness while these human atrocities continue to ravage our country and destroy our humanity.

I hope you will heed this call and engage in this work. Get solidarity and challenge yourself and other straight white men to advocate for social justice. It will be worth it, I guarantee it – for yourself, your loved ones, colleagues, friends, and future generations of you. Better yet, your engagement will lend a hand to individuals from minoritized backgrounds who have been oppressed for hundreds of years. It's high time straight white men developed responsibility to help end that oppression. I wish you all the best in these critically important endeavors.

Appendix A

Research Sites

Institution (Pseudonym)	Region	Type	Affiliation	Undergraduate Enrollment	Percent White Undergraduates	Percent Male Undergraduates
Callahan College	Midwest	B	Private	2,000	66	47
Danbury College	Midwest	B	Private	1,700	67	57
Lakeside State University	Midwest	M	Public	10,000	85	49
Lucas College	Midwest	B	Private	2,500	85	41
Mason College	Midwest	B	Private	2,000	66	40
Midwest University	Midwest	D	Public	36,000	74	49
Mountain State University	West	D	Public	30,000	75	49
Riverside State University	Midwest	M	Public	10,000	89	43
Southern State University	South	D	Public	15,000	70	45
St. Margaret University	West	D	Private	6,000	50	43

Note
Institutional type: B = Baccalaureate; M = Master's; D = Doctoral.

Appendix B

Sample Demographic Information

Demographics	Participants (n = 92)
Age (Average)	21.3
Contact (Hours/Week)	5.52
Intramurals (Percent)	62
Arts (Percent)	12
Student Organizations (Mean)	1.2
Office Hours (Hours/Year)	7.2
Diversity Programs (Average of all Participants/Year)	1.7
Diversity Electives (Average of all Participants/College)	0.6

References

Aboud, F. E. (2008). A social-cognitive developmental theory of prejudice. In S. M. Quintana & C. McKown (Eds.), *Handbook of race, racism, and the developing child* (pp. 55–71). Hoboken, NJ: Wiley & Sons Inc.

Adler-Bell, S. (2015, March 16). Why white people freak out when they're called out about race. Retrieved May 30, 2017, from www.rawstory.com/2015/03/why-white-people-freak-out-when-theyre-called-out-about-race/

Alimo, C. J. (2012). From dialogue to action: The impact of cross-race intergroup dialogue on the development of White college students as racial allies. *Equity & Excellence in Education, 45*(1), 36–59.

Allan, E. J., & Madden, M. (2006). Chilly classrooms for female undergraduate students: A question of method? *The Journal of Higher Education, 77*(4), 684–711.

Allen, R. L., & Rossatto, C. A. (2009). Does critical pedagogy work with privileged students? *Teacher Education Quarterly*, 163–80.

Allport, G. W. (1954). *The nature of prejudice.* Cambridge, MA: Addison-Wesley.

American Civil Liberties Union (2007). ACLU calls on Department of Justice to explain omissions in report [press release]. Retrieved September 8, 2017, from www.aclu.org/news/department-justice-statistics-show-clear-pattern-racial-profiling

American Civil Liberties Union (2011). Combating mass incarceration: The facts [infographic]. Retrieved from incarceration-facts?redirect=combating-mass-incarceration-facts-0

Andersen, M. L., & Collins, P. H. (Eds.) (2010a). *Race, class, and gender: An anthology* (7th edn). Belmont, CA: Wadsworth Cengage Learning.

Andersen, M. L., & Collins, P. H. (2010b). Why race, class, and gender still matter. In M. L. Andersen, & P. H. Collins (Eds.), *Race, class, and gender: An anthology* (7th edn) (pp. 1–15). Belmont, CA: Wadsworth Cengage Learning.

Anderson, C. E. (2016). *White rage: The unspoken truth of our racial divide.* New York, NY: Bloomsbury USA.

Applebaum, B. (2005). In the name of morality: Moral responsibility, whiteness and social justice education. *Journal of Moral Education, 34*(3), 277–90. https://doi.org/10.1080/03057240500206089

Applebaum, B. (2010). *Being white, being good: White complicity, white moral responsibility, and social justice pedagogy.* Lanham, MD: Lexington Books.

Aran, I. (2013, December 2). *Black professor rebuked for teaching white students structural racism.* Retrieved from http://jezebel.com/black-professor-rebuked-for-teaching-white-students-str-1475090370.

Asante-Muhammed, D., Collins, C., Hoxie, J., & Nieves, E. (2016, August 8). *Without change, African-American and Latino families won't match current average white wealth for centuries.* Retrieved March 24, 2017, from www.ips-dc.org/without-change-african-American-latino-families-wont-match-current-average-white-wealth-centuries/

Astin, A. W. (1993). *What matters in college? Four critical years revisited* (Vol. 1). San Francisco, CA: Jossey-Bass.

Banaji, M. R., & Greenwald, A. G. (2016). *Blindspot: Hidden biases of good people.* New York, NY: Bantam Books.

Banks, K. H. (2009). A qualitative investigation of white students' perceptions of diversity. *Journal of Diversity in Higher Education, 2*(3), 149–55. http://doi.org/10.1037/a0016292

Banyard, V. L., Plante, E. G., & Moynihan, M. M. (2005). Rape prevention through bystander education: Bringing a broader community perspective to sexual violence prevention [report]. U.S. Department of Justice. Retrieved from: www.mcrdpi.marines.mil/Portals/76/Docs/SAPR/SAPR_Bystander%20Research.pdf

Banyard, V. L., Moynihan, M. M., & Plante, E. G. (2007). Sexual violence prevention through education: An experimental evaluation. *Journal of Community Psychology, 35*, 463–81.

Bekiempis, V. (2015, May 14). The new racial makeup of U.S. police departments. Retrieved September 28, 2016, from http://europe.newsweek.com/racial-makeup-police-departments-327312

Bell, L. A. (2007). Theoretical foundations for social justice education. In M. Adams, L. A. Bell, & P. Griffin (Eds.), *Teaching for diversity and social justice* (pp. 1–14). New York, NY: Routledge.

Bergerson, A. A. (2003). Critical race theory and white racism: Is there room for white scholars in fighting racism in education? *International Journal of Qualitative Studies in Education, 16*(1), 51–63. https://doi.org/10.1080/0951839032000033527

Bergo, B., & Nicholls. T. (Eds.) (2015). *I don't see color: Personal and critical perspectives on white privilege.* University Park, PA: The Pennsylvania State University Press.

Berkowitz, A. D. (2004). *The social norms approach: Theory, research, and annotated bibliography.* Retrieved March 10, 2019, from www.alanberkowitz.com/articles/social_norms.pdf

Bitterman, A., Goldring, R., Gray, L., & Broughman, S. (2013). *Characteristics of public and private elementary and secondary school principals in the United States: Results from the 2011–12 Schools and Staffing Survey.* Washington, DC: U.S. Department of Education. Retrieved from https://nces.ed.gov/pubs2013/2013313.pdf

Blau, P. (1977). *Inequality and heterogeneity: A primitive theory of social structure.* New York, NY: Free Press.

Boatright-Horowitz, S. L., & Soeung, S. (2009). Teaching white privilege to white students can mean saying good-bye to positive student evaluations. *American Psychologist, 64*, 574–5. Retrieved from http://psycnet.apa.org/journals/amp/64/6/574/

Bondi, S. (2012). Students and institutions protecting whiteness as property: A critical race theory analysis of student affairs preparation. *Journal of Student Affairs Research and Practice, 49*(4), 397–414. https://doi.org/10.1515/jsarp-2012-6381

Bonilla-Silva, E. (2014). *Racism without racists: Color-blind racism and the persistence of racial inequality in the United States* (4th edn). Lanham, MD: Rowman & Littlefield Publishers.

Boutte, G. S., & Jackson, T. O. (2014). Advice to White allies: Insights from faculty of Color. *Race Ethnicity and Education, 17*(5), 623–42.

Brayboy, B. M. J. (2003). The implementation of diversity in predominantly white colleges and universities. *Journal of Black Studies, 34*(1), 72–86.

Brooks, G. B., & Elder, W. B. (2015). History and future of the psychology of men and masculinities. In Y. J. Wong & S. R. Wester (Eds.), *APA Handbook of men and masculinities* (pp. 3–22). Washington, DC: American Psychological Association.

Broido, E. M. (2000). The development of social justice allies during college: A phenomenological investigation. *Journal of College Student Development, 41*(1), 3–18.

Broockman, D., & Kalla, J. (2016). Durably reducing transphobia: A field experiment on door-to-door canvassing, *Science, 352* (6282), 220–4. doi: 10.1126/science. aad9713

Brown, A. L., Banyard, V. L., & Moynihan, M. M. (2014). College students as helpful bystanders against sexual violence: Gender, race, and year in college moderate the impact of perceived peer norms. Psychology of Women Quarterly, 38(3), 350–62.

Brown, A. L., & Perry, D. (2011). First impressions: Developing critical consciousness in counselor training programs. *Journal of Feminist Family Therapy, 23*(1), 1–18. https://doi.org/10.1080/08952833.2011.548699

Brown, E. L. (2004). What precipitates change in cultural diversity awareness during a multicultural course: The message or the method? *Journal of Teacher Education, 55*(4), 325–40. http://doi.org/10.1177/0022487104266746

Brown, K. T., Brown, T. N., Jackson, J. S., Sellers, R. M., & Manuel, W. J. (2003). Teammates on and off the field? Contact with black teammates and the racial attitudes of white student Athletes. *Journal of Applied Social Psychology, 33*(7), 1379–1403. https://doi.org/10.1111/j.1559-1816.2003.tb01954.x

Brown, R. D., Clarke, B., Gortmaker, V., & Robinson-Keilig, R. (2004). Assessing the campus climate for gay, lesbian, bisexual, and transgender (GLBT) students using a multiple perspectives approach. *Journal of College Student Development, 45*(1), 8–26.

Brown v. Board of Education of Topeka, 347 U.S. 483 (1954).

Cabrera, N. L. (2011). Using a sequential exploratory mixed-method design to examine racial hyperprivilege in higher education. *New Directions for Institutional Research, 2011*(151), 77–91.

Cabrera, N. L. (2012). Working through whiteness: White, male college students challenging racism. Review of Higher Education, 35(3), 375–401.

Cabrera, N. L. (2014). But we're not laughing: White male college students' racial joking and what this says about "post-racial" discourse. *Journal of College Student Development, 55*(1), 1–15.

Cabrera, N. L. (2019). *White guys on campus: Racism, White immunity, and the myth of "post-racial" higher education.* New Brunswick, NJ: Rutgers University Press.

Callner, M., & Rock, C. (2008). *Chris Rock: Kill the messenger* [DVD]. United States: HBO Home Video.

Capraro, R. L. (2010). Why college men drink: Alcohol, adventure, and the paradox of masculinity. In S. R. Harper & F. Harris (Eds.), *College men and masculinities: Theory, research, and implications for practice* (pp. 239–57). San Francisco, CA: Jossey-Bass.

Carlson, M. (2008). I'd rather go along and be considered a man: Masculinity and bystander intervention. *The Journal of Men's Studies, 16*(1), 3–17.

Chang, M. J. (2002). The impact of an undergraduate diversity course requirement on students' racial views and attitudes. *The Journal of General Education*, 21–42.

Charbeneau, J. (2015). White faculty transforming whiteness in the classroom through pedagogical practice. *Race Ethnicity and Education*, *18*(5), 655–74.

Cole, D., & Zhou, J. (2014). Do diversity experiences help college students become more civically minded? Applying Banks' multicultural education framework. *Innovative Higher Education*, *39*(2), 109–21. http://doi.org/10.1007/s10755-013-9268-x

Cole, E. R., Case, K. A., Rios, D., & Curtin, N. (2011). Understanding what students bring to the classroom: Moderators of the effects of diversity courses on student attitudes. *Cultural Diversity and Ethnic Minority Psychology*, *17*(4), 397–405.

Collins, P. H. (1993). Toward a new vision: Race, class, and gender as categories of analysis and connection. *Race, Sex, & Class*, *1*(1), 25–45.

Collins, P. H. (2008). Reply to commentaries: Black sexual politics revisited. *Studies in Gender & Sexuality*, *9*(1), 68–85. https://doi.org/10.1080/15240650701759292

Connell, R. (2003). *Gender and power*. Cambridge, UK: Polity Press.

Connell, R. W. (2014). *Gender and power: Society, the person and sexual politics*. San Francisco, CA: John Wiley & Sons.

Crenshaw, K. (1989). Demarginalizing the intersection of race and sex: A black feminist critique of antidiscrimination doctrine, feminist theory, and antiracist politics. *The University of Chicago Legal Forum*, 139–67.

Crenshaw, K. (1991). Mapping the margins: Intersectionality, identity politics, and violence against women of color. *Stanford Law Review*, 1241–99.

Creswell, J. W. (2014). *Research design: Qualitative, quantitative, and mixed methods approaches* (4th edn). Los Angeles, CA: SAGE.

Crew, D. F. (2005). *Hitler and the Nazis: A history in documents*. Oxford, UK: Oxford University Press.

Curry-Stevens, A. (2007). New forms of transformative education pedagogy for the privileged. *Journal of Transformative Education*, *5*(1), 33–58. Retrieved from http://tlc.oise.utoronto.ca/conference2003/Proceedings/Curry-Stevens.pdf

Czopp, A. M., & Monteith, M. J. (2003). Confronting prejudice (literally): Reactions to confrontations of racial and gender bias. *Personality and Social Psychology Bulletin*, *29*(4), 532–44.

D'Augelli, A. R. (1992). Lesbian and gay male undergraduates' experiences of harassment and fear on campus. *Journal of Interpersonal Violence*, *7*(3), 383–95.

Davis, T. L., & Laker, J. (2004). Connecting men to academic and student affairs programs and services. In G. E. Kellom (Ed.), *Developing effective programs and services for college men. New Directions for Student Services*, (106), 33–45.

Davis, T. L., & Wagner, R. (2005). Increasing men's development of social justice attitudes and actions. *New Directions for Student Services*, (110), 29–41.

Denson, N., & Bowman, N. (2013). University diversity and preparation for a global society: The role of diversity in shaping intergroup attitudes and civic outcomes. *Studies in Higher Education*, *38*(4), 555–70. http://doi.org/10.1080/03075079.2011.584971

DiAngelo, R. (2011). White fragility. *International Journal of Critical Pedagogy*, *3*(3), 54–70.

DiAngelo, R., & Sensoy, Ö. (2014). Getting slammed: White depictions of race discussions as arenas of violence. *Race, Ethnicity, and Education*, *17*(1), 103–28.

Dowd, N. E. (2010). *The man question: Male subordination and privilege*. New York, NY: New York University Press.

Dreher, T. (2009). Eavesdropping with permission: The politics of listening for safer speaking spaces. *Borderlands E-Journal*, *8*, 1–21.

Edmonds, C., & Killen, M. (2009). Do adolescents' perceptions of parental racial attitudes relate to their intergroup contact and cross-race relationships? *Group Processes & Intergroup Relations*, *12*(1), 5–21. https://doi.org/10.1177/1368430208098773

Edwards, K. E. (2006). Aspiring social justice ally identity development: A conceptual model. *NASPA Journal*, *43*(4), 39–60.

Ehrke, F., Berthold, A., & Steffens, M. C. (2014). How diversity training can change attitudes: Increasing perceived complexity of superordinate groups to improve intergroup relations. *Journal of Experimental Social Psychology*, *53*, 193–206. http://doi.org/10.1016/j.jesp.2014.03.013

Engberg, M. E. (2004). Improving intergroup relations in higher education: A critical examination of the influence of educational interventions on racial bias. *Review of Educational Research*, *74*(4), 473–524.

Evans, N. J., & Herriott, T. K. (2004). Freshmen impressions: How investigating the campus climate for LGBT students affected four freshmen students. *Journal of College Student Development*, *45*(3), 316–32.

Fabiano, P. M., Perkins, H. W., Berkowitz, A., Linkenbach, J., & Stark, C. (2003). Engaging men as social justice allies in ending violence against women: Evidence for a social norms approach. *Journal of American College Health*, *52*(3), 105–12.

Farkas, T., & Leaper, C. (2016). The psychology of boys. In Y. J. Wong & S. R. Wester (Eds.), *APA Handbook of men and masculinities* (pp. 357–88). Washington, D.C.: American Psychological Association.

Feagin, J. R. (2013). *The white racial frame: Centuries of racial framing and counter-framing*. New York, NY: Routledge.

Feagin, J. R. (2014). *Racist America: Roots, current realities, and future reparations* (3rd edn). New York, NY: Routledge.

Feagin, J. R., & Ducey, K. (2017). *Elite white men ruling: Who, what, when, where, and how*. New York, NY: Routledge.

Feagin, J. R., & O'Brien, E. (2003). *White men on race: Power, privilege, and the shaping of cultural consciousness*. Boston, MA: Beacon Press.

Feagin, J. R., Vera, H., & Imani, N. (1996). *Agony of education: Black students at white colleges and universities*. New York, NY: Routledge.

Fernandez, L. (2016, April 21). Empathy and social justice: The power of proximity in improvement science. Retrieved July 6, 2018, from www.carnegiefoundation.org/blog/empathy-and-social-justice-the-power-of-proximity-in-improvement-science/

Fisher, L. (2019, February 7). Should white boys still be allowed to talk? *The Dickinsonian*. Retrieved March 7, 2019, from https://thedickinsonian.com/opinion/2019/02/07/should-white-boys-still-be-allowed-to-talk/

Ford, Y., Barnes, J., & Ford, Y. (2017). *Strong Island* [motion picture]. New York, NY: Louverture Films.

Forster, K. (2017, March 24). Donald Trump meets 30 men to discuss future of maternity care under new healthcare bill. *The Independent*. Retrieved March 10, 2019, from www.independent.co.uk/news/world/americas/us-politics/donald-trump-obamacare-men-mike-pence-picture-no-women-freedom-caucus-repeal-healthcare-bill-a7647426.html

Foubert, J. D., & La Voy, S. A. (2000). A qualitative assessment of the "Men's Program": The impact of a rape prevention program on fraternity men. *NASPA Journal*, *38*(1), 18–30.

Foubert, J. D., & Perry, B. C. (2007). Creating lasting attitude and behavior change in fraternity members and male student athletes: The qualitative impact of an empathy-based rape prevention program. *Violence Against Women, 13*(1), 70–86.

Freire, P. (1970). *Pedagogy for the oppressed.* New York, NY: Continuum.

Frey, W. H. (2015). *Diversity explosion: How new racial demographics are remaking America.* Washington, D.C.: Brookings Institution Press.

Gerwarth, R. (2016). *The vanquished: Why the First World War failed to end.* New York, NY: Farrar, Straus and Giroux.

Goodman, D. J. (2011). *Promoting diversity and social justice: Educating people from privileged groups* (2nd edn). New York, NY: Routledge.

Greif, G. (2009). *Buddy system: Understanding male friendships.* Oxford, UK: Oxford University Press.

Gulati-Partee, G., & Potapchuk, M. (2014). Paying attention to white culture and privilege: Missing link to advancing racial equity. *Foundation Review, 6*(1), 25–38. https://doi.org/10.9707/1944-5660.1189

Guttmacher Institute. (2016, March 14). *Requirements for ultrasound.* Retrieved February 25, 2017, from www.guttmacher.org/state-policy/explore/requirements-ultrasound

Hagerman, M. A. (2017). White racial socialization: Progressive fathers on raising "antiracist" children. *Journal of Marriage and Family, 79*(1), 60–74. https://doi.org/10.1111/jomf.12325

Hallinan, M. T., & Williams, R. A. (1989). Interracial friendship choices in secondary schools. *American Sociological Review, 54*, 67–78.

Harper, C. E., & Yeung, F. (2013). Perceptions of institutional commitment to diversity as a predictor of college students' openness to diverse perspectives. *The Review of Higher Education, 37*(1), 25–44.

Harper, S. R., & Harris, F. (Eds.) (2010). *College men and masculinities: Theory, research, and implications for practice.* San Francisco, CA: Jossey-Bass.

Harper, S. R., & Hurtado, S. (2007). Nine themes in campus racial climates and implications for institutional transformation. *New Directions for Student Services,* (120), 7–24.

Harper, S. R., Harris, F., & Mmeje, K. C. (2010). A theoretical model to explain the overrepresentation of college men among campus judicial offenders. In S. R. Harper & F. Harris (Eds.), *College men and masculinities: Theory, research, and implications for practice* (pp. 221–38). San Francisco, CA: Jossey-Bass.

Harris III, F., & Harper, S. R. (2014). Beyond bad behaving brothers: Productive performances of masculinities among college fraternity men. *International Journal of Qualitative Studies in Education, 27*(6), 703–23.

Harris, V., & Ray, D. (2014). Hate speech & the college campus: Considerations for entry level student affairs practitioners. *Race, Gender & Class, 21*(1/2), 185–94.

Hart Research Associates (2015). *Falling short? College learning and career success. Selected findings from online surveys of employers and college students* (conducted on behalf of the Association of American Colleges & Universities). Washington, DC: Hart Research Associates. Retrieved March 10, 2019, from www.aacu.org/sites/default/files/files/LEAP/2015employerstudentsurvey.pdf

Harvard College (2017). Mission, vision, and history [website]. Retrieved May 4, 2017, from https://college.harvard.edu/about/mission-and-vision

Heinze, P. (2008). Let's talk about race, baby: How a white professor teaches white students about white privilege & racism. *Multicultural Education, 16*(1), 2–11.

Helms, J. E. (1984). Toward a theoretical explanation of the effects of race on counselling: A black and white model. *The Counseling Psychologist, 12*(4), 153–65. https://doi.org/10.1177/0011000084124013

Helms, J. E. (1990). *Black and white racial identity: Theory, research, and practice.* New York, NY: Greenwood Press.

Hinchey, P. H. (2004). Understanding our own thinking: Developing critical consciousness. In P. H. Hinchey (Ed.), *Becoming a critical educator: Defining a classroom identity, designing a critical pedagogy* (pp. 23–45). Bern, Switzerland: Peter Lang Publishing.

Hirschfeld, L. A. (2008). Children's developing conceptions of race. In S. M. Quintana & C. McKown (Eds.), *Handbook of race, racism, and the developing child* (pp. 37–54). Hoboken, NJ: Wiley & Sons.

hooks, b. (1984). *Feminist theory: From margin to center.* Cambridge, MA: South End Press.

Hoxmeier, J. C., Flay, B. R., & Acock, A. C. (2016). Control, norms, and attitudes differences between students who do and do not intervene as bystanders to sexual assault. *Journal of Interpersonal Violence, 33*(15), 2379–401.

Hu, S., & Kuh, G. D. (2003). Diversity experiences and college student learning and personal development. *Journal of College Student Development, 44*(3), 320–34.

Hudson, K. D., & Mountz, S. E. (2016). Teaching note – third space caucusing: Borderland praxis in the social work classroom. *Journal of Social Work Education, 52*(3), 379–84. https://doi.org/10.1080/10437797.2016.1174633

Hughey, M. W. (2012). *White bound: Nationalists, antiracists, and the shared meanings of race.* Stanford, CA: Stanford University Press.

Human Rights Watch (2009). *Decades of disparity: Drug arrests and race in the United States.* New York, NY: Human Rights Watch. Retrieved March 10, 2019, from www.hrw.org/sites/default/files/reports/us0309web_1.pdf

Hurtado, S. (1992). The campus racial climate: Contexts of conflict. The Journal of Higher Education, 63(5), 539–69.

Hurtado, S. (2005). The next generation of diversity and intergroup relations research. *Journal of Social Issues, 61*(3), 595–610.

Hurtado, S., Clayton-Pedersen, A. R., Allen, W. R., & Milem, J. F. (1998). Enhancing campus climates for racial/ethnic diversity: Educational policy and practice. *The Review of Higher Education, 21*(3), 279–302.

Hurtado, S., Mayhew, M. J., & Engberg, M. E. (2012). Diversity courses and students' moral reasoning: A model of predispositions and change. *Journal of Moral Education, 41*(2), 201–24. http://doi.org/10.1080/03057240.2012.670931

Iati, M., & Paul, D. (2019, May 17). Everything you need to know about the abortion ban news. *Washington Post.* Retrieved from www.washingtonpost.com/health/2019/05/17/havent-been-following-abortion-ban-news-heres-everything-you-need-know/?noredirect=on&utm_term=.0456fd004140

Iceland, J., & Sharp, G. (2013). White residential segregation in U.S. metropolitan areas: Conceptual issues, patterns, and trends from the U.S. Census, 1980 to 2010. *Population Research and Policy Review, 32*(5), 663–86. https://doi.org/10.1007/s11113-013-9277-6

Iceland, J., Sharp, G., & Timberlake, J. (2013). Sun Belt rising: Regional population change and the decline in black residential segregation, 1970–2009. *Demography, 50*(1), 97–123. https://doi.org/10.1007/s13524-012-0136-6

Irvin, J. (2016, April 1). *I know why poor whites chant Trump, Trump, Trump.* [blog post. Retrieved March 24, 2017, from www.stirjournal.com/2016/04/01/i-know-why-poor-whites-chant-trump-trump-trump/

Johnson, A. G. (2000). *Privilege, power, and difference*. New York, NY: McGraw-Hill.

Johnson, A. G. (2010). The social construction of difference. In M. Adams et al. (Eds.), *Readings for diversity and social justice* (2nd edn) (pp. 15–20). New York, NY: Routledge.

Johnson, J. R., Rich, M., & Castelan Cargile, A. (2008). "Why are you shoving this stuff down our throats?": Preparing intercultural educators to challenge performances of White racism. *Journal of International and Intercultural Communication*, 1(2), 113–35. http://doi.org/10.1080/17513050801891952

Jones, R. P. (2014, August 21). Self-segregation: Why it's so hard for whites to understand Ferguson. *The Atlantic*. Retrieved from www.theatlantic.com/national/archive/2014/08/self-segregation-why-its-hard-for-whites-to-understand-ferguson/378928/

Jones, S. R., & Abes, E. (2013). *Identity development of college students: Advancing frameworks for multiple dimensions of identity*. San Francisco, CA: John Wiley & Sons.

Jordan, N. A., & Luzader, J. (2016). The Boys' Club: Borrowing a feminist lens to critique men-only groups in the fight against gender oppression. *Journal of College and Character*, 17(2), 130–5. https://doi.org/10.1080/2194587X.2016.1159225

Kantrowitz, M. (2011, September 2). The distribution of grants and scholarships by race. Retrieved March 10, 2019, from http://racialequitytools.org/resourcefiles/Distributionracescholarships.pdf

Kastner, G. (2002). Adolf Eichmann, German citizen. *Austrian History Yearbook*, 131.

Keddie, A. (2006). Negotiating and enabling spaces for gender justice. *Issues in Educational Research*, 16(1), 21–37.

Kehler, M. D. (2007, June). Hallway fears and high school friendships: The complications of young men (re)negotiating heterosexualized identities: *Discourse: Studies in the Cultural Politics of Education*, 28(2). Retrieved June 18, 2018, from www.tandfonline.com/doi/abs/10.1080/01596300701289375

Kellom, G. E. (Ed.) (2004). Developing effective programs and services for college men. *New Directions for Student Services*, *107*.

Kimmel, M. (2002, December). Toward a pedagogy of the oppressor. *Tikkun Magazine*.

Kimmel, M. (2008). *Guyland: The perilous world where boys become men*. New York, NY: Harper Collins.

Kimmel, M. S. (2010). Masculinity as homophobia. In M. Adams et al. (Eds.), *Readings for diversity and social justice* (2nd edn) (pp. 326–31). New York, NY: Routledge.

Kimmel, M. S. (2013). *Angry white men: American masculinity at the end of an era*. New York, NY: Nation Books.

Kimmel, M. S. & Ferber, A. L. (Eds.) (2014). *Privilege: A reader* (3rd edn). Boulder, CO: Westview Press.

Kiselica, M. S., Benton-Wright, S., & Englar-Carlson, M. (2016). Accentuating positive masculinity: A new foundation for the psychology or boys, men, and masculinity. In Y. J. Wong & S. R. Wester (Eds.), *APA Handbook of men and masculinities* (pp. 123–43). Washington, D.C.: American Psychological Association.

Krakauer, J. (2015). *Missoula: Rape and the justice system in a college town*. New York, NY: Doubleday.

Kroll, D. (2013, July 7). *State-mandated transvaginal ultrasounds: Where are the medical societies?* Retrieved February 25, 2017, from www.forbes.com/sites/david-kroll/2013/07/07/state-mandated-transvaginal-ultrasounds-where-are-the-medical-societies/

Krueger, R. A., & Casey, M. A. (2000). *Focus groups: A practical guide for applied research* (3rd edn). Thousand Oaks, CA: SAGE Publications.

Kuh, G. D., Nelson Laird, T. F., & Umbach, P. D. (2004). Aligning faculty activities & student behavior: Realizing the promise of greater expectations. *Liberal Education, 90*(4), 24–31.

Kurtz, A. (2012, November 15). Bernanke: Minority homebuyers face housing discrimination. Retrieved November 10, 2017, from http://money.cnn.com/2012/11/15/news/economy/bernanke-housing-discrimination/index.html

Kurtz, K. (2015). *Demographics: Who we elect*. National Conference of State Legislatures. Retrieved from www.ncsl.org/Portals/1/Documents/magazine/articles/2015/SL_1215-Kurtz.pdf

Landreman, L. M., Rasmussen, C. J., King, P. M., & Jiang, C. X. (2007). A phenomenological study of the development of university educators' critical consciousness. *Journal of College Student Development, 48*(3), 275–96.

Larke, P., & Larke, A. (2009). Teaching diversity/multicultural education courses in the academy: Sharing the voices of six professors. *Research in Higher Education Journal, 3*, 1–8.

Lazar, M. M. (2014). Doing "critical" in a postfeminist era: Reviving critical consciousness through peer dialog. *Discourse: Studies in the Cultural Politics of Education, 35*(5), 733–48. https://doi.org/10.1080/01596306.2014.931115

Lemert, C. (2007). Mysterious power of social structures. In B. A. Arrighi (Ed.), *Understanding inequality: The intersection of race/ethnicity, class, and gender* (pp. 19–26). Lanham, MD: Rowman & Littlefield Publishers.

Lewin, T. (2012, March 6). Black students face more harsh discipline, data shows. *New York Times*. Retrieved from www.nytimes.com/2012/03/06/education/black-students-face-more-harsh-discipline-data-shows.html

Lewis, V. A., Emerson, M. O., & Klineberg, S. L. (2011). Who we'll live with: Neighborhood racial composition preferences of whites, Blacks and Latinos. *Social Forces, 89*(4), 1385–407. https://doi.org/10.1093/sf/89.4.1385

Lichter, D. (2013). Integration or fragmentation? Racial diversity and the American future. *Demography, 50*(2), 359–91. https://doi.org/10.1007/s13524-013-0197-1

Lieberman, M. D. (2013). *Social: Why our brains are wired to connect*. Oxford, UK: Oxford University Press.

Lind, D. (2014, August 21). The FBI is trying to get better data on police killings. Here's what we know now. Retrieved September 8, 2017, from www.vox.com/2014/8/21/6051043/how-many-people-killed-police-statistics-homicide-official-black

Linder, C., & Johnson, R. C. (2015). Exploring the complexities of men as allies in feminist movements. *Journal of Critical Thought and Praxis, 4*(1), 1. Retrieved March 10, 2019, from https://lib.dr.iastate.edu/jctp/vol.4/iss1/2/

Lim, F., Johnson, M., & Eliason, M. (2015). A national survey of faculty knowledge, experience, and readiness for teaching lesbian, gay, bisexual, and transgender health in baccalaureate nursing programs. *Nursing Education Perspectives, 36*(3), 144–52.

Littleford, L. N., Ong, K. S., Tseng, A., Milliken, J. C., & Humy, S. L. (2010). Perceptions of European American and African American instructors teaching race-focused courses. *Journal of Diversity in Higher Education, 3*(4), 230–44. http://doi.org/10.1037/a0020950

Ludeman, R. B. (2004). Arrested emotional development: Connecting college men, emotions, and misconduct. In G. E. Kellom (Ed.), Developing effective programs and services for college men. *New Directions for Student Services, 107*, 75–86.

Lyons, C. J., & Pettit, B. (2011). Compounded disadvantage: Race, incarceration, and wage growth. *Social Problems*, 58(2), 257–80. https://doi.org/10.1525/sp.2011.58.2.257

McCann, P., Plummer, D., & Minichiello, V. (2010). Being the butt of the joke: Homophobic humour, male identity, and its connection to emotional and physical violence for men. *Health Sociology Review*, 19, 505–21. https://doi.org/10.5172/hesr.2010.19.4.505

McGee, E. O., & Kazembe, L. (2015). Entertainers or education researchers? The challenges associated with presenting while black. *Race Ethnicity and Education*, 19(1), 96–120.

McIntosh, P. (2004). White privilege: Unpacking the invisible knapsack. In P. S. Rothenberg (Ed.), *Race, class, and gender in the United States: An integrated study* (pp. 188–92). New York, NY: Worth Publishers.

McKay, A., & Ferrell, W. (2004). *Anchorman: The Legend of Ron Burgundy* [motion picture]. Los Angeles, CA: Apatow Productions

McKinney, K. D. (2005). *Being white: Stories of race and racism*. New York, NY: Routledge.

McMahon, S., Banyard, V. L., & McMahon, S. M. (2015). Incoming college students' bystander behaviors to prevent sexual violence. *Journal of College Student Development*, 56(5), 488–93.

Manning, J. E. (2016, July 1). *Membership of the 114th Congress: A profile*. Retrieved September 28, 2016, from www.fas.org/sgp/crs/misc/R43869.pdf

Martin, K. J. (2010). Student attitudes and the teaching and learning of race, culture and politics. *Teaching and Teacher Education*, 26(3), 530–9. http://doi.org/10.1016/j.tate.2009.06.018

Matias, C. E., & Mackey, J. (2016). Breakin' down whiteness in antiracist teaching: Introducing critical whiteness pedagogy. *The Urban Review*, 48(1), 32–50.

Mazur, E. (1989). Predicting gender differences in same-sex friendships from affiliation motive and value. *Psychology of Women Quarterly*, 13(3), 277–91.

Mezirow, J. (1981). A critical theory of adult learning and education. *Adult Education*, 32(1), 3–24.

Mezirow, J. (1991). *Transformative dimensions of adult learning*. San Francisco, CA: Jossey-Bass.

Mezirow, J. (2000). *Learning as transformation: Critical perspectives on a theory in progress*. San Francisco, CA: Jossey-Bass.

Moody, J. (2001). Race, school integration, and friendship segregation in America. *American Journal of Sociology*, 107(3), 679–716.

Mouilso, E. R., Calhoun, K. S., & Rosenbloom, T. G. (2015). Impulsivity and sexual assault in college men. In M. Roland (Ed.), *Perspectives on college sexual assault* (pp. 137–50). New York, NY: Springer Publishing Company.

Munniksma, A., & Juvonen, J. (2012). Cross-ethnic friendships and sense of social-emotional safety in a multiethnic middle school: an exploratory study. *Merrill-Palmer Quarterly*, 58(4), 489.

Musu-Gillette, L., de Brey, C., McFarland, J., Hussar, W., Sonnenberg, W., & Wilkinson Flicker, S. (2017). Status and trends in the education of racial and ethnic Groups 2017 (NCES 2017–051). U.S. Department of Education, National Center for Education Statistics: Washington, DC. Retrieved March 19, 2019, from http://nces.ed.gov/pubsearch

Nash, R. J. (2010). "What is the best way to be a social justice advocate?": Communication strategies for effective social justice advocacy. *About Campus*, 15(2), 11–18.

National Archives (2018). *Vietnam War U.S. military fatal casualty statistics.* Washington, D.C.: The U.S National Archives and Records Administration. Retrieved from www.archives.gov/research/military/vietnam-war/casualty-statistics

National Sexual Violence Resource Center (2016). *Statistics about sexual violence.* Enola, PA. Retrieved October 20, 2016, from www.nsvrc.org/sites/default/files/publications_nsvrc_factsheet_media- packet_statistics-about-sexual-violence_0.pdf

National Student Clearinghouse Research Center (2017, April 26). Completing college: A national view of student attainment rates by race and ethnicity – Fall 2010 cohort. Retrieved September 15, 2017, from https://nscresearchcenter.org/signaturereport12-supplement-2/

National Survey of Student Engagement (2014). *Bringing the institution into focus – Annual results 2014.* Bloomington, IN: Indiana University Center for Postsecondary Research.

National Survey of Student Engagement (2017). NSSE report builder. Retrieved May 31, 2017 from http://nsse.indiana.edu/html/report_builder.cfm

Nelson Laird, T. (2011). Measuring the diversity inclusivity of college courses. *Research in Higher Education, 52*(6), 572–88. https://doi.org/10.1007/s11162-010-9210-3

Nelson Laird, T. F. N., Engberg, M. E., & Hurtado, S. (2005). Modeling accentuation effects: Enrolling in a diversity course and the importance of social action engagement. *The Journal of Higher Education, 76*(4), 448–76.

Neville, H., Poteat, V., Lewis, J., & Spanierman, L. (2014). Changes in White college students' color-blind racial ideology over four years: Do diversity experiences make a difference? *Journal of Counseling Psychology, 61*(2), 179–90.

Newsom, J. S., Congdon, J., Anthony, J., Scully, R. K., Ehrmann, J., Kimmel, M. S., Heldman, C. et al. (2015). *The mask you live in* [motion picture]. Ross, CA: Representation Project.

New York Civil Liberties Union (2017). Stop-and-Frisk data. Retrieved September 15, 2017, from www.nyclu.org/en/stop-and-frisk-data

New York Times (2016, October 8). Transcript: Donald Trump's taped comments about women. Retrieved from www.nytimes.com/2016/10/08/us/donald-trump-tape-transcript.html

Norton, M. I., & Sommers, S. R. (2011). Whites see racism as a zero-sum game that they are now losing. *Perspectives on Psychological Science, 6*(3), 215–18.

Nurenberg, D. (2011). What does injustice have to do with me? A pedagogy of the privileged. *Harvard Educational Review, 81*(1), 50–64.

Obergefell v. *Hodges,* 576 U.S. __ (2015).

OECD (2013). Education at a glance 2013: OECD indicators. Paris: OECD Publishing. http://dx.doi.org/10.1787/eag-2013-en

Orfield, G. (2015). Education and civil rights: Lessons of six decades and challenges of a changed society. In K. L. Bowman (Ed.), *The pursuit of racial and ethnic equality in American public schools: Mendez, Brown, and beyond* (pp. 405–30). East Lansing, MI: Michigan University Press.

Ortiz, A. M., & Patton, L. D. (2012). Awareness of self. In J. Arminio, V. Torres, & R. L. Pope (Eds.), *Why aren't we there yet? Taking personal responsibility for creating an inclusive campus* (pp. 9–32). Sterling, VA: Stylus.

Pager, D., Western, B., & Bonikowski, B. (2009). Discrimination in a low-wage labor market: A field experiment. American Sociological Review, 74(5), 777–99. https://doi.org/10.1177/000312240907400505

Park, J. J., & Chang, S. H. (2015). Understanding students' precollege experiences with racial diversity: The high school as microsystem. *Journal of College Student Development, 56*(4), 349–63.

Parker III, E. T., Barnhardt, C. L., Pascarella, E. T., & McCowin, J. A. (2016). The impact of diversity courses on college students' moral development. *Journal of College Student Development, 57*(4), 395–410.

Pascarella, E. T., & Terenzini, P. T. (2005). *How college affects students* (Vol. 2). San Francisco, CA: Jossey-Bass.

Pascoe, C. J. (2007). *Dude, you're a fag: Masculinity and sexuality in high school.* Berkeley, CA: University of California Press.

Patton, L. D., & Bondi, S. (2015). Nice white men or social justice allies? Using critical race theory to examine how white male faculty and administrators engage in ally work. *Race Ethnicity and Education, 18*(4), 488–514. https://doi.org/10.1080/13 613324.2014.1000289

Perry, G., Moore, H. A., Edwards, C., Acosta, K., & Frey, C. (2009). Maintaining credibility and authority as an instructor of color in diversity-education classrooms: A qualitative inquiry. *The Journal of Higher Education, 80*(1), 80–105.

Perry, S. L. (2014). Hoping for a godly (white) family: How desire for religious heritage affects whites' attitudes toward interracial marriage. *Journal for the Scientific Study of Religion, 53*(1), 202–18. https://doi.org/10.1111/jssr.12079

Pew Research Center (2015, December 9). *The American middle class is losing ground: No longer the majority and falling behind financially.* Retrieved from www.pewsocial trends.org/2015/12/09/the-American-middle-class-is-losing-ground/

Pica-Smith, C. (2009). Children speak about interethnic and interracial friendships in the classroom: Lessons for teachers. *Multicultural Education, 17*(1), 38–47.

Picca, L. H., & Feagin, J. R. (2007). *Two-faced racism: Whites in the backstage and frontstage.* New York, NY: Routledge.

Piccigallo, J. R., Lilley, T. G., & Miller, S. L. (2012). "It's Cool to Care about Sexual Violence." *Men and Masculinities, 15*(5), 507–25. https://doi. org/10.1177/1097184X12458590

Pittman, C. T. (2010). Race and gender oppression in the classroom: The experiences of women faculty of color with white male students. *Teaching Sociology, 38*(3), 183–96. https://doi.org/10.1177/0092055X10370120

Planty, M., Langton, L., Krebs, C., Berzofsky, M., & Smiley-McDonald, H. (2013). *Female victims of sexual violence, 1994–2010. Special Report (No. NCJ 240655).* Washington, DC: Bureau of Justice Statistics, US Department of Justice.

Plaut, V. C., Garnett, F. G., Buffardi, L. E., & Sanchez-Burks, J. (2011). "What about me?" Perceptions of exclusion and Whites' reactions to multiculturalism. *Journal of Personality and Social Psychology, 101*(2), 337–53. http://doi.org/10.1037/ a0022832

Pleasants, R. K. (2011). Men learning feminism: Protecting privileges through discourses of resistance. *Men and Masculinities, 14*(2), 230–50.

Pollack, W. (1998). *Real boys: Rescuing our sons from the myths of boyhood.* New York, NY: Holt.

Porter, C. (2013). U.S. news: Bias incidents shake campus. *Wall Street Journal*, p. A.2. New York, NY.

Posey, K. G. (2016). *Household income: 2015.* United States Census Bureau. Retrieved from www.census.gov/content/dam/Census/library/publications/2016/demo/ acsbr15-02.pdf

Priest, N., Walton, J., White, F., Kowal, E., Baker, A., & Paradies, Y. (2014). Understanding the complexities of ethnic-racial socialization processes for both minority and majority groups: A 30-year systematic review. *International Journal of Intercultural Relations, 43*, 139–55. https://doi.org/10.1016/j.ijintrel.2014.08.003

Rankin, S. R. (2004). Campus climate for lesbian, gay, bisexual and transgender people. *The Diversity Factor, 12*(1), 18–23.

Rankin, S. R. (2005). Campus climates for sexual minorities. *New Directions for Student Services, 2005*(111), 17–23.

Rankin, S., & Reason, R. (2008). Transformational tapestry model: A comprehensive approach to transforming campus climate. Journal of Diversity in Higher Education, 1(4), 262–74.

Reardon, S. F., Fox, L., & Townsend, J. (2015). Neighborhood income composition by household race and income, 1990–2009. *The ANNALS of the American Academy of Political and Social Science, 660*(1), 78–97. https://doi.org/10.1177/0002716215576104

Reason, R. D. (2013). Infusing social responsibility into the curriculum and cocurriculum: Campus examples. *New Directions for Higher Education, 2013*(164), 73–81. https://doi.org/10.1002/he.20076

Reason, R. D., Broido, E. M., & Davis, T. L. (Eds.). (2005). Developing social justice allies. *New Directions for Student Services*, (110).

Reason, R. D., Roosa Millar, E. A., & Scales, T. C. (2005). Toward a model of racial justice ally development. *Journal of College Student Development, 46*(5), 530–46. http://doi.org/10.1353/csd.2005.0054

Reilly, K. (2016, September 10). Read Hillary Clinton's "basket of deplorables" remarks on Trump supporters. *Time*. Retrieved from http://time.com/4486502/hillary-clinton-basket-of-deplorables-transcript/

Renn, K. A., & Reason, R. D. (2013). *College students in the United States: Characteristics, experiences, and outcomes*. San Francisco, CA: Jossey-Bass.

Rich, M. D., Utley, E. A., Janke, K., & Moldoveanu, M. (2010). "I'd rather be doing something else:" Male resistance to rape prevention programs. *The Journal of Men's Studies, 18*(3), 268–88. https://doi.org/10.3149/jms.1803.268

Rivera, L. A. (2015). *Pedigree: How elite students get elite jobs*. Princeton, NJ: Princeton University Press.

Robbins, C. K., & Jones, S. R. (2016). Negotiating racial dissonance: White women's narratives of resistance, engagement, and transformative action. *Journal of College Student Development, 57*(6), 633–51.

Roe v. Wade, 410 U.S. 113 (1973).

Romero-Sánchez, M., Durán, M., Carretero-Dios, H., Megías, J. L., & Moya, M. (2010). Exposure to sexist humor and rape proclivity: The moderator effect of aversiveness ratings. *Journal of Interpersonal Violence, 25*(12), 2339–50.

Roper, L. D. (2004). Do students support diversity programs? *Change, 36*(6), 48–51.

Ryan, K., & Kanjorski, J. (1998). The enjoyment of sexist humor, rape attitudes, and relationship aggression in college students. *Sex Roles, 38*(9–10), 743–56.

Sahl, A., & Batson, C. (2011). Race and religion in the Bible Belt: Parental attitudes toward interfaith relationships. *Sociological Spectrum: The Official Journal of the Mid-South Sociological Association, 31*(4), 444–65.

Sax, L. J. (2008). *The gender gap in college: Maximizing the developmental potential of women and men*. San Francisco, CA: Jossey-Bass.

Sax, L. J. (2009). Gender matters: The variable effect of gender on the student experience. *About Campus, 14*(2), 2–10.

Schueths, A. M., Gladney, T., Crawford, D. M., Bass, K. L., & Moore, H. A. (2013). Passionate pedagogy and emotional labor: Students' responses to learning diversity from diverse instructors. *International Journal of Qualitative Studies in Education*, *26*(10), 1259–76.

Segal, E. A. (2011). Social empathy: A model built on empathy, contextual understanding, and social responsibility that promotes social justice. *Journal of Social Service Research*, *37*(3), 266–77.

Seidman, I. (1998). *Interviewing as qualitative research: A guide for researchers in education and the social sciences* (2nd edn). New York, NY: Teachers College Press.

Shih, D. (2015, April 1). What comfort tells us about racism. Retrieved from http://professorshih.blogspot.com/2015/04/what-comfort-tells-us-about-racism.html

Silver, B. R., & Jakeman, R. C. (2016). College students' willingness to engage in bystander intervention at off-campus parties. *Journal of College Student Development*, *57*(4), 472–6.

Sinclair, S., Dunn, E., & Lowery, B. (2005). The relationship between parental racial attitudes and children's implicit prejudice. *Journal of Experimental Social Psychology*, *41*(3), 283–9. https://doi.org/10.1016/j.jesp.2004.06.003

Smiler, A. P., & Heasley, R. (2016). Boys' and men's intimate relationships: Friendships and romantic relationships. In Y. J. Wong & S. R. Wester (Eds.), *APA Handbook of men and masculinities* (pp. 569–89). Washington, D.C.: American Psychological Association.

Smith, J. A., McPherson, M., & Smith-Lovin, L. (2014). Social distance in the United States. *American Sociological Review*, *79*(3), 432–56. https://doi.org/10.1177/0003122414531776

Soble, J. R., Spanierman, L. B., & Liao, H.-Y. (2011). Effects of a brief video intervention on White university students' racial attitudes. *Journal of Counseling Psychology*, *58*(1), 151–7. http://doi.org/10.1037/a0021158

Solórzano, D., Ceja, M., & Yosso, T. (2000). Critical race theory, racial microaggressions, and campus racial climate: The experiences of African American college students. *Journal of Negro Education*, 60–73.

Spanierman, L. B., Neville, H. A., Liao, H.-Y., Hammer, J. H., & Wang, Y.-F. (2008). Participation in formal and informal campus diversity experiences: Effects on students' racial democratic beliefs. *Journal of Diversity in Higher Education*, *1*(2), 108–25. http://doi.org/10.1037/1938-8926.1.2.108

Spanierman, L. B., & Smith, L. (2017). Roles and responsibilities of White allies: Implications for research, teaching, and practice. *The Counseling Psychologist*, *45*(5), 606–17.

Spielberg, S., Krieger, K. M., Pascal, A., & Spielberg, S. (2017). *The Post* [motion picture]. United States: 20th Century Fox.

Stachowiak, D. M. (2015). Re-envisioning diversity in higher education: From raising awareness to building critical consciousness among faculty. *Thought & Action*, *31*(2), 117–28.

Stainback, K., & Tomaskovic-Devey, D. (2009). Intersections of power and privilege: Long-term trends in managerial representation. *American Sociological Review*, *74*(5), 800–20. https://doi.org/10.1177/000312240907400506

Steele, C. (2011). *Whistling Vivaldi: How stereotypes affect us and what we can do*. New York, NY: W. W. Norton & Company.

Stewart, D-L (2017, March 30). Colleges need a language shift, but not the one you think. Insidehighered.com. Retrieved March 10, 2019, from www.insidehighered.com/views/2017/03/30/colleges-need-language-shift-not-one-you-think-essay

Stotzer, R. (2010). Sexual orientation-based hate crimes on campus: The impact of policy on reporting rates. *Sexuality Research and Social Policy, 7*(3), 147–54. https://doi.org/10.1007/s13178-010-0014-1

Strayhorn, T. L. (2012). *College students' sense of belonging: A key to educational success for all students.* New York, NY: Routledge.

Strayhorn, T. L., & Johnson, R. M. (2014). Why are all the White students sitting together in college? Impact of *Brown* v. *Board of Education* on cross-racial interactions among Blacks and Whites. *The Journal of Negro Education, 83*(3), 385–99. https://doi.org/10.7709/jnegroeducation.83.3.0385

Sue, D. W. (2010). *Microaggressions in everyday life: Race, gender, and sexual orientation.* Hoboken, NJ: Wiley.

Svoboda, V., & Vianden, J. (2015). Challenging straight White college men (STR8WCM) to develop positive social justice advocacy. *ACPA Developments, 12*(4).

Swan, E. (2017). What are White people to do? Listening, challenging ignorance, generous encounters and the "not yet" as diversity research praxis. *Gender, Work & Organization, 24*(5), 1–17. doi: 10.1111/gwao.12165

Synnott, A. (2009). *Re-thinking men: Heroes, villains and victims.* Burlington, VT: Ashgate.

Tatum, B. D. (2004). Defining racism: "Can we talk?" In P. S. Rothenberg (Ed.), *Race, Class, and Gender in the United States: An Integrated Study* (pp. 124–31). New York, NY: Worth Publishers.

Tatum, B. D. (2017). *Why are all the Black kids sitting together in the cafeteria: And other conversations about race.* New York, NY: Basic Books.

Taylor, E. W., & Cranton, P. (2012). *The handbook of transformative learning: Theory, research, and practice.* San Francisco, CA: John Wiley & Sons.

TED Talk (2012, November). *Jackson Katz: Violence against women – It's a men's issue* [video file]. Retrieved from www.ted.com/talks/jackson_katz_violence_against_women_it_s_a_men_s_issue?language=en

TED Talk (2013, November 26). *Ryan McKelley: Unmasking masculinity – Helping boys become connected men* [video file]. Retrieved from www.youtube.com/watch?v=LBdnjqEoiXA

Tice, D. M., & Baumeister, R. F. (1985). Masculinity inhibits helping in emergencies: Personality does predict the bystander effect. *Journal of Personality and Social Psychology, 49*(2), 420–8.

Tomlinson, M. J., & Fassinger, R. E. (2003). Career development, lesbian identity development, and campus climate among lesbian college students. *Journal of College Student Development, 44*(6), 845–60.

Tran, A. G., Mintert, J. S., & Jew, G. B. (2016). Parental ethnic–racial socialization and social attitudes among ethnic–racial minority and white American emerging adults. *American Journal of Orthopsychiatry.* Retrieved from http://psycnet.apa.org/psycarticles/2016-39467-001.pdf&productCode=pa

Trout, J. D. (2009). *The empathy gap: Building bridges to the good life and the good society.* New York, NY: Viking.

Tyson, A., & Maniam, S. (2016, November 9). Behind Trump's victory: Divisions by race, gender, education. Washington, DC: Pew Research Center. Retrieved from www.pewresearch.org/fact-tank/2016/11/09/behind-trumps-victory-divisions-by-race-gender-education/

Ukpokodu, O. N. (2007). Preparing socially conscious teachers: A social justice-oriented teacher education. *Multicultural Education, 15*(1), 8–15.

Umbach, P. D., & Kuh, G. D. (2006). Student experiences with diversity at liberal arts colleges: Another claim for distinctiveness. *Journal of Higher Education*, 169–92.

U.S. Census Bureau (2017a). *Quick facts: United States*. Washington, DC: U.S. Department of Commerce.

U.S. Census Bureau (2017b). *United States median household income*. Retrieved from www.census.gov/search-results.html?q=median+income&page=1&stateGeo=none &searchtype=web&cssp=

U.S. Department of Education (2016a). *Digest of education statistics, 2015*. Washington, DC: National Center for Education Statistics.

U.S. Department of Education (2016b). *The state of racial diversity in the educator workforce*. Washington, DC: U.S. Department of Education.

Vaccaro, A. (2010). What lies beneath seemingly positive campus climate results: Institutional sexism, racism, and male hostility toward equity initiatives and liberal bias. *Equity & Excellence in Education*, *43*(2), 202–15. http://doi.org/10.1080/ 10665680903520231

Van Dyke, N., & Tester, G. (2014). Dangerous climates: Factors associated with variation in racist hate crimes on college campuses. *Journal of Contemporary Criminal Justice*, *30*(3), 290–309.

Van Gorder, A. C. (2007). Pedagogy for the children of the oppressors liberative education for social justice among the world's privileged. *Journal of Transformative Education*, *5*(1), 8–32.

Vianden, J. (2009). Exploring college men's perceptions about interacting with faculty beyond the classroom. *Journal of College Student Affairs*, *27*(2), 224–41.

Vianden, J. (2018). "In all honesty, you don't learn much": College student perceptions of diversity requirements and instructors. *International Journal of Teaching and Learning in Higher Education*.

Vianden, J., & Gregg, E. A. (2017). What's my responsibility? Undergraduate White men in sport management discuss increasing diversity in sport. *Sport Management Education Journal*, *11*, 88–101. http://dx.doi.org/10.1123/smej.2015-0023

Vianden, J., Kuykendall, J., Mock, R., & Korb, R. (2012). Exploring messages African American men receive about attending a predominantly White university. *New York Journal of Student Affairs*, *12*(2), 23–39.

Villalobos, J. (2015). Applying white followership in campus organizing: A leadership tool for Latinx students working for racial justice. In A. Lozano (Ed.), *Latina/o college student leadership: Emerging theory, promising practice*. Lanham, MD: Lexington Books.

Waldron, T. (2012, November 16). *Discriminatory lending made housing crisis worse for minorities*. Retrieved November 10, 2017, from https://thinkprogress.org/federal-reserve-chair-discriminatory-lending-made-housing-crisis-worse-for-minorities-50629acc12b4/

Wallace, D., Budden, M., Juban, R., & Budden, C. (2014). Making it to the top: Have women and minorities attained equality as higher education leaders? *Journal of Diversity Management*, *9*(1), 83–8.

Walters, A., & Sylaska, K. (2012). Gender in motion: Developmental changes in students' conceptualizations of gender through participation in a first-year seminar course. *American Journal of Sexuality Education*, *7*(2), 89–109. http://doi.org/10.108 0/15546128.2012.680856

Watt, S. K. (2015). *Designing transformative multicultural initiatives: Theoretical foundations, practical applications, and facilitator considerations*. Sterling, VA: Stylus.

Wellman, D. (1977). *Portraits of white racism.* Cambridge, UK: Cambridge University Press.

Whitt, E. J., Edison, M. I., Pascarella, E. T., Nora, A., & Terenzini, P. T. (1999). Women's perceptions of a "chilly climate" and cognitive outcomes in college: Additional evidence. *Journal of College Student Development, 40*(2), 163–77.

Wigg-Stevenson, N. (2016). White, privileged, fragile. *Sojourners Magazine, 45*(9), 22–6.

Wilkinson, R. G., & Pickett, K. (2009). *The spirit level: Why greater equality makes societies stronger.* New York, NY: Bloomsbury Press.

Williams, D. (1985). Gender, masculinity-femininity, and emotional intimacy in same-sex friendship. *Sex Roles, 12*(5–6), 587–600.

Winkler, E. N. (2009, August). Children are not colorblind: How young children learn race. *PACE: Practical Approaches for Continuing Education, 3*(3), 1–8.

Wise, T. (2003). *Cleaning up the funk: Commencement speech at Grinnell College.* Retrieved from www.timwise.org/2003/05/cleaning-up-the-funk-commencement-speech-at-grinnell-college-2003/

Wolf, A. (2016, June 22). *Massive database shows state judges are not representative of the people they serve.* Retrieved September 28, 2016, from https://news.vanderbilt.edu/2016/06/22/massive-database-shows-state-judges-are-not-representative-of-the-people-they-serve/

Wong, Y. J., & Wester, S. R. (Eds.) (2016). *APA handbook of men and masculinities.* Washington, D.C.: American Psychological Association.

Woodard, V. S., & Sims, J. M. (2000). Programmatic approach to improving campus climate. *NASPA Journal, 37*(4), 539–52. https://doi.org/10.2202/1949-6605.1117

Young, I. M. (2010). Five faces of oppression. In M. Adams et al. (Eds.), *Readings for diversity and social justice* (2nd edn) (pp. 35–45). New York, NY: Routledge.

Zúñiga, X., Lopez, G. E., & Ford, K. A. (2012). Intergroup dialogue: Critical conversations about difference, social identities, and social justice – guest editors' introduction. *Equity & Excellence in Education, 45*(1), 1–13. https://doi.org/10.1080/10665684.2012.646903

Zweigenhaft, R. L. & Domhoff, G. W. (2014). *The new CEOs: Women, African American, Latino, and Asian American leaders of Fortune 500 companies.* Lanham, MD: Rowman & Littlefield.

Index